5 part Gesso
1 part plaster of paris

Defend
Explain
Justify

CODEPENDENTS' GUIDE TO THE TWELVE STEPS

MELODY BEATTIE

PRENTICE
HALL
PARKSIDE

A Prentice Hall/Parkside Recovery Book

NEW YORK • LONDON • TORONTO • SYDNEY • TOKYO • SINGAPORE

Parkside Medical Services Corporation is a full-service provider of treatment
for alcoholism, other drug addiction, eating disorders, and psychiatric
illness.

Parkside Medical Services Corporation
205 West Touhy Avenue
Park Ridge, IL 60068
1-800-PARKSIDE

PRENTICE HALL PRESS
15 Columbus Circle
New York, NY 10023

LC No. 90-52819

ISBN 0-13-140054-1

Designed by Robert Bull Design

Manufactured in the United States of America

10 9 8 7 6 5 4 3 2 1

First Edition

This book is dedicated to the people working the Twelve Steps
and to the Higher Power that helps us do that

ACKNOWLEDGMENTS

For their contributions to this book, I acknowledge and thank the many recovering people who openly and willingly talked about their experiences with the Twelve Steps and codependency. They made it possible for this book to be representative of the group consciousness.

I also acknowledge and thank:

The Twelve Step groups, who cooperated in providing the information we needed for an accurate directory.

Beatrice Pieper, my research assistant and on-staff freelance writer. Bea diligently conducted the interviews with recovering people and compiled the directory of Twelve Step programs and the book reviews. Her efforts, contributions, and encouragement were vital to this book.

Jonathon and Wendy Lazear of The Lazear Agency, whose professional and personal contributions were invaluable from beginning to end of this project.

Ann Poe, whose editorial contributions were efficient, helpful, timely, and delivered with speed and grace under pressure.

My children, Shane and Nichole. Shane makes me laugh, accepts me when I'm busy, and welcomes me when I'm not. Nichole is my inspiration and a gift.

And my mother, who bought me my first word processor years ago and told me to get to work.

CONTENTS

OUT THERE

Out there
you'll see it all.
The floating ends
will meet and mend,
and you will be yourself;
your fully-formed,
though always changing,
self of selves.
Every clumsy backward look
will pay for itself.
Every tear you've cried,
or wanted to cry,
will set your broken bones.
The rips in your heart
will no longer
need to be guarded
by steel girders,
banyan trees,
or even rice paper.
Not so much as a
dragonfly's wing
will you need
to cover the bludgeoned place,
to protect the private you
you love so much
and hope to save intact
from what has seemed years
of relentless pummeling.

Go and live and love
in peace, my friend,
for surely there is love
to enfold you,
and life to be feasted upon:
your portion is boundless.
Love will be the more
you've wanted.
You will know it
when you see it.
You will love yourself
as no lover
has ever had the courage
to love;
and the warmth you've wanted
will line your pillowcases,
dance upon your windowsill,
and hide
at the ends of your socks
awaiting your toes.

—DEBORAH MEARS

INTRODUCTION

The first time I was exposed to the Twelve Steps, I was forced into a state hospital to recover from chemical addiction. I didn't want to be there; I didn't want to get sober. But I had to stay in treatment to avoid legal problems.

As part of the treatment agenda I had to attend a peculiar session in the hospital auditorium. Twice weekly, people from the community came in, walked onstage, and talked about themselves. They said how awful life used to be when they were drinking, what had happened, and how good life was now. They had gone from trouble and pain to living happily ever after.

I sat in the back row, as far away from these people as possible. One day, a man said something that hit me right in the solar plexus. He was no longer talking about himself. He was talking about *me*—my pain, my struggles, the fears I had hidden, even from myself. Something changed despite my agenda. I got sober.

Seven years and several relationships with alcoholics later, I knew I needed something more than sobriety. I wasn't on my way to living happily ever after; I was on my way to codependency recovery.

I found myself again facing these Twelve Steps, this time from a different point of view. This time I was being affected by *another person's* alcoholism. Before long, I learned the truth. It wasn't about the other person; it was about me and my codependency issues—which I now believe were present from age four.

I wasn't happy to be facing these Steps again. I didn't like being in so much pain that I needed another recovery. I thought one big problem was all one person should have to face in one lifetime.

But I'm grateful now. The first time I was exposed to these Steps, they gave me sobriety. The second time I was exposed to them, they gave me a *self* and a *life*. They gave me recovery from codependency.

This is a book about the Twelve Steps and how these principles can be applied to codependency recovery, regardless of which Twelve Step group you now regularly attend.

Many of us have looked for magic. We've payed, waited, prayed, searched, longed, and hoped for the key that would unlock the mystery of recovery in our life. We've looked for the person, place, or thing that would make us feel better, that would stop our pain and change us.

How many times have we attended a seminar, bought a book, or gone to a therapist, hoping to be transformed? Those activities help. They're valid tools on this journey.

But there's more.

I regularly receive letters from people asking when I'm going to lead a seminar or asking if the person could consult with me. "If I could just talk to you, then I'd get better. You hold the key, the magic to my recovery."

I know the feeling well because I've had it about others. If only I could stand in the presence of Earnie Larsen, or Anne Wilson Schaef, or any of the other teachers long enough, then I'd be changed. I'd be transformed.

We know that's not true. We each have our own key, our own magic. We each have the power and the ability to discover that magic and tap into our own healing process, regardless of our present circumstances.

The way to do that is by working the Twelve Steps. These are the basic principles of recovery from our codependency. By working these Steps, we will be led, at the right time, to the people, seminars, helping professionals, and books that we need.

But the Steps are the core of transformation. They are the path to recovery.

That's why I'm writing a book about them.

Many Twelve Step groups related to codependency recovery have sprung up across the nation. Many of these groups are inundated with new members and have a shortage of old-timers, people with practical experience working the Steps. Sometimes, group members practice in group what they are there to recover from: caretaking, shame, controlling, obsessing, victimization, and neglect of self-responsibility. For lack of knowing what else to do, many find themselves sitting in group focusing on the problem instead of the solution—the Steps.

This is my gift to those of you recovering from codependency while this multitude of codependency groups travels from infancy into coming-of-age. It is also a gift to myself. Writing this book has renewed and refreshed my belief in these Steps and their ability to facilitate recovery in anyone's life, including my own.

To write this book, I've interviewed many people attending a variety of groups—from CoDA (Codependents Anonymous) to Al-Anon (for those affected by a loved one's drinking) to Families Anonymous (people concerned about chemical or behavioral problems in a loved one, usually a child) to Co-SA (Codependents of Sex Addicts). And more.

I've talked to people recovering from multiple addictions—combinations such as an eating disorder, chemical dependency, and codependency. I've talked to people recovering from incest or abuse issues and codependency. I've talked to people who consider themselves "just codependent."

I've talked to people from the straight and gay communities.

I've talked to people from all parts of the country who, in a variety of dialects, are learning to stop asking "How can I help you?" and start asking "How can I help myself?"

The common denominator of the people I've talked to is that regardless of the Twelve Step group they attended, they considered codependency an important recovery issue and were willing to talk about how the Twelve Steps applied to codependency issues.

The people interviewed were not talking to me on behalf of any particular group. This book is not endorsed, sponsored by, or affiliated with any particular Twelve Step group; it does not represent the opinions of any Twelve Step group. It is not written to promote a Twelve Step group. It is written to spark and trigger individual thinking about how these Steps can facilitate healing from codependency.

Then, you can show others how these principles are working for you.

That's called recovery.

The anonymity of people interviewed has been protected.

Included in this book is a list of the Twelve Step programs that people are using to recover from codependency and related issues. You will also find a list of books that people have found helpful at different times in their recovery. Some of these are recovery books; others are treasures, little gifts that have helped along the way. It is a list of the classics and the favorites.

You can use this book any way you choose. It is not intended to be read cover to cover; you can dive in at any chapter or Step that feels right for you. This is not The Book on the Steps. As with my other writings, it is my personal and prejudiced opinion.

At the end of each chapter I have included suggested activities to trigger thinking about how each Step might apply to your life. You can read the questions and think about your answers. Or, you may want to write your answers in a journal or notebook. To help clarify your thinking and facilitate your recovery, you may want to discuss your answers with a trusted friend.

It is with the greatest respect that I write about these Twelve Steps, originally designed for recovery from alcoholism. In this book, I've tried to capture how these Steps work for recovery from codependency issues. Yet writing about these Steps is a weak reflection of what these Steps are and what they can do. The magic, the mystery, the power in these Steps can only be understood when each of us personally applies these Steps to our life. That's when they reveal themselves. That's when they become more than a list of twelve suggestions.

"I really think these Steps are freedom," said Jody. "They give me clues to what freedom can really be about. They do it in a way that challenges my already existing beliefs about what freedom is, about what being human is, about what being spiritual is. And I need that."

Read about what these Steps have done for us, then capture their mystery and magic in your life.

A note here for beginners. It can often be confusing to hear recovery jargon, such as "working a Step." What does it mean to work a Step? Some people think about, write about, and work on the Steps in the same way they would work on school homework or tax returns—in a disciplined, dedicated manner. Some work on the Steps with their sponsor, another person in the program they choose as their mentor. Others go to meetings, listen, and let the Steps sink in. Others find a course somewhere in the middle.

We are each free to find our own version of what it means to work a Step. I find it helpful to think about these Steps before, during, and sometimes after an incident where I would normally lapse into a codependent behavior, such as controlling or not taking care of myself. I think about the Steps when I'm in emotional pain, when I get stuck, and during those times I find myself running from my feelings.

A natural process takes over, and many of us find ourselves instinctively focusing on these Steps during the course of our lives. We start working the Steps, and soon the Steps begin to work on us. Sometimes they've worked on me when I've resisted. They change us, transform us, in ways that must be experienced, not intellectualized.

Working the Steps means making a very human effort to apply a recovery principle in our lives, and very profound behavioral, emotional, and spiritual results occur. In the following chapters, we'll look at these efforts and the results.

"Surrender happens of its own accord. It just dawns on me. Then, peace of mind settles in, and my life starts to get more manageable."
—Bob T.

STEP ONE

"WE ADMITTED WE WERE POWERLESS OVER OTHERS—
THAT OUR LIVES HAD BECOME UNMANAGEABLE."
—Step One of CoDA

The first time I heard this Step, I didn't get it. I didn't understand. It felt dark, scary, and untrue.

Powerless over others? My life—unmanageable?

I thought I was in complete control of myself and others. I thought there was no circumstance too overwhelming, no feeling so great that I couldn't handle it by sheer force of willpower. I thought being in control was expected of me. It was my job. That's how I got through life!

And I thought my life looked so much more manageable than the lives of those around me—until I started looking within. That's when I found the undercurrent of fear, anger, pain, loneliness, emptiness, and unmet needs that had controlled me most of my life.

That's when I took my eyes off the other person long enough to take a look at the state of affairs in my life.

That's when I began to find a life and come alive.

"I didn't know about power and powerlessness," said Mary, talking about the First Step. "Being a victim and being in control was how I was in power. If I was powerless, then someone else was in control."

Now we are learning a better way to own our power than being victims and being controlling. It begins by admitting and accepting the truth about ourselves and our relationships.

We are powerless over others. When we try to exert power where we have none, our lives at some level may become unmanageable. Let's take a look at some ways unmanageability can present itself in our lives, and where our ideas about controlling others—or allowing them to control us—began.

MY STORY

I can still remember the scene vividly, even though it happened more than a decade ago. Someone I cared about a lot was drinking. He was an alcoholic. And he wouldn't stop. I had done everything I could to make him stop. Nothing worked.

Nothing.

Neither was I able to stop my efforts to control his drinking. After yet another round of promises, forgiveness, then broken promises, I settled on the ultimate plan to *make* him stop drinking. I would show him how it felt to love someone who was using chemicals. I would make it look like I had returned to drug usage. That would get his attention. That would show him how much I hurt. Then he would stop.

Carefully, I set the stage. Although I had been clean of drugs for years, I laid out the paraphernalia of a user: a small packet with white powder in it (I used sugar); a spoon, burnt on one side; a piece of cotton in the spoon. Then I lay down on the couch to make it look like I was under the influence of narcotics.

A short time later, the person who was the focus (at that time) of my control efforts entered the room. He looked around, saw the spoon, saw me, and started to react. I jumped off the couch and started lecturing.

"See!" I screamed. "See how it feels to love someone and see them using chemicals! See how much it hurts! See what you've been *doing to me* for these years!"

His reaction was not nearly as important as my neighbor's reaction later that evening. "What you're doing is really crazy," she said, "and you need to go to Al-Anon."

It took me months to learn the truth: I didn't need to prove to the alcoholic how much I hurt. I needed to become aware of how much pain I was in. I needed to take care of myself.

That's only one of many incidents that shows the lengths I went to to control people. I was so good at seeing the behaviors, especially the out-of-control behaviors, of another. Yet I couldn't see unmanageability in my own life. I couldn't see myself. And I was trapped, locked into the victim role. People didn't just do things. They did things *to me*. No matter what happened, each event felt like a pointed attempt to do me in.

My ability to separate myself from others—to separate my issues, my business, my affairs, and my responsibilities from the issues, business, affairs, and responsibilities of others—was nonexistent. I blended into the rest of the world like an amoeba.

If someone needed something, I considered that need my personal and private responsibility, even if I was just guessing about what he or she needed. If someone had a feeling, it was my responsibility to work through it for him or her. If someone had a problem, it was mine to solve.

I didn't know how to say no. I didn't have a life of my own. I had a backlog of feelings from childhood, and chances were great that whatever I was reacting to today was probably a patterned reaction from childhood. Two weeks after I got married, I raced home from work, flung open the closet doors, and checked to see if my husband's clothes were still in the closet. I was certain I was going to be abandoned, left. I felt totally unlovable. And I didn't have the foggiest idea what it meant to own my power.

The base I operated from was fear, coupled with low self-esteem. I spent most of my time reacting to other people, trying to control them, allowing them to control me, and feeling confused by it all.

I thought I was doing everything right. Aren't people supposed to be perfect? Aren't people supposed to be stoic? Shouldn't we keep pushing forward, no matter how much it hurts? Isn't it good to give until it hurts, then keep giving until we're doubled over in pain? And how can we allow others to go about their life course? Isn't it our job to stop them, set them straight? Isn't that the right way, the good way, the Christian way?

The codependent way.

As many others have said about themselves, I wasn't me. I was whoever people wanted me to be. And I felt quite victimized and used up by it all. After years of practicing hard-line codependency, the unmanageability in my life was overwhelming. Some of my codependency I didn't understand until well into recovery.

When I began recovery I was more than $50,000 in debt, as a result of the unmanageability in my financial affairs. No amount was too great to be borrowed if it would help someone else.

My spirituality had been taxed to the limit. How many times had I prayed for God to change other people? How often had God refused? I thought God had abandoned me. I didn't know that I had abandoned myself. I didn't know that now that I was an adult, people couldn't abandon me. All they could do was leave.

In some instances, I may have been better off if they had.

My relationships with my children were chaotic. It's hard to be an effective parent when you're bound up in pain, denial, and repressed feelings and are regularly wishing for death.

My relationships with friends were strained. I had little to offer friends, except my perpetual complaints about the misery in my life. Most of my friendships centered around shared stories of victimization, interspersed with Rabelaisian humor to make it bearable.

"Guess who used me today?"

I had no feelings that I was aware of. I had no needs that I was aware of. I prided myself on my ability to endure needless suffering, deprive myself, and go without.

I neglected my career.

My health was failing. I spent years seeking medical treatment for nonspecific viruses. I had a hysterectomy. I had viral meningitis. I had gastritis. My back hurt. My head ached. Arthritis was beginning to settle in.

And I was only thirty-two years old.

Codependency is a powerful force. So is denial and the ability to ignore what is before our eyes. What's there has the power to hurt, especially when we feel helpless, vulnerable, frightened, and ashamed by it all.

STANLEY'S STORY

Stanley is a successful architect in his fifties. It took him sixteen years to notice the unmanageability and chaos in his life— sixteen years of denying, putting up with, pretending, and going deeper into hiding within himself before he saw the truth.

Stanley's father is an alcoholic. Stanley's wife's father died of alcoholism. And after sixteen years of trying to control his youngest son, Stanley reached the point of emotional collapse.

"By the time our youngest son, John, was six, I knew we were in trouble," Stanley said. "He constantly fought at school. He was belligerent and refused to do his homework. At home, he caused problems. He hollered at his mother, swore at her, and sometimes hit her.

"My wife and I fought all the time. I tried to be understanding. She had special circumstances. She had been in the camps during World War II, and she believed children should be loved and adored. She didn't want us to discipline John.

"John caused complete chaos at home. He was bright. He knew how to push everyone's buttons. He had my wife and I fighting, his siblings and I fighting. He even had his grandparents going at it."

When John was ten, Stanley gave his wife an ultimatum: Either they sought professional help for John and the family or Stanley was moving out. They went to a psychologist who told them not to worry. John, the psychologist said, was a bright child, a bit precocious, but he'd grow out of this *stage*.

That session was the beginning of $20,000 (after insurance coverage) of fruitless family counseling.

When John was eleven, Stanley's wife threw up her arms in despair and walked out of a school counseling session. She was tired. She had given all she could to the situation. She vowed never to set foot inside a school again. A short time later she moved out, leaving Stanley to raise the three children alone.

By the time John was twelve, Stanley was spending more time in school than John. Stanley was there three days a week, explaining why John was only there two days a week.

"The only way I could get John graduated from ninth to tenth grade was by promising to leave that school system," Stanley said. "How codependent is that? I sold our home and moved to another school system so the school would graduate John."

On one occasion, Stanley came home to find his middle son, Jeremy, choking John. Jeremy had his hands around John's neck and had lifted him off the ground. Jeremy quietly said that he had put up with John for twelve years and could do it no longer.

Another time, Stanley walked into a room just as John was throwing a knife at another child. Stanley was able to deflect the course of the knife, causing it to pierce a window screen instead of the boy.

When John was sixteen, things came to a head. By then, Stanley's wife had moved back home. One Sunday, Stanley was in the den watching football, and his wife was in the kitchen preparing brunch. John walked into the kitchen and began arguing with his mother. Stanley listened, as their discussion escalated and their voices grew louder.

"I was afraid," said Stanley. "John still acted abusively toward his mother, hollering at her and sometimes hitting her. I wasn't going to let that happen again."

Stanley walked into the kitchen just as John was about to strike his mother. Stanley grabbed John and restrained him in a bear hug. When he did this, his wife came to John's rescue. She started pulling at Stanley, trying to get him to let John loose.

Then Jeremy, the middle son, walked into the kitchen. He started pulling at his mother, trying to get her to leave Stanley alone, so he could restrain John.

The four of them toppled to the floor. Stanley cut his head open. Blood gushed out. Stanley let John loose, ran to the car, drove to the emergency room at the hospital, received forty-five stitches, and drove back home.

There in the living room stood Jeremy and John, toe to toe. They were still going at it.

"They were ready to duke it out," said Stanley. "My wife was standing next to them, watching. She didn't know what to do. The boys were fully grown. John was six feet tall and weighed 175 pounds. Both of them had been trained in martial arts.

"Damn it," Stanley said. 'If there's going to be any fighting around here, I'm going to do it."

Then Stanley stepped in between the two boys and punched them both.

The next day Jeremy moved out. A few weeks later, the oldest sister moved out. Two weeks after that, Stanley moved out. Two months later, Stanley's wife moved out.

"A sixteen-year-old boy had gained complete control of the house and two dogs," Stanley said. "That was it. I moved back in."

Two weeks later, a school counselor called Stanley. "I think you've got a problem," she said. The counselor then informed Stanley that John was using drugs and had been since he was eight years old—a fact that $20,000 worth of counseling and therapy had failed to reveal.

By then, when he wasn't dealing with the school or police officials, Stanley was spending his days locked in his office, head down on his desk, crying.

"I was drained, and felt totally devoid of any worth as a human being," Stanley said.

Stanley began attending Al-Anon, then Families Anonymous. He was ready to face and accept his powerlessness and the unmanageability in his own life. He was ready to detach and begin taking care of himself.

(The epilogue to the story is this: John went to treatment but wasn't successful. Later on, after going to jail on a narcotics sale charge, he began a true recovery. He is now a successful businessman and has a close relationship with his father. Stanley and his wife divorced. Jeremy and the oldest sister are not yet in recovery for codependency. Stanley has lost one hundred pounds, exercises regularly, feels peaceful and hopeful about life, and takes care of himself daily.)

OTHER STORIES OF UNMANAGEABILITY

But I'm not in that much trouble, you might be thinking. My response is: good. You don't have to be in a lot of trouble to recognize unmanageability and begin recovering from codependency. It takes many of us much pain to become ready for recovery. Others do not need as much chaos.

Mike's awareness of the unmanageability in his life was a quiet one.

"I came home from work one night, and I could no longer stand my usual system of sitting in front of the television, staring at it, and escaping from myself by reading the newspaper. My sister, who has always been borderline psychotic, called. She started going on and on, giving fifteen different reasons for why she had lost her job. It was about the fifteenth one in a row she had lost. And the thought occurred to me that I could either go on and on with my life as it was, being bored and quietly escaping through the television, or I could start doing something different. Someone had given me the address of a Twelve Step group for adult children of alcoholics. I got up, turned off the television, and went to a meeting. I was ready to take this First Step—out of sheer boredom."

Karen's unmanageability with her codependency became apparent while she was in recovery from addiction to drugs and alcohol.

"I had been recovering from chemical addiction for fifteen years. I was doing everything everyone told me to. I was going to five meetings a week. I was *helping* people constantly, whether they wanted it or not. But inside, I was just as ashamed of myself as I was the day I got sober. I had no self-worth. I couldn't tell people 'no.' I couldn't say what I thought. And everything I did, I did to make people like me—from the way I dressed, to the way I combed my hair and put on my makeup, to the way I sat, and the things I did for people. I felt so victimized. I never felt good enough. If I ever did say no or take care of myself with people, I felt so guilty. And, I felt angry and resentful, because my days and hours were consumed with doing things for people I felt I had to do, and people never seemed to appreciate what I did for them.

"I felt so bad about myself, I hoped that if I helped enough people, God would start treating me good. That's when it dawned on me that I needed to start treating myself good. God wasn't making me do all these things. God wasn't stopping the good from happening in my life. I was.

"I knew I needed, wanted, and deserved more from my sobriety than what I was getting. I came to understand that to get that 'more,' I had to begin addressing my codependency. It was time."

To use author Charlotte Kasl's phrase, Karen was constantly "giving more than she could afford" to others and not giving to herself—a codependent behavior that ultimately creates unmanageability. We can give more of ourselves than we can afford financially or emotionally. Any time our giving begins to get compulsive or is induced by feelings of guilt and obligation or leaves us feeling victimized, we are in danger. Any time we're uncomfortable with what we're doing because it goes against our own truth and what we want, we are in danger.

Consistently giving more than our share and not getting our needs met in relationships can create unmanageability.

After ending a relationship and staying away from love relationships for a while, Martha met Jack. He really charmed her one evening in the early days of their relationship when he drove her to the train station and carried her bags to the platform for her.

"No man had ever done anything like that for me in my life," she said. "It was love at first sight."

The problems began subtly and were hard to identify. Jack told her early on that once she got to know him, she wouldn't like him. Jack was right.

"He seemed to want to control my opinions and thinking," Martha said. "Whenever I voiced an opinion that was different than his, even if it was about a piece of art, he would argue with me until I gave in and agreed with him."

Whenever it came time to be close, Jack withdrew. He would have sexual relations with Martha, but he refused to spend the night with her. He would go for long periods without seeing her, then make a date, and at the last minute, cancel.

The relationship evolved into long conversations on each other's answering machines.

"My friends kept telling me this relationship was no good," Martha said, "but I had a hard time seeing it. I couldn't break loose. I got stuck, trapped in it. It caused me a lot of pain. My self-esteem dropped. I cried a lot and sat waiting by the phone. I stopped trusting myself."

Finally, Martha began attending meetings of CoDA. Soon she was able to terminate the relationship and begin taking care of herself. Martha learned that giving away her power and allowing herself to be victimized created unmanageability in her relationship and her life. She also began to look at and change some of the underlying reasons she had done this. (We will, too, in the chapters on the Fourth and Fifth Steps.)

OUR LIVES HAD BECOME UNMANAGEABLE

Our codependency, and our unmanageability, doesn't always surround addicts and alcoholics. Many of us discover that our efforts to control another's behavior extend beyond that of controlling one person's addiction. Many of us get caught up in overt, and subtle, gestures to control many people—what they do, think, feel, and how and when they change.

Many of us find ourselves trying to control others well into recovery. I have come to recognize that my need to control, or take care of another, is instinctive. It's my first reaction to people. It's no longer as obvious as it once was, but it's still there.

We can try to control people we love, people we work for, people who work for us, friends, enemies, relatives, children, neighbors, and even strangers.

Controlling and caretaking don't work. Codependency doesn't work. It makes us feel crazy. It makes us feel like people and circumstances are driving us crazy. Our lives become unmanageable. *Controlling and caretaking create unmanageability.*

And we don't see clearly *what* is going on *while* it is going on. It is as though we are in a fog.

This unmanageability can be external, internal, or both. We may become so enmeshed in other people and their issues, so focused on them and out of touch with ourselves, that we lose control of the external affairs in our life. Unmanageability may creep into our relationships, our spirituality, health, employment, recreational activities (or lack of them), home life, community involvement, and finances.

Our internal affairs—our feelings, thoughts, and reactions to others and ourselves—may become unmanageable. Depression, fear, anger, sadness, and a whirlwind of chaotic thoughts may overtake us. Or we may become so consumed with thoughts of another and with wondering what that person is feeling, that we lose touch with ourselves and our own thoughts and feelings.

Our mental energy, our minds, our intellects, may be in an unmanageable state, clouded by denial, fear, and attempts to control another. We may be caught in a torrent of obsessive thinking. Or, we may get stuck in negative thought patterns, patterns detrimental to our health and well-being.

We may neglect our careers and our creative gifts and talents.

Our financial affairs may be unmanageable. We may be overspending, or underspending and depriving ourselves.

We may deprive ourselves so badly our martyrdom and self-sacrifice create ongoing feelings of victimization. We may allow others to victimize us; we may victimize ourselves. We may subject ourselves unnecessarily to other people and their inappropriate, abusive, or out-of-control behaviors. We may feel victimized by our inability to set the boundaries we need to set.

Our behaviors may be out of control. The behaviors we use to control another may be as crazy as the behaviors of the person we're trying to control.

We may feel compelled to take care of others in a way that diminishes their ability to take responsibility for themselves. When we do this overtly, taking responsibility for the consequences of another's addictive behaviors, we feel angry and used. When we are covert caretakers, walking through life feeling responsible for the feelings and needs of others, we neglect our own feelings and needs.

Not saying no, not saying what we mean, not being in touch with what we want and need, not living our own lives, creates unmanageability.

We may become so controlled by the expectations and desires of others that we feel like puppets on a string with no lives of our own.

Some of us become trapped in unhealthy relationships, unable to extricate ourselves. Some of us become isolated, terrified of risking further involvement with people because we feel so unable to take care of ourselves in relationships and so frightened of being disappointed or hurt again.

If codependency goes untreated long enough, the results can be serious, even deadly. We may begin using alcohol or drugs to stop our pain. We may get caught up in other compulsive behaviors. We may develop physical illnesses from stress and from not dealing with our emotions. We may end up thinking about, or actually attempting, suicide.

Or, we may become terminally miserable, enduring life, getting through, waiting for our reward in heaven, not knowing that there is a reward each day in being alive and living our own lives.

Unmanageability can creep into our recoveries, no matter how long we've been recovering. It happens whenever we try to control something we cannot control. It happens when we allow our fear and panic to control us. It happens when we allow others' expectations, demands, agendas, problems, and addictions to control us.

It happens when we neglect our responsibility to take care of ourselves lovingly. It happens when we try to exert power where we have none, then continue trying ferociously, even though what we're doing isn't working. Whenever we try to have power where we have none, we forfeit our personal power. Our real power is to think, feel, make choices, live our own lives, and take care of ourselves.

Unmanageability occurs when we stop owning our power and start believing that we do not have choices about how we want to act, regardless of what another person is or isn't doing.

Perhaps the relationship most affected by our attempts to control or change what we cannot, is our relationship with ourselves. We become frustrated, confused, and often immersed in negativity, self-hatred, repression, and depression. We stop loving and caring about ourselves because we have cared about others too much or in ways that don't work for them, for us, or for the benefit of the relationship.

We may have developed a life pattern of self-neglect. If so, we can now learn how to take care of ourselves in a loving, gentle manner that feeds our soul and makes life worthwhile.

Many of us develop new definitions of unmanageability after we've been recovering for a while. We begin to expect more from our lives.

When I lose my peace and serenity, when I become excessively frightened, panicky, guilty, or ashamed, I consider my life unmanageable. When I stop dealing with my feelings, when I stop nurturing and caring for myself, when I stop listening to myself, when I get caught up in trying to control events and people, I consider my life unmanageable. The solution is to return to Step One.

So much of what we call codependency is simply human attempts to avoid, deny, or divert our pain. Taking this Step means we become ready to face and feel our pain. Be gentle with ourselves and others as we move from denial into the acceptance generated by this Step.

THE ROOTS OF CONTROL

The belief that we have power over other people is a powerful belief—a destructive illusion that many of us learned in childhood.

Listen to how some recovering people were trained to believe they had control over others.

"When I was in high school, my mother started the habit of trying to kill herself," said Marcia, a grown woman now recovering from codependency. "She kept trying to gas herself in the oven. I was terrified for her. Every day at school I'd call her between classes. When she didn't answer the phone, I knew she was doing it again. I'd race home, turn off the oven, air out the house, put Mother to bed, and race back to school.

"At a young age, I learned I had an enormous amount of power over people. I learned I had power over my mother's life or death."

A twist to this story is that Marcia's mother also believed she wielded power over Marcia's life. When Marcia was sixteen, her mother parked her car on the railroad tracks on Easter Sunday morning. Then, she waited for a train to hit her, which it did.

Marcia's mother escaped with only a few cuts and bruises, but she was committed to a mental institution for four years because of that suicide attempt. While Marcia's mother was in the hospital, she told Marcia that she wanted her (Marcia) to have a better life, so she was sending her to another city to live with her Uncle Charly.

"Later on, when I was in college, my mother got out of the hospital. She told me that she never intended me to live with Uncle Charly; she had wanted me to live with her *cousin* Charly. I laughed at the irony of control: to almost kill yourself so your child could have a better life, then find out that the child was sent to the wrong Charly and had a horrible life because of it," Marcia said.

Some of us were raised with more subtle, but equally powerful, illusions about control.

"From the time I was a young child, about three, my mother ingrained in me the idea that 'I made her miserable,' " said Jackie. "I grew up honestly believing that I had this power over her. I also came to believe that I held the power to make her happy. Then, I spent my life alternating between the two ideas: acting out to make her miserable or turning myself inside out to make her happy, which I never succeeded at. I felt guilty, trapped, and in bondage by both ideas.

"As an adult, I lived with this belief for years. And it wasn't just about my mother. It spread to everyone I had contact with. I really believed I had the power to make people miserable, make them happy, make them feel. It was a tremendous responsibility, an inaccurate one, and it kept me walking on eggshells and feeling crazy most of my adult life, until I began recovering from codependency. I turned myself inside out to control how others felt or to avoid making them feel a certain way. I got so I hated to be around people, because controlling their feelings felt like such a big, tiresome job. I couldn't relax and enjoy being with people. My energy was out there—trying to make them feel, trying to control them. And I was out of touch with what I was feeling.

"I didn't know it was okay to have feelings," said Jackie.

Many of us grew up believing it wasn't okay to have feelings. That was part of the control we were taught to have—repression of our emotions. Now we are learning that whatever we try to control gains control of us. If we try to control our feelings in an unhealthy way—which many of us were taught to do and learned to do to survive—our feelings will gain control of us and create unmanageability.

"From the time I was old enough to listen, I was told not to feel," said Jackie. "It didn't take me long to begin telling myself that. I was told to stand tall, sit straight, and ignore my feelings.

"Actually, this advice was helpful. I lived in a cold, sterile environment. I received no nurturing and little love. From the time I was born, the people I expected to love me, disappointed me. I wasn't hugged. I wasn't told I was beautiful. I wasn't allowed to be afraid, to be angry, and of course, I didn't feel joy. I was told to be more, be better, try harder, and be stronger. Be in control.

"I learned that no situation merited falling apart or indulging in feelings. Feelings were a waste of time, a childish, weak, human, unnecessary display.

"By not feeling, I survived in this family. I survived life. And in short order, I learned to treat myself as I had been treated— neglecting, avoiding, criticizing, demeaning, and berating myself for having feelings and needs, for being human.

"Shutting off this part of myself made me strong, stronger than I knew. It helped me endure and survive the fact that my needs weren't being met. But my feelings, needs, and humanness caught up with me. That part of me refused to be ignored any longer.

"Now I've been recovering for a while. As I look back, I can see that although I didn't feel my feelings—*because* I didn't feel them—they, and my unmet needs, controlled me. They drove me, they propelled me. I lived in fear, and my response to that fear was to try to control everyone and everything around me."

Fear is the undercurrent, the force, for much of what we do that we call control—control of others, ourselves, situations, circumstances, and timing.

"In this past year of attending CoDA," said Jane, "I got to see how terrified I've been all of my life. All that time, I've lived through fear."

Sometimes, this fear is expressed as anger.

"I've been alone, disconnected from people most of my life," said Brad, whose father is an alcoholic. "I was always lonely, stressed out, stretching too much. I couldn't make a relationship work. I think I was really angry for most of my life before recovery. Anger was my source of life energy. I didn't *get angry*. But it was an underflow that ran my life."

For some, this undercurrent escalates into panic, sometimes terror—of life, people, circumstances, ourselves, and our feelings. We don't know how to relax and detach. Some of us aren't aware of how afraid we are. I can now see how much fear I lived with for most of my childhood and adult life. I didn't see or feel it at the time, but it controlled most of my actions.

What I did was focus on others: caretaking, controlling, and obsessing about them. What I didn't do was take care of myself in a loving manner.

Step One gives us permission to relax, stop controlling, deal with our fear, and take care of ourselves.

Not being able to take care of ourselves with people gives them control over us. Just as many of us have learned well how to try to control others, we have also learned to allow them to control us.

"I was raised with the belief that I would be killed if I said no," said Marcia, who talked earlier about rescuing her mother from suicide attempts. "I was raised Catholic. I was taught to honor my father and mother. And a great deal of fear was instilled in me about ever telling anyone no. From television, I learned that you follow people around and do for them. I learned the concept 'Love thy neighbor and forget thyself.' I learned that if I did what was expected of me, I would be loved and taken care of."

Sherri explains her version of codependency: "I believe much of what I call codependency in my life is a result of feeling frightened, trapped, and stuck in relationships because I don't know how to take care of myself with people."

When we love others too much, when we so desperately want and need what they have—whether that is acceptance, approval, love, or friendship—we may forfeit our ability to take care of ourselves with them, out of fear that we may not get what we need. We may hope that if we hold things in place by willpower, we will finally be safe and get what we need.

We won't.

These ideas are illusions. We aren't defective. Most of us have simply been doing what we learned, sometimes at a young age: protecting ourselves by trying to control others or by allowing others to control us. We grow up to be caretaking, controlling adults who have lost touch with a true and appropriate goal: loving and accepting ourselves and trusting the flow of life and goodness.

We grow up to do codependent behaviors.

It may be normal to want to control people and events and cut our losses, but it is not necessarily healthy. It's not good for us; it's not good for others.

And we may be so shut off from ourselves that we barely notice until life comes tumbling down around us. Our lives become unmanageable.

The First Step gives us permission to stop controlling and taking care of others and begin taking care of ourselves.

"I was angry when I started attending Al-Anon and people told me I needed to start taking care of myself," said Joannie. "I had been taking care of myself and everyone around me all my life!"

That's not the kind of self-care we're talking about in recovery. The kind of self-care that accompanies recovery and these Steps is gentler, more loving, more freeing, and more focused on tending to our own responsibilities. It's a healing, rejuvenating, renewing kind of self-care, one with room for feelings, needs, wants, desires, goals, plans, and lives of our own—lives with meaning and purpose, ones that make sense.

ACCEPTING POWERLESSNESS

Some of us have an easy time accepting the premise in this Step: that we are powerless over others. By the time we get to this Step, we're ready to give up and give in. Others have a struggle accepting powerlessness.

I love this Step. But I hate that I can't control. I hate being vulnerable and helpless. I don't like feeling uncomfortable or being in emotional pain. I get sick of having to detach and surrender. But the love affair with this Step comes in when I admit the truth. I am powerless over much in life, and when I try to have power where I have none, I get crazy. I can't control others, no matter how much I want to, no matter how much better I think I know what's right for them.

I can't control what others do, think, or feel, whether or how they choose to interact with me, whether or when they choose to grow and change, and whether or when they choose to recover from their addictions.

Sometimes I can't control myself.

I'm powerless over the backlog of feelings and negative beliefs I've accumulated. I'm powerless over my own and other people's addictions, including addictions to alcohol and misery. I can't control my children or other people's children. I'm powerless over results, life, circumstances, events. I can't control the course of relationships. I can't control timing.

God, I wish I could control timing.

But I can't.

When I try to control myself by rigidly repressing my thoughts and feelings, I lose myself. I fall deeper into the pit of myself and the morass of codependency.

When I try to control other people, I make them and myself crazy. When I try to control addictions, the addictions control me. When I try to control what others think of me, I turn into a puppet on strings. Controlling makes me and others crazy. It puts me under the control of whatever I'm trying to influence. I lose myself. I lose touch with myself.

And other people get angry with me and tend to back off.

When I try to control situations and circumstances, I set up blocks to events moving forward. When I spend my time and energy trying to have power when I have none, I lose my ability to live my own life.

Controlling sets up a peculiar energy. People can feel it—even if we're just thinking about it and not acting on it. People react to it—sometimes by deliberately doing what we are trying to make them stop doing, or not doing what we are trying to make them do. It's an energy controlled by fear.

It's natural to want to control others, especially when they're hurting themselves or us, or when things aren't working out to our liking. But it isn't our job to take care of others—to take care of their feelings, thoughts, decisions, growth, and responsibilities. It is our job to do that for ourselves.

Step One does not imply irresponsibility or helplessness. We are not saying, "I can't help myself because of what others are doing or have done to me." We are saying the opposite: that we are responsible for ourselves and our affairs. Others are responsible for themselves and their affairs—whether or not we like how they are handling them.

We are responsible for ourselves, for directing our life energy toward our path, for creating a wholesome, fulfilling life for ourselves. When we become open to allowing that to happen, then it will.

We are responsible for stopping our own pain, facing and dealing with our own fears, saying no, giving ourselves what we need, setting boundaries we need to set, and making choices and decisions we need to make to take care of ourselves—in any circumstance or situation.

We are not victims.

When we accept powerlessness, we will become empowered to take care of ourselves. When we begin taking care of ourselves, we will begin living our lives, and all that is meant to come to us will be ours. When we stop controlling others, we can allow and trust them to live their lives.

This Step grounds us in reality and in ourselves. It centers us. It balances us. It brings us back home to ourselves.

When we stop controlling, things fall into place. And we find that our place in this world is a good place. Eventually, we become grateful for the way things work out because it's better than what we could have accomplished with our controlling behavior.

We are powerless over so much more than anyone taught us. Accepting that means we're free to own our true power in life, which is also so much more than anyone told us. We have power to think, feel, solve problems, set boundaries, set and reach goals, create, heal, take care of and love ourselves unconditionally, and love those around us unconditionally.

What am I powerless over? Almost everything I want to control.

THE DETACHMENT STEP

The First Step is the Step that helps us begin detaching—a recovery concept that means we release and detach from others—lovingly, whenever possible.

This Step helps us begin to identify the proper use and abuse of willpower. We begin feeling instead of running from our emotions. We identify how we have neglected ourselves, so we may better love ourselves in any circumstance.

It is the first step toward removing ourselves as victims—of others, of ourselves, of life.

This is the Detachment Step.

This Step is about boundaries. We learn the limits and extent of ourselves and our responsibilities. We learn to identify what we can and cannot do. We learn to identify when we're trying to do the impossible or trying to do that which is not our job.

Then, we stop doing the impossible and focus our attention on the possible—living our own lives, taking care of ourselves, feeling and responding appropriately to our feelings. We can love ourselves and others without feeling the overwhelming need to control and manipulate them and their situations to our liking.

Often, this Step puts us in touch with our feelings—feelings of fear, hurt, or shame. It puts us in touch with grief. At first, this Step can feel dark and frightening. It doesn't have to, not for long. It renders us powerless over what we cannot control, so we can become empowered. Once we accept whatever loss or area of powerlessness we're facing, we're free to feel and deal with our feelings, then move forward with life.

We'll take this Step when we're ready. When we're worn out, when we've exerted all our attempts to manage and control, when we're tired of feeling crazy and fighting battles we cannot win, we'll surrender. When it's time, this Step will find us and do its work.

Let it. Let it bring us home. Let it take the burden of controlling and feeling so responsible for others off our backs. Let the peace, relief, and comfort of this Step sink in.

Detach. Detach from the fear. Detach from the need to control. Focus on ourselves, and let ourselves be. Stop trying so hard and doing so much, when doing so much doesn't work.

Love and accept ourselves, as is, no matter what our present circumstances. The answer will come. The solution will come. But not from trying so hard.

The answer will come from detachment.

We are powerless over others, and our lives have become unmanageable. And for now, that's all we need to be. That's who we are, and it's good enough.

Become sensitive to feelings of powerlessness and unmanageability. Become sensitive to what it feels like—on the overt and the more subtle levels.

Take this Step in the beginning of recovery. Then take it again as needed. Take it whenever the codependent crazies set in. Take it whenever we believe that things are out of control and our lives are a mistake. Take it when we find ourselves taking care of others and wondering if we have a right to take care of ourselves. Take it when we start ignoring our feelings. Take it when we start obsessing about others or worrying about our future or the future of another. Take it when we start believing others control our happiness.

Take it when we neglect ourselves.

Take it when we get stuck.

When we don't know what to do next, we can take this Step.

Think about it. Let it sink in. Let it define us, and our present and past circumstances. Let it heal, help, and comfort. It always brings us home—to ourselves, to reality, and to mastering the spiritual lesson in our current circumstances.

The first word in this First Step is *we*. Self-acceptance, based on this simple definition of ourselves, feels good. We are not alone, not anymore. There are many of us practicing this Step daily. There are many of us who share the problem. We may have felt alone, but we are not unique in our pain or our dilemma. Neither are we isolated in our solution. There is power in the community of recovery, power in taking this Step in the privacy of our own homes, and in group settings with others. We come together in this Step, as a "we," to share our common problem and solution. The sharing in community makes the problem grow smaller and the solution more imminent.

There is a place I get to in my relationships with people, and life, that is dark and ineffective. It is a place ruled by fear and an instinctive desire to control.

I have done it overtly—trying to control an alcoholic's drinking by focusing my life around that person.

I have done it quietly—trying to control and repress my feelings, trying to control a particular situation, ferreting into myself until I barely existed, repeating unsuccessful similar efforts to solve a problem, or pretending a particular problem doesn't exist. I get to that dark place when I allow others to control me or when I allow negative beliefs or unresolved feelings from my past to control me.

I get to that place when I don't do what I need to do to take care of myself with people, because I am afraid to do so.

This Step takes me out of that dark place. It helps me remember who I am. I can't control others, and I get crazy when I try to. I don't have to control others. I don't have to take care of them. I don't have to control life, or situations, for life to work.

It is safe now to trust. It is safe now to detach. I can accept myself, my problems, my current situation, and all my unmanageability. I can detach, because holding on so tightly doesn't work. I relax and just be me. And I can love, accept, and take care of myself.

The first time I took this Step on my codependency issues, when it really sank down from my head to my soul, it brought freedom and the gift of detachment. For the first time, I understood, in my heart, that I could not control another. This Step brought relief and the ability to begin tending to the affairs of my own life.

This Step still brings relief, each time I take it.

This Step gives us permission to be who we are. This is the

Step where we accept ourselves, our powerlessness, and our present circumstances, in peace, grace, and trust that all is, and will be, well.

We surrender. Then we watch as manageability sets in.

This Step takes us to a safe place, a comfortable place. Let ourselves go there, as often as we need to. We can trade in lives based on fear, control, and shame for lives that are manageable.

Each Step has its own work to do in our lives. Each Step is important.

The work, the healing, begins with the First.

ACTIVITIES

1. Have you been trying to exert power or influence where you may, in reality, have none? Have you been trying to control someone or something, trying harder and harder with less and less beneficial results?

2. Who or what in your life is making you feel crazy and causing you stress? Whom do you feel victimized by? Who do you feel is now controlling you, your emotions, or some other area of your life? What situations, feelings, or realities have you been running from, denying, or avoiding?

3. What would you have to face in your own life if you stopped trying to control someone or something? What might happen if you stopped allowing someone or something to control you?

4. What are some areas in your life that may reflect unmanageability? What is your current condition in these areas: emotions, finances, spirituality, physical health, career? What are you doing for fun, pleasure, and enjoyment?

5. What is the current state of your relationships with these people: family, friends, co-workers. Do you have any relationships, or are you feeling alone and isolated?

6. Does your mind feel clear and consistent? Who are you holding responsible for your emotions, finances, and health? Who are you holding responsible for the state of your relationships?

7. What are you doing in your life that you feel resentful about? What do you feel you have to do but don't want to? In what areas of your life do you feel you have no choices, no options? Who or what is trapping you? Whom do you most want to say something to? Why do you feel you can't say it?

8. What is the particular incident that propelled you to begin attending a Twelve Step group? If attending for a time, what is the issue that has been plaguing you most recently? Who or what are you most worried about? When was the last time you did something loving and nurturing for yourself? Is there someone in your life that you feel is causing you misery? Do you feel that if he or she behaved differently, you would be happy?

STEP TWO

"CAME TO BELIEVE THAT A POWER GREATER THAN OUR-SELVES COULD RESTORE US TO SANITY."
—Step Two of CoDA

I love the Second Step. When I began recovery from code-pendency, I was devastated by the behavior of people around me. I had abandoned my own life and myself. The things I was doing to make people "see the light" were insane.

I was out of control.

After I surrendered to the First Step by accepting and admit-ting my powerlessness and unmanageability, the Second Step brought fresh air and hope.

Now I've been recovering for a while, but I still love this Step. On those days when I forget what I know about recovery, when my mind whirls, when shame returns, when anger, resentment, or old messages begin controlling me, when I forget it's okay to be who I am and that it's okay to own my power, when I panic or become fearful, when I start obsessively looking to others to make me feel or make me real, I know what to do.

I go back to the First Step to get my bearings and remember who I am. Then I go on to the Second Step to become all I'm capable of becoming.

The Second Step puts us on track—a new track—a course that holds more power and direction than we have on our own. It is the transition Step. It takes us from where we are to where we want to go.

All we are asked to do now is believe. In fact, all we are asked to do is "come to believe." We do that by opening our minds and hearts and connecting with other recovering people.

RESTORED TO SANITY

Sarah is a striking woman who dresses colorfully and speaks with a strong East Coast accent. Six years ago her life and relationships were out of control. Today she has a good relationship with herself and is director of a codependency treatment program.

Sarah began her recovery journey sixteen years ago by attending Twelve Step meetings of Overeaters Anonymous. Although she worked hard at that recovery program, something was missing in her life.

"I came in as an overeater, then picked up bulimia and anorexia. I became a sex addict, a relationship addict, and a pill addict," Sarah said.

"I lost my excess weight. I looked good. But I felt empty, as I had many times before. I thought that emptiness had something to do with things outside of myself. My husband was an alcoholic. My friends in Overeaters Anonymous said I had the best of both worlds: I was married and I was also out there having affairs with vulnerable men in the program. I felt empty, lonely, ashamed, and guilty. But I didn't know then what shame and guilt were. I now call it the 'hole in the soul complex,' " Sarah said.

Seven years later, the first crash came in Sarah's life. She was placing her mother in a nursing home and preparing to ask her husband for a divorce because she was having a "hot-and-heavy affair." The night she was going to ask him for a divorce, she had a heart attack on the dance floor. She promised God that if God helped her live through this, she would make some changes in her life.

Sarah did make some changes. She stayed with her husband and went on to become addicted to alcohol, sleeping pills, and Xanax, the tranquilizer her doctor prescribed to help her heart condition. Before long, she began having affairs again.

"I was still attending Overeaters Anonymous," Sarah said. "I used pills, food, and alcohol, and I was silently screaming for help in the O.A. meetings. People thought I was doing so well. I wouldn't divulge exactly what was going on in my life, but I would get up at meetings and say, 'I'm hurting; there are problems in my life; pinch me; I'm real; I hurt.' I think people were frightened about what was happening to me. They didn't want to think I could be recovering that long and still have problems. They didn't know what to say to me."

Then Sarah attended school to be an alcoholism and drug recovery counselor. She separated from her husband and had an affair with one of the patients. When he was discharged, he moved in with her. He was black; Sarah was white—a fact she said further isolated her from people. Soon her boyfriend began using cocaine again.

"It was insane," Sarah said. "I was totally codependent, trying to save him and fix him. By the time I finished school to be an alcoholism counselor, I was drinking and using pills heavily. My boyfriend had been through two more treatment centers and was still using drugs."

Sarah then checked herself into treatment for alcoholism and relationship addiction. After finishing treatment, she went to work at a treatment center for eating disorders, renewed her relationship with her cocaine-addict boyfriend, and brought him to live with her in the southern town where she worked.

"Here we are. I'm Jewish and white, from the North living with a black man in a Southern town. I knew I had three strikes against me when I moved down there, but I said I was going to make it, no matter what. I did make it, but I got caught up in the relationship again. My boyfriend kept relapsing. I was working at the treatment center. I was clean, but not from the crazy relationship.

"There was physical and sexual abuse in the relationship, but I was the perpetrator," Sarah said. "I was so full of rage and anger that each time he went into his crazy behavior, I'd go at him in such rage that it terrified me. I'd claw him and pull his shirt off. The only way he could stop me was by picking me up and holding me on the bed. In my insanity, I'd free myself from his hold. Then, I'd call the police on *him.* The police would take him away. And I'd take him back."

Finally, Sarah checked herself into a codependency treatment center.

"The thing that got to me was the thought that I could purposefully hurt another human being," Sarah said. "It was terrifying. I saw my mother in me, but I was worse than my mother. And I had always said, "Dear God, don't ever let me be like her.""

After codependency treatment, Sarah began attending CoDA meetings and started private therapy sessions.

"If it wasn't for the Twelve Step program, I'd probably be dead today," Sarah said. "Insane, if not dead. I've made my amends for the rage I showed toward my ex-boyfriend, and he truly is an ex now. I'm not in a relationship and haven't been, but I believe I could have a healthy relationship with someone today because I have a healthy relationship with myself.

"I've established good relationships with my children and made amends to them. They haven't changed, but I have. I see them differently.

"I've opened my own center for codependency treatment because I see it as the prevention for relapse of other addictions. I believe that I was codependent long before I was any of the other things," Sarah said.

"I know that I, and nobody else, am responsible for what I think and feel. I believe in me and what I'm doing today. If I believe in me, then I can believe in what I'm doing. I used to seek validation from everybody and everything. I'd go to ten people and ask them if what was going on with me was okay. Today I don't need to do that. I trust myself.

"I know I am enough."

Sarah is one person whose life has been transformed by working the Twelve Steps on her codependency. She has been restored to sanity. Although the details of our insanity and how we define being restored to sanity vary, there are millions, like Sarah, who have taken this Step and have seen its power to work.

After five years of working at his Twelve Step program of recovery, Craig has been transformed from a frightened, angry, insecure man to a confident, peaceful, relaxed man. Craig is an adult child of an alcoholic and is also an incest victim. He is now able to express feelings. He has close friends. His biggest complaint before recovery was feeling isolated and disconnected from people. That is also the area in his life where he feels he has been restored to sanity.

Although we share codependency issues, each of us has a personal version of how codependency manifested itself in our lives and what being restored to sanity means.

Ten years ago, Jane was on the verge of emotional collapse. Her father was an alcoholic, but no one in the family, including her father or herself, had identified his problem as alcoholism.

Jane was chronically depressed, crying or on the verge of tears most of the time. She overate, withdrew from people, and couldn't bring herself to look for work or hold a job. She spent years living a hand-to-mouth existence in an efficiency apartment, believing she deserved no better.

"I felt afraid constantly, but I didn't know that's what I was feeling," Jane said. "My fear expressed itself more as 'I don't want; I don't want; I don't want.' Nothing interested me. I didn't think about suicide, but I hated where I was in life. I felt that my life would never change.

"I kept wanting to go completely crazy. I never did, but I thought it would feel good because then I could express all the stuff inside me. I didn't know that's exactly what I needed to do."

Then Jane began attending Twelve Step meetings. First she attended Overeaters Anonymous; group members soon suggested she needed Al-Anon. At first, Jane didn't understand why people thought she needed Al-Anon. She didn't understand what being codependent meant.

Now, ten years later, Jane's life has changed. And she understands.

"I feel at home. I feel safe at my groups and with myself," said Jane. "It was hard. It was a struggle. But slowly, my hope came back. My 'wanting' for life and myself came back."

Jane obtained a master's degree and works full-time for a government agency. She has a nice home, a car, and herself back. Her beliefs about what she deserves from work, relationships, and life have changed. Although she is still struggling with relationships, she has finally found the courage to participate in one and works toward getting her needs met. She has a support system and feels connected to people and herself.

"The biggest thing the Twelve Steps have done is put me in

conscious contact with the empowerment, the freedom, and the goodness of my own life. The hardest thing for me to grasp is that I'm not in control of others—how they feel, what they do, and how they respond to me. I'm learning what it means to love and care about someone I have no control over. I want people to be like me, so I can feel safer, acknowledged, and affirmed. To me, recovery is about feeling safe with myself.

"By keeping open to the Steps and figuring out what they mean to me, surprises are revealed to me. The Twelve Steps have been a structure, a container. Not a container that binds me, but one that allows me to feel safe while I discover the various mysteries in life."

Dan is a minister. His codependency issues centered around not being able to express anger in his marriage, not setting limits with clients, and not seeing the good in himself.

"I attracted sick and needy people," Dan said. "I was a wonderful listener who couldn't set limits with people. They just lopped onto me."

Dan's idea of being restored to sanity was learning balance: expressing his anger appropriately, without becoming either enraged or passive; balancing listening, which he considers a gift, with the ability to assert himself; and noticing his gifts and strengths as well as his faults.

"The Steps help me be more in touch with who I am, what I want, and what I need," said Dan.

"Crazy things still happen to me," Dan said, "but I'm learning to respond sanely. My recovery program continually reminds me that life is good. It surprises me with goodness and change. I've seen some people much more wounded and bruised than I am, making amazing progress in their recoveries. It gives me a lot of hope for my own recovery."

Not only do we each have our own ideas of what it means to be restored to sanity but these ideas may change as we change. In the beginning of recovery, I needed to be restored from chasing alcoholics around, trying to make them stop drinking, to the sanity of living my own life. I needed to be restored from continual self-neglect to learning to pay daily, loving attention to myself and my needs. I needed to be restored from believing I had to, and could, control others to a place of letting go of others and allowing life to unfold.

Sometimes I need to be restored from shame, fear, and suppressed feelings to peace, confidence, and good feelings about myself. Sometimes I need to be restored from negative, hopeless thoughts to a positive, hopeful outlook.

Sometimes I get stuck and need help extricating myself. Or, I get obsessed and need my mind and soul back. Sometimes I revert to believing that others hold the key to my happiness and destiny, and then I need help remembering that I possess that key. Other times my insanity means I hold back, cowering within myself. I need my fears healed so that I can live life, be fully alive, and trust the flow.

My idea of being restored to sanity centers around owning my power in relationships—learning how not to let others have all the power, learning not to allow others to control me, no matter how healthy or well intentioned the people I'm dealing with. To me, sanity is when I am at peace with myself and take care of myself with others, instead of taking care of them.

Living with insanity or allowing others to treat us badly, living life as victims, is insane. Living in denial, telling ourselves other people are fine—people who are abusing us and treating us poorly—telling ourselves that there is something wrong with us for not liking this abuse, is insane.

Believing that we deserve so little from life is insane.

Believing that we have to do it alone, whatever *it* is, is unnecessary.

Many of us find that as our recovery progresses, our definition of sanity changes. Initially, many of us come to recovery thinking that it is reasonable to repress our feelings, dislike ourselves, stay immersed in shame, and feel trapped and hopeless. We may come to recovery thinking it normal that people endure being alive and slog through a miserable form of existence. We may think it normal to deny and deprive ourselves. We may think expecting perfectionism of ourselves is reasonable!

We may look upon victimization as a normal day-to-day event, a reasonable reaction to most of life's circumstances.

But this viewpoint changes for many of us when we begin to identify those past behaviors as codependent.

Later, we may look upon any return to the unpleasant and negative thought patterns and emotions that accompany codependency as undesirable, and a reason to use this Step. We do not blame ourselves or expect to be free of tangles. Tangles can be beneficial and growth-producing. We do not look upon emotions as insanity, but rather as healthy expressions of healthy living. But most of us prefer to stay balanced. In fact, feeling good—and for us that means feeling all our emotions—eventually begins to feel good.

Some of us are looking for more from this Step and from recovery as a whole than being restored. Many of us feel that we have never experienced the kind of life we want for ourselves. We feel we are beginning for the first time to develop a manner of loving and living that is healthy.

This program can do that for us. It can restore us if we are seeking restoration. It can also make us new.

CAME TO BELIEVE

We do not begin by believing a Power greater than ourselves can restore us to sanity. We work into it. We grow into our belief. We *come to believe.*

"I wasn't alive when I started attending Al-Anon," said Margaret. "I was emotionally and spiritually dead. I didn't know how I felt. I was abusive, and I was being abused. A friend introduced me to Al-Anon. I found many bones to pick with the Twelve Step program. But I found something to hang on to, so I kept coming to meetings because of Step Two. I didn't believe. And I needed to be restored to sanity. I felt insane. I wanted to be healed and restored, so I faked it and kept coming until I believed, until the restoration began."

Many of us find that we come to believe by seeing other people with problems similar to ours restored to sanity as a result of working these Steps. For us, seeing is believing.

And coming to meetings is how we come to believe.

"I learned how to let go by watching others who were dealing with the same type of problems and noticing that they looked okay. They were doing something to deal with it better. I drew strength from their strength," said Stanley, the architect whose life had been controlled by an addicted son for sixteen years.

I didn't know there was any other way to react, to live life, or to feel until I began listening to other people who had been recovering from codependency. I saw others with similar circumstances, behaving in a sane manner, looking happy and healthy. When I saw it, I could believe it. Initially, all I could do was believe it had worked for them. Slowly, I came to believe that recovery could work for me. I believed because I saw other people; then I believed because I began to see small changes in myself.

Seeing other people change, seeing the Steps work in their lives, seeing their lives restored to manageability, peace, and joy, is how we come to believe that it is possible for us. Sometimes listening to stories of how others have been changed in major ways helps us. Sometimes listening to the smaller words of wisdom, the daily examples of how others are learning to take care of themselves and live life differently, can be just as important.

We get our messages in many ways.

Many of us have little difficulty working this Step, once we begin attending meetings. It is difficult *not* to come to believe if we listen and watch.

It was revolutionary to me that people could actually behave differently from the ways I had. I thought I had to control. I felt trapped in my depression. This Step was a step out of my darkness and my codependency. It was my Step into healing and learning I had choices.

Perhaps the greatest offering of this Step is that no matter what we want and need done in our lives, we do not have to do it by ourselves. We don't have to use our will to change ourselves. For once, we don't have to try so hard.

We can turn to a Power greater than ourselves.

A POWER GREATER THAN OURSELVES

We don't have to begin with a complex understanding of a Power greater than ourselves. We don't have to begin with detailed ideas about what we want accomplished in our lives and how that should happen.

We don't even have to know what we're going to be doing tomorrow.

We can start where we are, with whatever amount of belief or disbelief we have at the moment. We start by believing that we can and will be restored to sanity—whether that restoration is a brief event, such as handling a momentary feeling, or a larger event, such as the restoration we need when we begin recovery or go through a traumatic experience.

We open ourselves to the help, loving care, guidance, and power of God. We come to believe we will be healed and that the tools we need to be healed will come into our lives. Our faith is not misplaced when we come to believe that recovery will work for us.

God was inserted into this program of recovery because God is fundamental to recovery and fundamental to the psychic and soul-level change and healing we're seeking. We do certain things to change, but essentially, we *are changed*. It is a spiritual process.

The decision to refer to God as a "Power greater than ourselves" and to allow people to develop their own understanding of this power was intentional.

This program is spiritual, not religious. The Steps were written to be compatible with all religious and denominational beliefs. They were also intended to be accessible to those without religious or denominational beliefs.

Many of us come to recovery with contorted, fearful, and sometimes rigid and shame-based understandings of God. We may fear God. We may fear that God despises us or has abandoned us. We may have had unpleasant dealings with certain religious denominations. Some people come to this program because a religious system had the same destructive impact on them as a dysfunctional family system.

Great care must be taken to allow individuals the freedom to explore and determine their own spiritual beliefs.

Because of the great amount of physical and sexual abuse that many of us have suffered, some Twelve Step programs have removed any gender reference to God. Some people don't want to identify God as a male-gender Being; some don't want to refer to God as a female-gender Being. Some don't want to call God "Father," because of the abuse suffered at the hands of an earthly father.

Some of us are comfortable embracing a traditional concept of God. That's fine, too.

These Steps allow us each to get our needs met by a God of our understanding. We can come to these Steps with our fears, prejudices, needs, and desires, and still find recovery.

It is not our job to impose any religious, denominational, or spiritual beliefs on another human being. Nor do we need to accept another's beliefs.

"These steps were so confusing to me in the beginning," said Tim, who attends Adult Children of Alcoholics meetings. "I kept telling myself, 'I don't get it. I don't get it. I don't get it.' Now, I'm beginning to connect spiritually with these Steps. I've learned that parents are representative of God, and my parents were so dysfunctional that I had said, 'To hell with God.' Now, I'm using these Steps to redo God in my life."

Struggle with the Higher Power concept. Struggle all you need to. Most of us have.

Struggle until you find your Higher Power and know your God cares about the largest and most minute details of your life.

When we take this Step, we begin to learn through personal experience. Then, others come to believe through our example of how we have been healed and helped. This program is a never-ending chain of healing.

By believing and staying open to this healing process, we will become changed, in a natural, manageable fashion.

This is the most exciting part of recovery for me. It's also a part I need to remember. I don't have to force or control my recovery. I can do my best to work the Steps and peacefully allow change to happen.

We can use this Step to help us get through difficult situations around us, within us, or both.

We can use this Step to help us come to believe that we can develop a sane, loving approach to ourselves, life, and others—no matter what our past or present circumstances. This Step means we no longer have to limit our futures by our pasts.

THE HOPE STEP

Once upon a time, I found myself in treatment for chemical-dependency issues. My life was a mess; I was a mess. When I finally faced and accepted that fact, despair overwhelmed me.

Years later, I found myself facing my codependency. Again, my life was unmanageable. I was depressed and embroiled in rage and self-hatred. I was consumed with thoughts of controlling others. The idea of focusing on myself and my own issues was foreign to me. It made no sense at all. After spending years denying reality, I finally began to see, admit, and accept the truth: I had lived with and around crazy people so long I had become one of them. My illusion of moral superiority was becoming more difficult to maintain. In spite of momentary bursts of feeling more sane than those around me, in truth I suspected I was crazy, too.

Both times—in both those periods of absolute despair that had been created by accepting reality—this Second Step gave me hope and light.

Both times this Step occurred to me. It happened to me through no effort of my own. When I was about to begin recovery from chemical dependency, a person came to me who had problems similar to mine and had been restored to sobriety and sanity. I recall thinking that it was possible. It could happen. It had happened to her. Maybe it could happen to me.

When I began recovering from codependency, *people* brought me the message of this Step. I was in a group of recovering people, and although I was in a crabby, distressed state, I saw out of the corner of my eye cheerful, peaceful people who looked healthy and happy, even though they had lived through similar or worse circumstances than mine. A small part of me registered this. *It is possible,* I thought. Those people are handling the same situation I'm facing, only they're handling it differently. Maybe that could happen for me.

Now I come joyfully to this Step, when I have the presence of mind to remember to practice it. And for me, practicing it means simply thinking about it. I let it pass through my mind and give it whatever degree of validity I can at the moment.

I use it when old, negative beliefs and fears begin to control my life.

I use it when I get tangled up in my shame and self-hatred and begin seeking a way to tunnel into the dark recesses of myself. I use it when I get absorbed in other people and their issues—what they're doing or not doing, and how angry or hurt that makes me feel.

I have learned to accept my anger and hurt, but dwelling on them to the point of losing focus with myself, dwelling on them to the point of obsession, dwelling on others to the degree that I lose my balance and my thoughts are not my own, can be a form of insanity in my life.

I no longer want to lose my balance, at least not for long.

I take this Step. I think about it for a moment. After identifying that my life has again become unmanageable, on whatever level, this Step still brings me hope. It tells me I can and will be restored to sanity.

It tells me I do not and cannot restore myself. I love to control and manage—not because I am bad and defective, but because I am protective and feel so afraid of letting go—but I can't restore myself. I must muster enough faith and humility to trust that a Power greater than myself can and will do this for me.

I have learned that this faith is well placed, far better placed than looking to my own resources.

There is a gentleness, a harmonic flow that sweeps me up after I take this Step. It sweeps me into a way out of my confusion, even when I cannot see that way.

It takes me out of my internal chaos and my stubborn insistence that I must continue in the old way, even though that way is destroying my spirit.

It opens me to a better way.

When I tire of efforts that do not work, when I am hopeless, when I am tangled up in unmanageability or compulsive efforts to control something that I cannot, then I become ready to take this Step. I become ready to accept and admit the truth: that I am powerless. Things appear unmanageable—either in work, family relationships, love, finances, or any area of my life. And it's time to come to believe. It's time to turn to a Power greater than myself for help.

I have been using this Step for seventeen years now. It has never failed to work for me. In fact, I'm not certain that I turn to this Step. Often, it turns to me. It settles into my awareness like a gift, a way out of my chaos—like a loving Father saying: "Child, would you like to try this? It might help you feel better."

The thought comes gently, sometimes in the form of, "Why don't I get myself to a meeting?" Sometimes it appears as a friend calling, gently talking about the program. Sometimes I pick up the phone and call someone. Sometimes it is a personal affair between that Power and me.

A tremendous battle takes place within me on a regular basis. That battle is between the part of me that insists that if I try harder, I can control things and extricate myself from any mess, and the part of me that knows there is a Higher Way, a Way that will lift me to levels of thinking, feeling, and behaving beyond what I could accomplish on my own.

This Step works whenever I turn to it, whenever I let it. And sometimes when I don't turn to it, it finds me anyway.

Breathe deeply. Believe that a Power greater than ourselves can restore us to sanity. Be grounded on that new level. By believing, we create the space for that to happen. We stop empowering the problem and begin to empower the solution, one that will be given to us.

Do not worry about how it will happen. Do not worry about when it will happen. All we need will be given to us, done for us. We are in the process of becoming changed. All we need to do is believe.

Most of us find we don't have to work too hard at this Step. Coming to believe is a gift. It will be given to us when we are ready for it, and we will receive as much belief as we can handle as we are ready.

We are asked to have faith—not forever, but for one day. At times, we may need to take it one hour at a time. We believe that all is well, that all will be well, that things in the universe are on track, and we are right where we need to be, for the moment.

The transformation will take on a life of its own if we let it.

Take care not to confuse unmanageability or insanity with the deep grief many of us experience when we come to this program. Many of us are facing losses and feel pain about these losses. This pain, this grief, is a healthy, normal response to our circumstances. We can allow ourselves to go through it without making ourselves miserable by blaming ourselves for grieving.

The purpose of this program is to help us develop a sane, spiritual approach to any life situation—whether that means addressing insane or objectionable behavior in those around us or in ourselves; getting through unpleasant or painful situations; dealing with loss or change; functioning within the realm of normal situations; or creating a better "normal" for ourselves. This program can assist us in breaking off our unhealthy ties with others. It can teach us to have healthy connections to ourselves, our Higher Power, and other people.

In the First Step we surrendered to powerlessness. That was the beginning. Now we are on the way to becoming empowered by a Power greater than ourselves. This Power responds quickly and greatly to the slightest movement forward, the smallest indication of belief on our part.

Sometimes all we have to do is go to a meeting or think about this Step.

We will be restored. We will be renewed. We will be lifted out of our present circumstance and into a solution, whether that involves a change of heart, a change of attitude, a new path, a new feeling, or a new vision of what we are to do. Sometimes this happens quickly. Sometimes it takes a while.

Open ourselves to the belief that a new and better way will appear, and it will. Open ourselves, for one moment, to the possibility that a Higher Power can create a new way or a new situation or a solution, and we have set the stage for that to happen. Open ourselves to the possibility that we can be restored, and we shall begin that journey.

For many of us, taking the First Step—facing and admitting the unmanageability, pain, and loss in our lives—felt dark and hopeless. The Second Step takes us out of the darkness and into the light of hope and promise.

This Step offers hope, not the false hope many of us have clung to for years, but real hope in a real recovery. Take it whenever we need to.

ACTIVITIES

1. What are the activities that bring you hope and help you believe things are okay and will be okay? Going to meetings? Talking with recovering people? Reading recovery literature? Name those who have helped you to believe the most in your future.

2. How have your ideas changed about what it means to be restored to sanity? Have your expectations about recovery changed? What do you expect from recovery now that is different from what you expected when you first began recovering?

3. For now, how do you define a Power greater than yourself? Do you believe that Power cares about you?

4. What is a reasonable plan of self-care for you to help you continue to believe that recovery can, and will, work for you? Look again at your ideas in question 1 above.

5. What has been done for others in recovery that you would like to happen for yourself? Do you believe this is possible?

6. Make a list of the areas in your life where you would like to be restored. Your goals will be more effective if they center around restoring your own life rather than someone else's.

*"Infinite goodness means creating
a being that you know in advance
is going to complain."*
—William Peter Blatty

STEP THREE

"MADE A DECISION TO TURN OUR WILL AND OUR LIVES
OVER TO THE CARE OF GOD AS WE UNDERSTOOD GOD."
—Step Three of CoDA

Before recovery from codependency, I spent most of my life turning my will and my life over to the care of other people. The rest of the time I tried to get others to turn their will and lives over to me.

Now, I've learned to do something different: turn my will and life over to God. While it's important to grow in my understanding of God, I'm learning it's more important to know that God understands and cares about me.

I had many confused notions about God and about this Step that have changed as I've changed. I imagined God's will to be a place where I was expected to be more, do more, give more, and not ask for anything in return. For a while I called every unpleasant, distressful circumstance that happened to me "God's will."

Now I've learned that my ideas about God and God's will for my life had little to do with God and recovery and much to do with the deprived, restricted way I had learned to treat myself. It had to do with my codependency issues.

Many of us have confused ideas about what it means to surrender to the care of God. Anyone who has battled with control issues may have a hard time giving up, giving in, and letting go. Sometimes we surrender too much. We become victimized, we refuse to take care of ourselves, and we blame that on God.

I was afraid to take this Step. I was afraid I'd lose myself again, as I had so often in the past. What I learned was that I didn't lose myself by taking this Step: I found myself. The Third Step set me free. The Third Step is the "God and us" part of the program.

TURNING OVER OUR LIVES AND WILLS

Before I began recovery, I was convinced my life was a mistake. Not only did I believe that I had little business being here, I didn't believe there was any purpose for my life.

This Step tells us differently.

Making a decision to turn our will and our lives over to the care of God, as we understand God, is making a decision to live our life with God's help, and we each have a life to live.

We make a conscious decision to place ourselves and our lives, our internal affairs and external circumstances, over to the care of God. Then, we take responsibility for our lives and allow others to do the same for themselves.

In Step Two, we acknowledge that a Power greater than ourselves can restore us to sanity. In this Step, we do what needs to be done to let God do that. We turn ourselves over to God's care. Then we do our part by learning to take care of ourselves.

TO THE CARE OF GOD

Some of us struggle with the concept of God as a result of what we have been through before finding our way to these Steps. "I was really confused about God and the God part of this program," said Mary. "I kept wondering how a loving God could have allowed this to happen in my life."

Most of us find that if we stay open, we find our own path to spirituality. Most of us find things work out if we begin with whatever amount of belief, or disbelief, we possess.

"When things started to change for me in Al-Anon was when I began to conceptualize that surrendering wasn't failure," said Marcia. (Marcia is the woman whose mother kept attempting suicide.) "At first I intellectualized that, then I moved into the emotional phase of surrender. When I did, I was flooded by memories—of home, of all the times I wanted to say no, but was afraid to. I started off easy. I started to say no, stand up for myself, and gradually began to see that lightning didn't strike me and I wasn't killed when I did. I moved into listening to other people and realized that many had gone through the same things I had. I used the power of the program and the fellowship. I figured that I wasn't any better than these people; I figured I could be no worse than them, either, which led to the idea that maybe I could do this—recovery—too.

"Once I surrendered, things got easier. The Third Step became beneficial, I was able to take it, once I saw the word *care* in there.

"My life has changed. I can say no and not be afraid. The fear of being alone has passed. I was alone for seven years before marrying again. My relationship with my Higher Power has a lot to do with feeling better about myself and not feeling alone. I used to be afraid, now I take risks to go places and do things that are new.

"Sometimes, I ignore the Steps in my daily life. Then I get into trouble, which for me means I butt into other people's lives. I revert to caring about what is happening to others more than caring about myself. I can go through the day and not know what I felt or what I cared about.

"I get into trouble when I think I'm the power. In my childhood, I was the power in my mother's life. I get into the intellectual thinking that I'm all powerful. When I let go, life is much better. I ask God to help me to do His will. I believe that my inborn reaction is to lie or maneuver my way out of situations. If I am working my program, then I take the time to ask myself what I really feel, and what I really need."

There is a great deal of relief in taking this Step. God is going to help us take care of ourselves.

It is safe, now, to let go of our need to be in control.

We can go to God as our source, our Creator, our inspiration, our guidance, our direction. And we hold ourselves responsible for our behavior and choices.

It is a relationship based on trust—trust in God and trust in self.

AS WE UNDERSTOOD GOD

This Step declares that God is an important part of our recovery and our lives. It also states specifically that we are each free to understand God as we choose. This Step is not about religion— although a particular religion may be important in our lives. This Step is about coming to terms with a personal relationship with God, as we understand and define God.

God is not malicious. Not punitive. Not a trickster. Not out to play jokes on us. God may ask us to wait longer than we want, but only if waiting is in our best interests.

God knows our hearts and God understands our healing needs. God understands the good that is waiting around the corner for us, the good that we can't see yet. God sees the benefit in the lessons we're learning, not just the turmoil, which is what we so often focus on.

God can help us bring out the healer in ourselves.

TURNING IT OVER

This Step is about willpower, and the limits and the consequences of plowing our way through life running on our own fuel. Many of us have found that we haven't gotten too far or have not arrived at a destination we liked by using our own will.

How can we tell when we're forging ahead on our own steam or when it may be time to surrender? We'll learn.

Claire is a teacher, a mother of two, and divorced. She has attended Al-Anon meetings for five years, Adult Children of Alcoholics meetings for two years, and CoDA meetings for a year and a half.

"As I changed, all hell broke loose in my marriage," said Claire. "My husband and I began to fight a lot. My changes threatened him. I kept getting better, but the healthier I got, the worse it got at home."

After attending CoDA, it took Claire four months to leave her husband.

"I got into a lot of my family stuff, living with him those years I was in recovery. My parents had been emotionally unavailable to me all my life. My husband's stuff was emotionally abusive, but subtle. It was hard to let go of control because I felt that if I did, something bad would happen to me. I didn't know I deserved the good stuff.

"I talked with a lot of people about getting a divorce, and I waited until I was ready. I consider filing for divorce a real triumph in my recovery.

"I had no conscious resistance to the Steps when I came to the program," Claire said. "Basically, my recovery happened by this method: I call you up, you tell me what to do, and I will do it. A lot of people tell me that I listened and did everything I was supposed to.

"I feel like I really own my life for the first time—my sexuality, my time, my rules, my attention to my kids, my attention to me. I love my job, and I'm good at it. It's pretty new still, and I'm still trying to do things six months before I'm ready. I'm less angry and resentful. And I'm still accepting the realities of my relationship with my parents.

"A sponsor used to say to me, 'Trust God, trust me, and do the dishes.' I'm a great analyzer. So now I trust, I pray, and I do what's in front of me. I trust my recovery people to give me reality checks.

"And I trust me."

We do not have to look around us too long or too hard to find God's will for us and our lives today. It is not hidden from the eye. God's plan for us today is taking care of ourselves the way we want and choose, within the framework of what's happening in our lives today. When it's supposed to be something different, we'll know. We'll get interrupted. We'll be lead into a new circumstance. Or a new circumstance will find us.

Usually we find God's will by becoming quiet, trusting God, and listening to and trusting ourselves. It is a place found in peace and trust, not urgency and intensity.

It is by surrendering to the present moment that we reach the next moment in our lives.

ACCEPTANCE AND GRATITUDE

Two concepts help me work this Step: acceptance and gratitude. When I can't surrender, when I can't stand what is going on in my life, when I resist or deny reality, I can practice gratitude.

When I cannot see the good in what's happening, when I think I know best and no one is listening, when I don't know what to do next, or when I know what I want to do next but can't do it, I can practice gratitude.

When I feel deprived, unloved, uncared for, abandoned, and left out of life, I can practice gratitude.

And I can practice self-care.

Gratitude has immense transformational powers—for ourselves, our lives, and our circumstances. I have used this tool over and again. It has taken me through many stressful circumstances— poverty, divorce, being alone, learning how to date, moves, overwhelming projects, overwhelming feelings, troubles with children, troubles with neighbors, fear, circumstances that perplexed me, and other unlit, foggy parts of this journey. Gratitude helps make things work out well. It helps us feel better while stressful things are happening. Then when things get good, it helps us enjoy the good.

Focusing on the negative, focusing on the "what's wrong with this picture" is a large part of our codependency. Gratitude empowers and increases what's right in our lives. It helps make things right.

We say thank you. We say thank you over and over again, whether or not we mean it, whether or not we feel grateful. We say thank you for every detail of our present circumstances, including what we're going through, who we are, where we are, what we're feeling, and what is frustrating us.

Gratitude can help bring us to a point of surrender. It can change the energy in us and our environment. Gratitude diminishes the power of the problem and empowers the solution. It releases us from the tight, negative grasp of our present circumstance. It releases fear. It helps us move out and move forward. It breeds acceptance, the magic that helps us and our circumstances change.

My first response to discomfort is to want the situation or the other person to change. When I take this Step, when I focus on taking care of myself, my circumstances change—usually because I change.

Force gratitude. Say thank you again and again for each circumstance. Say thank you even if you're not feeling grateful. Eventually the power of gratitude will take over, and joy and true gratitude will begin.

Next to the Steps and detachment, gratitude is probably the most helpful recovery tool available. Like any tool, thinking about using it isn't enough. It works only when we pick it up in our hands and actually begin using it.

THE FREEDOM OF SURRENDER

This is the surrender Step. Once we surrender, we become free to take care of ourselves, with the assistance of our Higher Power.

Surrender doesn't mean we're helpless. It doesn't mean we surrender to abuse or intolerable circumstances. It means we acknowledge these circumstances, then ask God to help us take care of ourselves in these circumstances.

We will learn how to say no; how to set boundaries; how to listen to our feelings, wants, and needs; and how to respond to others in a responsible, loving way. We will learn how to respond to external circumstances in a reasonable way, one that exhibits self-care, self-love, and respect for others.

Surrendering is how we become empowered to take care of ourselves.

Turning our will and life over to the care of God takes the control of our life away from others. It also takes the control of others' lives away from us. It sets us free to develop our own connection to our Source and to ourselves, a connection free of the demands, expectations, and plans of another person. It can even set us free from our own demands, expectations, and plans.

When we stop controlling others and allowing them to control us, we become free to take care of ourselves. The First Step is about powerlessness. This Step is about owning our power to take care of ourselves.

We become free to choose how we are to act, and to react, instead of believing that our actions need be controlled by the actions and life of another. So what if someone else is miserable? We can let them have their stuff. So what if someone else chooses not to be healthy? We can grieve for them and become as healthy as we want to. Once we take this Step, we no longer have to allow our self-esteem to be determined by the actions, words, feelings, or beliefs of others—people from our past or those in our present.

"The most significant way this Step has given me back my power is that I've learned to stop trying to do God's job," said Don. "Because I didn't have any healthy, accurate mirroring in my family and no respect, because there was almost no acceptance of who I was as a person, I got real confused about who I was and who God was. I think much of the difficulty I've had in my adult life is because of the draining of my energy trying to do God's work. Now it is a little clearer to me what my job is and what God's job is. This has helped me a lot with people in relationships and on the job."

We can use this Step when we are beginning recovery or when we run into an impasse. We can use it in the big moments of our lives or in the smaller, quieter moments. We can use it in times of confusion or despair, or when we feel stuck and trapped.

When I can see no way out, when I've tried everything I know and realize I don't know what I need to know, when I realize that I cannot plow and forge ahead any longer, when I can't stand 'it' any longer because I've exhausted myself trying to control 'it,' when I need help taking care of myself, it's time to surrender.

When I finally come to the realization that maybe life is trying to teach me something new and helpful, I take this Step. When I recognize that I need a change in thinking or in approach, I take this Step.

When I'm ready to become humble, I take this Step.

When we have neglected ourselves to the point of despair,

confusion, exhaustion, and sometimes self-abuse, we can take this Step. We can surrender to the Highest Plan and Purpose for our lives—the one that includes self-love.

There is another way besides ours, a better one. Taking this Step helps us find that way, even when the next move is a simple one like doing the dishes or watching television.

I spent years resisting, denying, trying to control the behavior of those around me, and neglecting myself. My efforts to control those around me produced not one iota of change in their behaviors, and they wore me out. I have finally learned this truth: My circumstances change only when I accept them and quietly figure out what it is I need to do to take care of me within the framework of reality.

We stop fighting it, whatever it is. We stop trying to force or superimpose our plan on the scheme of things. Then we allow circumstances—and our part in them—to unfold.

Things are being worked out in us. Things that we do not yet know about. Things we will see with the passage of time. Important changes are happening within us, as a result of our present circumstances. Important changes are taking place in others, right now.

How many times have I argued and fought with God over the way things are going? This is a mistake, I've screamed. This is wrong. This is not at all the way it should be. And then, a month later, sometimes a year later, I see the wisdom. I see the big plan, the one not limited by my vision. Then I thank God, truly thank God, for the way things worked out. Often I thank God for not letting things work out the way I wanted.

We do not know the whole picture, not yet. All we are seeing is a small area on a large painting. When we relax, trust, and back up, we will see more. We will gain perspective.

That does not mean we stop having feelings.

It means we allow ourselves to feel and listen to what our feelings are telling us.

It does not mean we say yes to all that comes our way. It means we learn to trust when we want to say no, and then we say no. It also means we learn to trust when we want to say yes.

When I first took this step, it frightened me. I thought it

required of me an unappealing passivity and mindlessness. I took this Step anyway, mostly because I had no other options. Willpower had led me deeper and deeper into a destructive lifestyle that I no longer wanted or could afford. I saw no way out on my own, and I was tired of what my efforts were able to produce.

Since then, I've learned some ideas about God's will for my life, about God, and about my relationship to God. God's will is not an outside, impossible, forced agenda for my life. If it's God's will, it happens. Usually, it happens naturally, without any control efforts required on my part.

At times, there have been hard lessons to learn. These lessons had to be learned, however, to work things out inside me so I could have the best possible life.

Usually, I have to wait longer than I want to. And much letting go is involved in the process.

God's love is immediate and powerful, yet gentle, healing, and nurturing. It takes into account what I want and need. God's will contains discipline, not deprivation. God isn't shame-based; people are. Yet, God holds me accountable for my actions.

When I first began recovering, I feared it was a brainwashing of sorts. Now I see that my life before recovery contained the brainwashing. This program has set me free.

This Step isn't about mindlessness or selflessness. It's about learning to trust my mind and trust that once I turn myself over to God, I will be guided by a Higher Power and Divine Wisdom. It's about finding, valuing, loving, and trusting *myself*.

Sometimes I still fear working this Step. But I know I no longer need to fear. It puts me back on track.

Taking this Step gets us into the flow for our lives. This flow will take us through discord in our relationships, healing within ourselves, problems at work, struggles in any area of our lives.

Stepping into God's care is a gentle step, one that brings peace and harmony. That doesn't mean our actions will never cause discord, hurt feelings, or a reaction in others. But there will be a rightness, a naturalness, and a harmony to what we do.

Surrendering cannot be forced or faked. It happens at a core, soul level—when whatever we've been trying to control, manipulate, influence, or resist becomes, at last, too much for us. We let go. We say, "That's it. I'm willing to let go of preconceived notions about what should happen. I'm willing to let go of my limitations, my agenda, my script, and my beliefs. I'm ready and willing to be open to what You have in mind for me. Now, just show me what that is. Let me know in a way I can understand."

We become ready to let God love us and help us love ourselves.

Taking the Third Step is a starting point for setting our new life in motion. We can do it when we begin recovery. Then we can do it as needed.

Once we have placed ourselves in the care of a Higher Power, the act is complete. Our lives and our wills belong to God.

People from our past may have abandoned us. God won't. When times get rough, we don't have to wonder whether God is there or whether God cares or whether God knows what is going on.

God is there. God cares. God's plan is one that we can participate in, one that lets us use each event and circumstance in our lives to bring about our highest good.

If we make mistakes, we don't have to worry that God will go away or reject us. God does not demand perfection of us. Others may have asked that of us; we may have expected that of ourselves. God doesn't.

We don't have to rely on our feelings. We can rely on fact. Even on those days when we feel like our lives or other people's lives might be a mistake, or when we feel timing is wrong, we can trust that we're not a mistake and all is coming to pass on schedule.

We don't have to rely on ourselves. We don't have to see clearly. We don't necessarily have to know what we're doing, or where we're going.

There will be times when we don't like it. Times we don't understand. Times we complain. That's okay. Complain, if we must. Get it out of our systems.

Then, become grateful.

If we have turned our lives and wills over to the care of a Higher Power, we can trust what we have done. We can trust ourselves to begin to understand what to do to take care of ourselves. We can trust God to oversee and help us with what we cannot accomplish.

We become open to a change of heart, a transformation of mind, and a transformation of our circumstances.

When we finally say and acknowledge that we give up, we give our Higher Power permission to do for us what we cannot do for ourselves.

Surrender renders us teachable. Humility and giving up make surrender possible. Becoming teachable allows us to learn what we could never have learned, had we not become willing to become students.

Sometimes we surrender to anything and everything and call it God's will, and then we feel angry and hurt and get mad at God. But this isn't about God, it's about our codependency.

When we use this Step, we understand that we cannot control others, so we stop trying. But we also realize that we no longer have to let them control us.

This is the freedom Step. In this Step we make a decision to live life differently. We make a conscious decision to begin taking care of ourselves with God's help. We start creating a life for ourselves, the life that we want to live.

This process of surrender happens not once, but again and again as we master a succession of lessons—lessons of healing, liberation, and love. Each time we may think: That's it. Now I've learned. It's free sailing from here on! Then we realize to our relief and delight that we are starting over as beginners again.

Situations will come to pass. People will come into our lives. Ideas will occur to us. Feelings will emerge. Old ways of thinking—negative, self-hating ways—will surface, then be taken from us and replaced by healthier ideas. These new ideas allow us to love ourselves and give and receive love from others. We will have no more than we can handle and as much as we need. Purposes, lessons, will make themselves clear. Our lives will begin to make sense, as will the events that come to pass—at least in retrospect. We will find ourselves being transformed and healed at the core of ourselves.

We will find that our faith has been well placed at last.

Some days it will feel as if nothing is happening; other days it will feel as though too much is happening. Know that each day all is well.

The journey is exciting. It holds secrets, mysteries, and lessons beyond our comprehension. It holds gifts bigger than our arms and hearts can hold.

Trust this process. It will take us where we truly want and need to go—in Divine and Perfect timing. Trust God's plan, for it is better than ours. Trust ourselves, for we have now tapped into a power and source infinitely more powerful than anything we've known.

Let this Step work its power. Let this Step take us where we need to go. Then watch and be open to the mystery that unfolds.

ACTIVITIES

1. To remember this Step, you may find it helpful to write it down in the form of an affirmation. For example: "I have turned my life and my will over to the care of God today. All is well."
2. If you knew that all was well and on schedule in your life today, how would you feel? If you knew that things were being managed by a Power greater than yourself in a way that would work out in your best interests, how would you act differently?
3. If you knew that you had no power to control events, outcomes, or a particular person, how would you behave differently? What would you say or do? What would you stop saying or doing? What would you do differently for yourself in order to enjoy your own life now, to live in the present moment?
4. If you weren't allowing someone else to control you, what would you be doing differently? What would you do today with your life? How would you feel?
5. If you weren't allowing a particular circumstance to control you, or if you weren't trying to control that circumstance—if you just let it be and accepted it as okay for the present

moment—how would you feel? If you weren't fighting with or resisting this circumstance, what would you be doing? How would you be feeling?

6. Taking this Step often puts you in touch with yourself. Listen to yourself. Write about what you feel, want, need, and think. Then pick up the phone and share who you are with someone safe, someone you trust. Talk in a way that reflects self-responsibility, not victimization. Don't ask them to rescue you. Ask them to listen and accept you as you are.

7. What is the most loving, most nurturing thing available to you right now that you can use to take care of yourself and enjoy life? What will you do with it?

*"Freedom is the ability to have or
to not have what you want
without it closing your heart."*
—Stephen Levine

STEP FOUR

"MADE A SEARCHING AND FEARLESS MORAL INVENTORY
OF OURSELVES."
—Step Four of CoDA

This is the scenario. It's time to go to your meeting. You're excited. Ready. Then you remember tonight's topic. The Fourth Step. Part of you goes, "Aaack." The other part goes blank. You wish the topic were different, something more pertinent to recovery. Something you had more to say about. Wish it were on the Second Step, you mumble to yourself.

Or you get to your meeting, all revved up for a night of healing conversation—until you discover the topic: the Fourth Step. Everyone passes, and the meeting, which usually lasts from an hour to an hour and a half, is over in thirty minutes.

Or, instead of passing, group members decide to talk about something else that evening. The Fourth Step barely gets mentioned. "I've been thinking about doing one." "I probably should." "It's getting around that time."

Maybe, just maybe, one person doesn't pass. That person talks straightforwardly about doing a Fourth Step. You sit in awe. That person has actually taken out paper and pencil and done an inventory.

You wonder how that person found the time and determination to actually *do* this Step. The concept seems mind-boggling and leaves you feeling guilty, confused, and wondering if you will ever get to this part of your recovery program. Yet, you look at that person who has taken the time to do this Step and notice something different about him or her. There is a comfort level with self that is appealing. That person has a recovery that is admirable. You feel somewhat, well, envious.

But actually tackling this Step still feels overwhelming.

This is the Step that brings fear, uncertainty, and guilt to those who have been around recovery meetings for a while and have not taken it—or to those who have gone a time without taking it again. It's housecleaning time. Healing time.

It's the dreaded Fourth Step.

"I've been in recovery and going to meetings for six years now," said Jody, "and I still haven't taken a Fourth Step. I just dread it. And I'm not sure why."

Many of us can identify with Jody. *I can identify with Jody.* Early in my own recovery, doing this kind of self-inventory felt overwhelming. I wasn't sure I had a self. I wasn't sure what I'd find. My self-worth was so low I wasn't sure I could handle any more self-criticism.

And I didn't know where to begin. I didn't know what I was looking for. I didn't know what I'd do with it when I found it. I didn't understand the purpose. And I didn't think I could do it well enough. It seemed like too much work, and it looked like roll-up-your-sleeves dirty work.

In this chapter, we'll look at this Step. We'll explore it with a fresh vision. We'll try to examine some simple ways of tackling this Step. And we'll look at some rewards from taking the time to look within.

LOOKING WITHIN OURSELVES

"Codependency hides under all my addictions," said Carol. "I avoid pain with something: relationships, substances, or work. I hid in a relationship so I didn't have to deal with me." Many of us hide from our pain. Many of us hide from ourselves. Perhaps the last, safest, and strongest holdout from looking at ourselves is blaming our circumstances and condition on others. Focusing on others will neither solve our problems nor bring relief from the pain. It will divert us, but it won't accomplish the work we are seeking. It won't bring healing. Focusing on others won't change our circumstances. Many of us make the mistake of stopping our recovery efforts before we work this Step. We recover long enough to identify the other person's problem and realize it's not our fault. But what we discover is this: If we do not use our present circumstances as a challenge, a trigger, and an invitation to look within, we will find ourselves dancing through a repeat performance.

We may leave one person because of their particular problem, only to find ourselves in another relationship with someone who has a similar, or perhaps identical, problem.

We are learning that these repeat performances are not coincidences. They are an an ongoing, continuous invitation to look inside ourselves and find the healing gift from our present circumstances.

We can welcome and embrace the challenge.

Many of us begin recovery from codependency by looking around and outside of ourselves. That's often how life gets our attention. We get mad, whine, rage, manipulate, attempt to control, and point the finger at the other person in absolute insistence that he or she is doing something inappropriate, something we do not like, something we want that person to stop doing.

This is what we call an "outward" focus.

Often, focusing on the behavior of others is justified, appropriate, and necessary. But when we tire of expending energy discussing the details of the other person, whether that person is a parent, child, friend, spouse, boyfriend, girlfriend, co-worker, boss, or employee, we face the Fourth Step questions: What's going on with me? What am I doing? What am I not doing? Why did I need to go through these circumstances? What are these circumstances triggering within me? What are the old memories, the old fears, the old tapes, being replayed? What's my agenda? What's *my* lesson from this experience?

What do I need to learn about taking care of myself? And what's stopping me from doing that?

In this Step, we begin the process of looking within as a response to our circumstances. We make a searching and fearless inventory of ourselves.

This Step doesn't tell us to make a critical, hostile, blaming inventory of ourselves. It doesn't tell us endlessly to find fault, hold ourselves irresponsible or overresponsible, or others unaccountable. It says: "searching and fearless."

We don't have to be afraid of what we will find. We simply decide to look within to find *ourselves*.

We don't take this step in lieu of setting boundaries. We don't take this Step to deny what another person is or isn't doing, and the impact of that on our families and our lives. We don't take this Step to deny what we are feeling.

We take this Step to get to the core of recovery: self-responsibility.

We are responsible for ourselves—our circumstances and whether we choose to remain in them and our attitude toward these circumstances. We are responsible for what we have created in our lives and what we will create. We are responsible for our feelings. They are ours.

The great codependency delusion is this: We would be feeling different if someone else would just do something, if we were somewhere else, if we had something we wanted. Not true. We could jet to every state and five foreign countries, and until we dealt with our feelings, we'd be feeling the same way in each location we visited.

If I feel miserable, it doesn't matter who calls or where I go—I'll feel that way until I face and deal with my feelings. If I'm feeling afraid, I'll feel afraid until I deal with my fear.

When we learn to look within and face what's there, we find ourselves less and less affected by external events and more and more empowered to deal appropriately with what is happening. Honestly facing ourselves and taking responsibility for ourselves is where our true power lies.

We take this Step to enable ourselves to take responsibility for ourselves within the framework of reality. A by-product of looking within is that we master the lesson of our present circumstances, so we avoid a repeat performance. And we become healed enough to enjoy life and love.

"Before I did my Fourth Step, I had this image of a cellar in a house," said Carol, who has been in Al-Anon for ten years. "The basement was dark. There were windows in it, but they were darkened with soot and covered with bushes. The cellar was a mess. Cluttered. Dirty. And no light filtered in.

"It scared me. That room in the house, my house, was frightening. I didn't want to look at it. I didn't want to go in it. Yet I was always aware of its presence.

"I've now done several Fourth Steps," said Carol. "Each time

I took one, the cellar became a little more orderly and organized. Cleaner. Now when I see the basement in that house, it's a nice room. It's redecorated and livable. The windows have been cleaned and polished—they're large and open—and the room is filled with golden light.

"I'm not scared of that part of my house anymore. It's comfortable for me to go into it and look around whenever I want to.

"That house is me."

It is common and natural to fear the unknown. It is common to fear dark, cluttered places. It is not in our best interests to have that unknown, dark, cluttered place be our soul.

"Before entering a Twelve Step program, I protected myself from negative emotions and fears," said Kathy. "I was living on other people's lives. I was always more concerned about others than myself. Inside was not a place that I looked. I didn't consider it. I felt empty, drab, and superficial. How I felt was similar to the way I kept house. The house was clean, but if you opened a closet, it would engulf you. Or if you moved the couch, tumbleweeds would surround you."

This Step is the beginning of our own housecleaning. It is where we begin looking within for the solution to our problems and pain. It is how we begin healing ourselves and our hearts.

In this Step, we begin to allow the light to come into ourselves.

A SEARCHING AND FEARLESS INVENTORY

What do we look for in our searching and fearless inventory? We look for what is right about ourselves and our values. We look for the wrongs we have done, too. But also included in this moral inventory are our self-defeating behaviors and the moral issue of whether or not we love ourselves.

We take stock of our behaviors—positive and negative. We look at the things we've done wrong—our big guilts and our little guilts. We look for those things we haven't done wrong but feel guilty about anyway. We ferret out all the guilt, earned and unearned, and get it into the light. We take a searching and fearless look at what bothers us now and what has bothered us in the past, a look that is free from the restrictions of denial, free from fear of speaking the truth.

We look for anger, fear, pain, rage, and resentment, including anger at God. We look for victimization—ways others have victimized us, ways we have allowed ourselves to be victimized by others, and ways we have victimized ourselves.

We look for painful repressed memories. We seek out our fears and our limiting beliefs, messages that aren't true and may be setting the stage for our life.

We look for the blocks that may be interfering with our ability to live and love.

We don't do this to criticize or further wound ourselves, or blame ourselves and others. We do this to heal from all that has taken place in our lives. We do this to set ourselves free from the past. We do this to hold ourselves accountable for our own healing and to achieve the highest level of self-responsibility and self-accountability possible.

Here are some ways people approach this Step:

1. An Inventory of Codependent Characteristics

We can list some of the codependent behaviors and characteristics we have been protecting ourselves with, the people involved with these behaviors, and our underlying feelings about them. The behaviors we may want to focus on are: caretaking; controlling; repressing feelings; not dealing with feelings appropriately; manipulation; self-neglect; not taking responsibility for ourselves (including emotional and financial responsibility); worrying; constantly criticizing ourselves and our efforts; feeling that we can't do "it" well enough (whatever "it" is); not liking and loving ourselves; not allowing others to like and love us; not nurturing ourselves or allowing ourselves to receive the nurturing we want and need; using denial as a coping tool; feeling victimized; allowing ourselves to be victimized; not setting boundaries; not trusting our feelings and instincts; not trusting God; not trusting life and recovery; feeling unsafe; lack of intimacy and fulfillment in relationships; earned and unearned guilt; sexual behaviors (including sexual codependency—having sex with people when we don't really want to or engaging in sexual behaviors we aren't comfortable with to please another); obsessing; being dependent on others; communicating poorly; dishonesty (including emotional dishonesty); not saying no when we mean no; not saying what we want and need; repressing our needs and wants; not feeling like we have a life of our own; low self-worth; believing we deserve little from people and life; perfectionism; unreasonable expectations of others; staying stuck or trapped in relationships; not owning our power with people (including family members); becoming rigid and inflexible; getting stuck in misery and negative thinking; not allowing ourselves to have fun; unnecessarily depriving ourselves; expecting others to be responsible for us; martyrdom; unclear or unrealistic thinking; lack of spontaneity; fear of or inability to tackle and solve problems; negative beliefs about ourselves and our abilities; shame; unresolved historical issues, particularly with nuclear family; unresolved abuse issues from our pasts; a sense of despair about our relationship history; confusing pain or longing with love; withdrawing from friendships; not tending to our daily and regular routine; being filled with fear and panic; a tendency to attract sick and needy people; a tendency to be attracted to dysfunctional relationships and employment situations; and resentments due to the characteristics listed above. In the latter stages of codependency, we may want to look for chronic depression; compulsive or addictive behaviors; self-neglect to the point of illness; and suicidal thinking.

"The big issues in my codependent inventory were manipulation and control," said Kevin. "Thinking I could control other people was really big, and trying to control other people's feelings so I felt safe. I was trying to be ahead of everybody. I was afraid of people being angry at me or being uncontrolled with me. I said I liked spontaneity, but I was afraid of it. I spent a lot of time worrying about what others thought of me, and I thought I could control that. I was fixated on other people."

2. A General Biographical Sketch
This is an easy way to dive into this Step. Sit down with pencil and paper and write about yourself. Start simple. Where were you born? Then let the process take over. Write what comes to

mind about yourself and your life—from childhood to present. Don't complicate it by telling yourself you have to write everything. Don't overwhelm yourself by trying to do it perfectly. After doing this first sketch, you may want to move on to the Fifth Step and talk to someone about what you've discovered. Or, you may want to move to the next layer of yourself.

Read your biography. Are there missing pieces? Are there parts you could write another paper about? What was it like in school? What was it like growing up in your family? What kinds of feelings did you have about yourself and others? What have you done well? Poorly? What have you wanted for yourself and your life? How do you feel about what you've done, what you've become so far? What did others expect of you? What do you expect of yourself? What are your secrets? What have you hidden from the world about yourself? Do you have some guilty "secrets" that are causing shame? Be honest. Now is not the time to mince words. What have you done wrong to others? What do you feel they've done wrong to you?

Remember, this Step is not about being nice and appropriate. It's about getting it all out. Your biography isn't going to be published. Let yourself go, and say what you need and want to say.

Write about your relationships, your feelings, your behaviors. How did you protect yourself? What did you do to survive? This exercise is an interesting one to do regularly over the years. We may be surprised to see how our perspective on ourselves and our lives changes as we change.

3. A Specific Biographical Sketch
Some people prefer to focus on one area of their lives, such as relationships, family, or work history. This can be useful if you find yourself blocked in a particular area. Write about your history in that one area, starting at the beginning. For example: What characterized that relationship? How did it begin? End? What were the good parts about the relationship? What were the traumatic events in that relationship? How did it end or how was it resolved? What is the status of that relationship now? How did you handle your feelings and needs in that relation-

ship? How did the other person? Did you feel victimized? Why? How did you protect yourself in that relationship? What did you learn from that relationship? Did you make any significant, self-defeating decisions about yourself or other people based on the course of that relationship, such as women (men, bosses, neighbors, relatives, etc.) can't be trusted? How do you feel about that person now? Is there peace in your heart toward this relationship? What was the good thing this relationship brought to your life? What were the painful things this relationship brought to your life? What is your belief now about yourself, the other person, and that relationship? What are your feelings?

We can do the same for employment. Write about your work history. This isn't a résumé, it's a personal review of ourselves and our life, behavior, and beliefs at work. This can help us identify self-defeating beliefs about ourselves and help us discover our talents and abilities. Write about your relationships with people at work, how you felt when you took the job, what happened, how you feel about that job now. What were the good things you gained from the experience? What were the negatives? What do you believe about yourself and your work abilities? Are there some things about your conduct that bother you about your work history? What are your feelings?

The more we can write about ourselves, our feelings, and our beliefs, the more helpful this work is.

4. A Big-Book Fourth Step

This approach (covered on pages 64 through 71 of *Alcoholics Anonymous*, "the Big Book") is the original approach suggested for a Fourth Step. This version calls for an honest stocktaking of ourselves. It is simple and straightforward. We write down the names of people we resent, and why. We write down what part of our lives we feel those people have affected or harmed. On our list of resentments, we include "people, institutions or principles with whom we are, or were, angry." For instance, "I'm resentful toward my friend because she doesn't call me often enough, and that affects my social life and my feelings of well-being."

We list our fears. Many of us learn that fear is an underlying motive in our codependency. This Step is a way to ferret it out. "Sometimes we think fear ought to be classed with stealing. It seems to cause more trouble," wrote the authors of the Big Book (p. 68).

We list our grudges and our injuries—real and imagined.

"It is plain that a life which includes deep resentment leads only to futility and unhappiness. To the precise extent that we permit these, do we squander the hours that might have been worthwhile," says the Big Book. "For when harboring such feelings, we shut ourselves off from the sunlight of the Spirit" (p. 66).

We don't squelch or repress our anger and resentments. Our feelings may be long overdue. The purpose of this process is to get out into the light our deeply rooted feelings, so we can feel them and be done with them.

In this Fourth Step, we may want to cover all the troublesome areas of our lives—anger, resentment, fear, sex, and money—reviewing each area thoroughly and with an attitude of self-acceptance, not shame.

5. Things We've Done Wrong

This can be an honest appraisal of the things we've done that we feel guilty about. This Step can help us clarify our own acts and words that cause guilt and shame, so we can be done with past guilt. It can also help clarify our inappropriate guilt—feelings of guilt that aren't really our own, but belong to others. We can be done with that, too. This is the place to let go of our rationalizations, our justifications, and look within.

Understand this: Treating ourselves badly is as much of a moral issue, a wrongdoing, as treating others badly. Believing that we're unlovable, stupid, unworthy, not good enough, inferior, or superior, is a moral issue. Not taking loving care of our feelings, our needs, ourselves, is a moral issue. Not setting boundaries and limits with people, allowing them to hurt or harm us, is a moral issue. It doesn't help them, and it hurts us. Telling ourselves it's okay to accept mistreatment is a moral issue. Neglecting ourselves is a moral issue. Expecting ourselves to be perfect is wrong. Not allowing ourselves to have fun and enjoy being alive is a moral issue.

Not listening to, not trusting, ourselves is a moral issue. Not liking and loving ourselves is a moral issue, and it is the heart and core of our codependency.

6. Wrongs Others Have Done to Us

Taking a Fourth Step from this vantage point can help us get it all out. We can list all our victimizations from day one. What people, institutions, places, and beliefs have victimized or hurt us? How or why? How did this affect our lives? How does this make us feel? Did we have any part in this? For instance, did we say yes to someone when we could have said no? Why didn't we? What did we fear might happen if we took care of ourselves? Why didn't we own our power with that person? What was the belief stopping us from taking care of ourselves?

Have a good gripe session on paper. Whine once and for all so we can be done with it and heal.

7. An Asset Inventory

So much of our codependency involves difficulty seeing what's good about ourselves and our lives. Seeing what's wrong can come so easily. It can be helpful to do a Fourth Step on our good qualities, our talents, our values, and what's right about us. It may also be, as one woman said, the hardest Fourth Step we've ever done.

8. A List of Anger, Fear—and Shame

Write a list of everyone we're mad at, everything we're afraid of, and everything we hate about ourselves. Dump it all. This is a simple approach to this Step. Just make a list of who or what, past and present, bothers you. *Bothers* means "causes you to feel upset, afraid, angry, helpless, outraged, indignant, hurt, ashamed, guilty, worried, or disturbed." *Bothers* also means "triggers any type of reaction in you, including caretaking or controlling." You can include things about yourself and your life that bother you. You can include things about others, relationships, or work that bother you.

Try to write your feelings and beliefs about each incident or person that bothers you. For instance, "Working with Marge bothers me. She is powerful and controlling, and I feel stupid around her." The more self-responsibility we can take with each incident, the better. This doesn't mean we blame ourselves; it means we attempt to get to the root of the problem. For instance, "Marge triggers my belief that I'm stupid." That understanding is the kind of work that helps us heal. If it is my belief that I'm stupid, if I learn that about myself, I can let go of the old belief and change it to a better one, such as, "I'm competent and capable. I'm intelligent. I can own my power with people."

But we won't know what to let go of and change until we do our Fourth Step work. The bottom line is this: If we believe we're unlovable, we won't let anyone love us. And if we believe people will hurt us and take advantage of us, they probably will.

The more childhood incidents we can include in this Step, the more we will heal. Much of what we are talking about in this Step includes a recovery concept called *family-of-origin work*. That means we look at what happened in our pasts, particularly when we were children, to see how that's affecting us today. We look at the pain, the incidents, and often the abuse we suffered as children, so we can heal and be freed from them.

We don't do this work to shame or to blame others and ourselves. But we may need to get angry for a while. An important part of this process is finally to feel as hurt and angry as we need to, so we can be done with these feelings. We need to get them out of our minds, bodies, and souls so we can be free from their control and influence.

We allow ourselves to grieve our losses fully. Our unresolved emotions may be motivating our behaviors today. Unfinished business does not go away. It keeps repeating itself until we are ready to deal with it. Often, acceptance is all that is required. Sometimes, we need more help healing from our pasts.

We look for denied addictions and problems from our past. If there was sexual addiction, alcoholism, unresolved codependency, or other problems in our family, we need to bring it into the open, identify it, and be honest about its impact on our lives.

We look for messages from our pasts that may be controlling our lives today: "Don't feel"; "Don't think"; "Don't be who you are"; "Don't feel good about yourself"; "Be perfect"; "Don't have fun"; "Take care of other people and don't take care of yourself." These are the generic codependent messages many of us received that control our behaviors and lives today. We look for other messages that may be interfering with the quality of our lives and relationships: "I'm not lovable"; "People aren't trustworthy"; "I'm stupid"; "I don't deserve to succeed"; "I'll never amount to anything"; "People always reject me"; "I'm better off alone."

These messages can be powerful, driving forces in our lives. If we believe we're stupid, that message can gain control of our lives. We may constantly be doing things to prove the message is true, or we may constantly be pressuring ourselves to prove the message isn't true. Our interactions with people may be driven by a conscious or subconscious need to prove we aren't stupid, and our fear that we are.

If we believe we're unlovable, that belief can affect the quality of our relationships, including our most important ones—our relationships with ourselves. Everything we do or don't do—with others or with ourselves—may be a result of that belief.

The potency of the "don't feel" message is apparent. If it's not okay to feel, we may spend most of our waking hours resisting, fighting off, not listening to, and repressing our feelings. If we have a feeling, we may spend more time being ashamed of it and feeling awkward about it than we do feeling it. Feelings are an important part of us. Not acknowledging them is a key issue in codependency. Feeling our feelings, allowing ourselves to have feelings, is a key to recovery.

One goal of this Step is to open up and heal the emotional part of ourselves.

"The Twelve Steps are affirmations to remind me that I have feelings," said Tim. "The Steps are a reminder to me to pay attention to my feelings, or to let my feelings be and not to forget or ignore them."

Many of us, including me, need that permission and that affirmation regularly. For years, professionals have called alcoholism "a feelings disease." Well, so is codependency. Feelings are not the disease; not feeling them, repressing them, holding back, is the problem.

Some experts now say that unfelt feelings cause disease— physical illness, sometimes death. I agree. And if we aren't feeling, we're not fully alive.

We can use this Step as a vehicle to achieve emotional honesty and to do an emotional inventory on ourselves. We grow so much when we take a moment to inventory ourselves for what we are really feeling. Are we trying to control because we're afraid? Are we in a rage because we're ashamed? Are we feeling sick because we're angry? What are we feeling?

Often, to discover our current emotions, we need to dig into our pasts and find our old feelings, the ones we didn't feel, but needed to, years ago. If we don't do this, these feelings get entangled and confused. We may be taking old anger at Mom and Dad and putting it on the people in our lives today.

Remember, our feelings are our responsibility. It doesn't matter who did what. Our feelings are our feelings. They'll be with us until we deal with them, whether or not the other person changes.

Unresolved feelings from the past don't disappear. Many of us find ourselves creating situations that trigger the feelings we were denying, until we feel safe enough to find a way to deal with those feelings. For instance, if someone important in our past rejected us, we may continually be drawn to and help create situations where we are rejected. We finish old business by acknowledging and releasing our old feelings and replacing negative beliefs with positive ones.

We can learn to let ourselves feel, and heal from the backlog of feelings from our pasts. We can learn to deal appropriately with our feelings. We can learn to live through the painful ones and get to the joyous ones.

These Steps will help us do that.

To open up to our hearts, our selves, and our feelings, we may need to do more than deal with minor unfelt emotions from our pasts. Some experts, such as Patrick Carnes, say an overwhelming majority of us in recovery from codependency, chemical dependency, or both, need to face and heal from unresolved abuse issues in our pasts. This can include physical abuse, sexual abuse, or emotional abuse. Many behaviors qualify as abuse, including neglect, covert abuse, and being shamed.

Using our recovery programs to identify, accept, and heal from abuse is no small part of our recovery process. Some recovering people believe this is a core part of the process. Understand, we do not do this to blame parents or any other persons. We do it to stop denying and begin healing from its impact. Many of us have lived with abuse for so long that we do not even identify abuse as such. We call it normal and make excuses for the perpetrator. Some of us were severely abused and may have complete memory blockage of the abuse.

That doesn't mean the abuse went away. It will haunt us until we are ready to deal with it. This type of work, this deep work, must be approached with caution. It is not to be handled casually or haphazardly. Seek professional help, if necessary. Use judgment and discernment in exploring this area. If this issue applies to you, it will surface in its time—when you are ready and when the time is right to face it.

As Louie Anderson, the comedian, has said, it's not about blame. Often, our parents were more abused than we were. But abused people abuse people. And they hurt themselves. We all need to begin identifying this problem and start healing from it, so it can stop.

Growing up in an addicted family is abusive, not normal. It doesn't produce health, self-esteem, and well-being among its members. Usually, it produces codependency. This condition we call codependency is not new. Addicted families are not new. Recovery is what's new.

We can finally do something to stop the family tradition of codependency, shame, and low self-esteem from being handed down generation to generation. We can begin our own healing process.

LEARNING TO LOVE OURSELVES

Besides identifying and healing from past feelings, incidents, and beliefs, there is another important benefit from working this Step. Some people call the Twelve Steps a "selfish" program. That's true. We do this program for ourselves, no matter whose problem got us into the Steps, no matter who we originally came to these Steps to help. But these Steps are also a self-esteem program. We work them to be done with shame, guilt, and low self-esteem. We work these Steps to learn how to love ourselves. Then we can learn how to love other people and let them love us.

Legitimate guilt means we feel badly about something we have done. If we feel badly about something we have done, we can remedy that and be done with the guilt. There is a solution, whether that involves changing our behavior or making an amend.

Shame means we feel badly about being who we are. Changing our behavior or making an amend doesn't make shame go away. Shame leaves us with the sense that all we can do is apologize for existing. Many of us have been controlled by shame. Sometimes it comes from others; sometimes it comes from within.

This Step helps us learn to switch from a shame-based system to a system of loving and accepting ourselves—as is. We are clearing up our guilt and shame.

An acceptance-based system means we love, cherish, nurture, and unconditionally accept ourselves and our histories. It means we allow ourselves to make mistakes and errors. This recovery program was designed for human, imperfect beings. Our new definition of perfection can mean embracing who we are at any given moment. Mistakes are what we do, not who we are.

When doing this Step, do not forget to list the wrongs we may have done to ourselves: telling ourselves that it is not okay to be who we are; punishing and rejecting ourselves for being that; treating ourselves in any manner that is less than what we deserve. Not loving, accepting, nurturing, and cherishing ourselves are some of the most abusive wrongs we can do.

People who love themselves don't stop growing and changing. People who love and accept themselves are the people who become enabled to change. That is what this Step is about—continuing the process of self-love and acceptance we began in Step One.

People who love themselves do not become self-centered. They become people able to love others because they love and accept themselves. If anyone told you it was bad or wrong to love yourself, don't believe them. It is the best, healthiest, and most loving thing you can do for yourself and all the people in your life.

This Step sets us on the track to doing that.

By the time we reach this Step, we are called upon to do some focused work. It can be intense. What are we searching for? The darker side, the side that prevents us from loving ourselves, loving others, and letting others love us—the side that blocks us from finding the love and happiness we want and deserve.

We look for fears, anger, hurt, and shame from past events—buried feelings that may be affecting our lives today. These feelings often have their roots in our relationships with our parents or with other significant people from our pasts. Often, present responses are connected to our unresolved feelings from the past. To free ourselves today, we must heal from yesterday's feelings.

We look for subconscious beliefs about ourselves and others that may be interfering with the quality of our lives and relationships today. We look at our behaviors and our patterns, with an eye toward discerning the self-defeating ones.

We look at our hidden agendas, the ones we sometimes hide even from ourselves.

We try to dig out all the guilt—earned and unearned—and get it into the light.

We do this without being afraid of what we will find. We perform this task with love and compassion for ourselves. We allow ourselves to have all the feelings about others we need to feel along the way, but our goal is to perform this task with as much love and compassion for others as possible—as long as that love and compassion doesn't reinforce our denial of reality.

We feel as angry, even rageful, as we need to feel at first, then we strive for forgiveness. We go back to the past long enough to be able finally to put it behind us and set ourselves free.

We often find a snowballing effect when we begin this process. The healing takes on a life of its own, if we are open and willing.

We talked in this chapter about some ways to do this Step. The different ideas mentioned are not all the ways. If you, or someone you know, has a suggestion for doing this Step that appeals to you, try it.

Al-Anon World Services publishes "Blueprint for Progress," a checklist that many find helpful in doing their Fourth Step. Some people, like Louie Anderson, find it helpful to write letters. *Dear Dad* is a sequence of letters he wrote to his deceased alcoholic father. In these letters, Anderson works through a range of emotions—from anger to confusion to love and acceptance—surrounding the impact his father's alcoholism had on him and their relationship.

Some people just take out pencil and paper and write.

"I've done three Fourth Step inventories now," said Jane. "I just sit down with a pad of paper, and I write and write and write. That works for me."

Some people say they've done this Step in bits and pieces, rather than tackling their entire histories at once.

Some people find it helpful, because of the severity of their backgrounds, to seek professional help.

Therapeutic massage can be helpful in exploring, identifying, and releasing stored memories and messages and in healing from them. So can other alternative forms of health care.

The feelings, beliefs, and pain don't go away just because we have denied and repressed them. They go deep within and are stored in the fiber and tissues of our bodies. Then they keep showing up in our behaviors until we heal. And yes, healing is possible. We can heal at as deep a level as we have been affected.

Don't worry about doing this Step perfectly. Don't worry about doing it well enough. This Step will work if we make an effort to work it. It will start a process. It will move us forward on our journey. Choose a way to do this Step, then do it. Be as honest as possible. Be open. Be willing to do what feels right for you, when it feels right to do that. You don't have to let it overwhelm you. Some people feel so critical of themselves when they begin recovery, they need to wait a year or two to work this Step.

If you don't feel ready, don't worry about it. Like the other Steps, this one will find you, when it's time. You'll *know* when it's time.

OPENING OUR HEARTS TO LOVE

It took me years to realize the power, the significance, and the potency of the Fourth Step of this program, as it applied to codependency recovery. Let me tell you what happened and what this Step accomplished in my life.

The first time I dared look within myself, I was terrified. I had made a life practice of avoiding myself, by any and all means. I craved and clung to any addiction, relationship, or outside distraction. I did this because I was afraid—afraid of what I would find, afraid of the emotional impact of searching out what had been long stored inside me. Maybe I was afraid I would find nothing inside or simply darkness.

I didn't know how to look within until I found this Step, this tool.

The first time I took an inventory of myself it was primitive and rudimentary. Thank God that's all this program asks, because my primitive and rudimentary experiment with self-examination was sufficient to propel me along the road to recovery.

It was enough.

I did an autobiography. I wrote what came to mind about myself. It was between eight and fifteen pages long. Tagged onto the autobiography was a list of my secrets that caused me the greatest shame. I did what I could at the time.

My next Fourth Step was more refined. I had spent an additional year in recovery circles. I became more aware of what bothered me and other secrets I felt badly about—things I had overlooked. These new insights were incorporated into my next Fourth Step.

Then the real work began. I entered a phase of looking within myself on a deep level. This wasn't a general sketch of my childhood, but a detailed sketch of my soul and mind and all that had gone into the making of them.

This process became experiential. I began to live a Fourth Step. Life prodded and poked me until I looked so deeply within that, at last, I could truly see *me*. I began to see more than the behaviors I had exhibited that had caused harm. The process of examining my behaviors in an autobiography was crucial. My first few Fourth Steps peeled away the outer layers of pain from my heart. But there was much more buried within.

This fearless searching, this looking within, became a forced process, imposed on me by recovery, life, and my Higher Power. I didn't like it, but I learned to accept it, to go through it. I wanted to use people, places, and diversions to stop myself from feeling what I felt. Even when I was forced to look within— because I had surrendered to a God that loved me enough to force me to do that—a small part of me clung to the belief that if I manipulated my circumstances—changed my location or present state of mind—my pain would stop.

It didn't. And I'm grateful. Because it was good pain—it was healing pain.

Finally, life got through to me. I learned that no matter how I rearranged my present circumstances, I would be feeling what I was feeling and facing what I was facing—because it was time to do that. It was time, finally, for me to become healed. I had asked for that to happen. Now I was receiving the gift of healing.

It hurt. The pain I was finally facing had been with me for a long time. It was so deep, as were the messages that accompanied it, that I hadn't recognized it as pain or negative messages. I was aware only of the dull and constant ache of being alive, or rather, being partially alive.

I had grief inside, so much grief and aloneness and pain. I had so many walls around my heart that I could not tolerate receiving love.

I had denied and blinded myself to my feelings for so long— feelings toward my father, my mother, friends, myself—that I lived in both illusion and delusion. The feelings of rejection and sadness were accompanied by beliefs that I was not good enough and never would be. And I masked it all in a strange dichotomy in which I vacillated between feelings of superiority and inferiority.

I had been neglected as a child, handed inaccurate beliefs about myself, abused, deprived, and denied of much that a child needs to become minimally healthy. To survive this, I had told myself terrible lies. I had bought into the brainwashing and had made one excuse after another for those I had lived with.

The ultimate pain came not from what I had experienced but from my reaction to those experiences: denial and self-rejection. I learned to accept so little from life because I believed I deserved so little.

I learned how afraid, how terribly afraid I was to live, to go freely through the motions of life, to dance the dance of life and love.

I said I wanted relationships, but I didn't really want intimacy. I wanted someone to buffer me. I wanted a fortress, a hiding place. But even in those hiding places of dysfunctional relationships, I couldn't hide. God kept shining a light on me, showing me, making me face the truth about myself.

I learned I could not own my power with a lover until I learned to own my power with a parent. I could not be free to love until I broke my original bondage and took my own freedom to be, to be alive, and to welcome myself into this world.

The grief from this process was enormous. Being forced to stand alone, own my power, feel my feelings, and go through life without a buffer caused overwhelming emotions. I had spent my whole life avoiding feelings, functioning off mental energy, protecting myself with intellect. Being forced into the emotional part of myself, which in essence is the heart, hurt so badly and felt so uncomfortable and awkward I screamed, whined, and bellyached about the whole thing for well over a year.

I writhed from the discomfort of feeling. I went through the entire grief process over and over again, breaking through denial on a particular issue, then ascending immediately into anger and rage, until I accepted the momentary piercing of pain and sadness. Then, for several days, I would have a reprieve—and the process would begin anew on another denied, repressed issue. Over and over again, I grieved one loss after another, from birth to the present.

Life continued to bring me the experiences I needed to trigger this looking inward. I felt rage I didn't know I had. Pages and pages—a torrent of fears and negative beliefs—spilled out of me.

Discomfort does not adequately describe this process of experientially living through this healing process. I began to believe that was all there was. I thought the most I could hope for was that someday this process would end and I would return to feeling as I had before. There was more to come, though. One night, in the privacy of my own home, a spiritual experience took place. It took place in my heart. Like a tidal wave, the realization that I needed to forgive all—every single person from my past—flooded through me. It was a spiritual thought, like Divine Guidance. It was also a human thought, like "It's time to go to the grocery store." It was an awareness. Immediately, the list of those I needed to forgive flooded through me. It went from my mind down to my heart, and a forgiving, loving thought went with each name. Forgiveness was a gift. All I needed to do was become willing, and I don't know how great a part I played in that.

For a while, I had assumed anger and acknowledgment was all there was to the process. Those ideas were important, but they were only part of the experience.

As each name, each person, and a forgiving thought for each passed through my heart, I felt my heart become lighter and lighter. I had a physical experience of feeling the heaviness, the pain, the steel girders around my heart melting. Great restricting bands around my chest were breaking loose, and a part of me that had been closed, opened.

That part was my heart.

At the end of this experience, I realized I had one more person to forgive. It took the most effort and most time to forgive and accept that person. That person was me.

For years, I kept myself protected—encased in steel. My heart is open now, open and able to love in a way it never has. My emotional center has become unclogged. Emotions cycle through me in waves—they come, they present themselves, they release.

And I am grateful to be freely feeling, experiencing, all of them. But the new one, the one I never had before, is love.

It is so powerful. For the first time in my life, I am experiencing unconditional love. I feel it from others. I feel it for others. It is so different from the way I have loved in the past. It is so big.

For the first time in my life, there is room, really room, to love myself and others and let others love me.

I still get afraid, but like other emotions, the fear passes through me, once I face and acknowledge it. My heart is opening to love, joy, peace, sadness, anger, fear—to all that hearts feel. The knives and burrs and thorns are being removed from it. It is a good heart, a nice heart. I can hear it beating, I can feel it now.

It's real. Sometimes I feel like the Tin Man from "The Wizard of Oz." I finally have a heart. I'm real and I can love. Maybe I had this heart all along, but it didn't become real until it healed.

Now, when I hear people balk about taking a Fourth Step, I chuckle. I haven't taken a formal one, they say. I probably should, they say, but I'm not really ready. I haven't gotten around to it, they mumble. I understand the fear, but I also understand the process. If they stick around life and recovery long enough, they'll probably end up taking one like I did, whether they're ready or not.

Then they'll be glad they did.

I remember asking God to help me heal and to help me really take a good Fourth Step, a deep one. God answers our prayers, the ones in our best interests, even when we forget we asked, even if we're afraid God will answer.

We work these Steps to heal from our pain, fear, guilt, and limiting beliefs, but to do that, we must first recognize them. That is our task in this Fourth Step. Those who find the courage to look within are the people most comfortable with themselves, and recovery.

This is the healing Step. This is the healing-the-heart Step. This Step can change lives. Go deep. Go as deep within yourself as you can. Start with the top layer, and let the process take you deeper. Do not be afraid of what you will find. The things that have happened to us may be dark, but our core is beautiful and good.

Take this Step once, twice, as often as we need. Let the process of looking within become a habitual response to life and life's situations. Not to blame. Not to hold ourselves responsible for the behavior of others. But to explore, understand, take responsibility for, and cherish who we really are. Take this Step to empower and enable ourselves to heal and to take care of ourselves in any circumstances.

If we don't know what our issue is to deal with, ask God to reveal it to us. Ask God to show us what it is we need to face within ourselves. God will answer.

When we find the courage to look within and discover what is really going on with us, when we accept who we are, including our darker side, we will find that what happens outside, around, and within us begins to change. Not facing our pain, not facing our fears, is often the great motivator to the behaviors we call codependency. Looking within is the key to releasing our pain and producing recovery and health in our lives.

Often, we need to begin our recoveries by pointing the finger at the other person. We need to get mad, indignant, and sometimes even blame, as we grieve. If we are seeking only the relief of being blameless, if we are seeking only the temporary relief and "high" of moral superiority, then we can continue doing that. But if we are looking for more from our recoveries and from our lives, looking within is the answer. We will stop looking to others to stop our pain and help us feel better. And we'll begin, with the help of our Higher Power, to do that for ourselves.

They say that alcoholics work these Steps passionately because their lives depend on it. Well, so do ours. When we discover what's really going on within us, we will soon learn what it is we need to do to take care of ourselves.

Be honest, but also be gentle and understanding with ourselves as we work this Step.

We have been doing what we believed we needed to do to survive. Now, we are on the way to becoming fully alive.

ACTIVITIES

1. Have you done any family-of-origin work yet? Have you identified any old beliefs or any feelings from the past?
2. Have you already done a Fourth Step? Do you feel up-to-date with your feelings and issues?
3. Did any of the suggestions for doing this Step provoke your curiosity? You may want to set a reasonable goal for doing this Step. You can write your goal down and give yourself as much time as you want. For instance, "I want to do a Fourth Step in the next eighteen months." Or, "I want to do a Fourth Step in the next three weeks."
4. Do you feel blocked in any area of your life? Do you think it might be helpful to do a Fourth Step on that area?

STEP FIVE

"ADMITTED TO GOD, TO OURSELVES, AND TO ANOTHER HUMAN BEING THE EXACT NATURE OF OUR WRONGS."
—Step Five of CoDA

Before I began recovery, the concept of being honest with anyone, including myself, never occurred to me. From the time I was old enough to talk, being honest about who I was, and what I thought, felt, believed, wanted, and didn't want, was out of the question.

I had no honesty training.

Taking my first Fifth Step in treatment was a breakthrough. The act of revealing myself honestly to another human being and to God, and then facing myself in an attitude of acceptance, nurturing, and forgiveness, changed my consciousness. The Twelve Step program, as the Big Book says, catapulted me into another dimension of living.

This act of honestly saying who I was did not stay limited to a one-hour Fifth Step confessional. It began to spread. I began to reveal myself to my counselor, to friends, in group. It changed me. This Fifth Step changed me. Reading the book *Why Am I Afraid to Tell You Who I Am* by John Powell changed me.

Saying what I thought or felt in group, telling a friend honestly who I was, was as frightening to me as going into a clergyperson's office and talking about the long list of my wrongs. Yet, going through with this self-revelation, this honesty business that the Twelve Steps called for, was truly a life-or-death matter.

And like other changes that have happened to me, I'm not certain how much of it I did. It happened to me, by my being willing, being open, by my showing up for my life. Honesty was a gift, and I participated in it by opening my mouth and making my first awkward attempts at revealing myself to people.

I can still remember that first Fifth Step. All I was able to find about myself were the negatives, the wrongs, the awful things I had done in my life, my weaknesses. And maybe that was what I needed to see at the time. But the clergyman who listened to my recital of errors was wise. He was compassionate. And he handed me one good quality about myself before I left that room.

"You know, Melody, you do have good qualities," he said.

"What?" I asked.

The man told me one good thing about me that he saw. I can't remember now exactly what it was. It may have been persistence or determination. But it felt so good to hear that there was something good about me. It was enough to keep me going for years, until I was able, slowly, to begin seeing some good things about myself.

It helped to have someone accept me and believe in me. It began my process of accepting myself and believing in me. It was not enough to *think* about who I was—whether that meant what I felt, what I had done, or what I believed. I needed to get it out into the open. I needed to tell God. I needed to accept and admit it myself. But I also needed to risk sharing it with another human being.

That was what set me free.

That is what this Step is about.

I believe this Step has two important implications: the focused Fifth Step confessional work we are called upon to do when we formally take this Step; and the practice of appropriate honesty and vulnerability with the people we relate to in our lives. Let's talk about both.

ADMITTED TO ANOTHER HUMAN BEING

Historically, religions have preached that confession is good for the soul. This is true. It is especially true for codependents, but let's reword it. Confession, honesty, and vulnerability are good for healing us and our souls.

Some call codependency a disease, an illness. Others call it a problem. Some don't know what to call it. Some don't even like to call it "codependency." But many, including some original Al-Anon members, call it a "soul-sickness." What we do in recovery is to practice the daily behaviors that we call "recovery." What we are seeking are psychic and soul-level changes in ourselves, changes that can be manifested in our lives and our relationships, beginning with our primary relationships with ourselves.

To begin that process, it is imperative that we unearth, release, get rid of, and be done with shame, fear, guilt, secrets, and anything else inside us that bothers us, causes us to feel less than, weighted down by, burdened by, and bad about ourselves. The way to do that is by opening our mouths and getting it out. It is a simple but effective way to begin healing ourselves. We simply tell the truth about ourselves to ourselves, to another person, and to God in an attitude of self-responsibility, acceptance, and forgiveness.

There is something magical, but frightening, about opening our mouths and telling the truth. There is also something healing about it. An important part of this healing process we're going through is reconnecting to ourselves, our Higher Power, and other people. Being honest about ourselves is how we do that.

If we have done the work called for in the Fourth Step, if we have sat down and inventoried ourselves, we have started to shake up our souls. We have reached in with a Brillo pad and begun to scrub loose the debris and film within, those things blocking us from living the life we want. No matter what form of Fourth Step we use, no matter if we do a small, medium, or large one, we have loosened some things that need immediately to be washed away.

Once we start this process of loosening the "stuff" within, we will often notice it more. We may feel the weight of it all. We may begin to *notice* the feelings, needs, guilt, and burden of what we have carried around. We need to set up an appointment to talk about this soon. We need to move quickly on to this Step to do the washing away and cleansing of all that has been loosened.

It's important to take a Fifth Step soon after completing our

Fourth Step inventory. Some people suggest making an appointment to take a Fifth Step before we begin working on the Fourth, giving ourselves about two weeks. They suggest beginning on deadline to do the Fourth and going immediately in for the "cleansing" part. However we do it, we can do ourselves a favor and move quickly to this Step. With many of the Steps there is no rush to move on to the next. This one is an exception.

A traditional Fifth Step means that we make an appointment with someone trained in hearing Fifth Steps as soon as possible after we have done our Fourth Step. We sit in a room, face to face with this person, and begin talking about what we have discovered in our Fourth Step work.

We start talking with an attitude of humility, openness, self-responsibility, and honesty. Then the process takes on a life of its own. We begin to get to the core, the heart, of what's bothering us. For many of us, this is the first time in our lives we have done this.

This Fifth Step usually takes about an hour. Sometimes it takes longer. Sometimes that great sense of relief does not come immediately. For many it does. When they leave the conference room, their hearts have been permanently lightened. Some do not receive this sense of immediate lightening but gradually find that this Step, like the others, has done its work. They were moved forward on their journey, even though they did not notice a revolutionary change in the way they were feeling.

Some find revelations, insights, and buried guilts coming out, ones they had forgotten or never intended to discuss.

Some people find it a relief just finally to be heard.

"It was wonderful that someone could listen to eighty-four pages of my story and not fall asleep or be shocked," said Jane. "I think God was real gentle with me. I wasn't ready for much. I didn't see much, then."

Sometimes, people don't get to the core of the issue during the first hour. They need to go back to Step Four, do a little more digging, and schedule another appointment.

Sometimes, like Jane, we find that the longer we're in recovery, the more we see about ourselves and our issues. It can be helpful to take a Fourth and Fifth Step every so often, as our insights about ourselves and our behaviors increase and as our denial gradually and gently lifts.

However it happens, whatever the results, we can trust the process that is taking place when we make our efforts to work this Step. All we ever need to do with the Steps is make our best effort, the best we can do at that time, for them to work in our lives.

Many of us, myself included, find that we need to work on ourselves in layers, taking one Fourth and Fifth Step one year, doing our best, then moving on to another layer the next year. I was in such a fog about myself when I began recovery, there were issues, secrets, shames, and guilts I didn't even recognize at first. I needed more time recovering before I even noticed these issues. I needed to peel off one layer at a time, then deal with the next when it emerged.

Just as it's important to do our Fifth Step soon after we write our inventory, it's also important to choose carefully the person with whom we take our Fifth Step. Some people choose to do Fifth Step work with clergy. Others prefer not to. Some people choose a trusted program sponsor to do this work with. Others search around until they find the right person. An important criterion is that we take the Fifth Step with someone experienced in listening to Fifth Steps, someone who has done it before, and knows what we're looking for, someone who can assist and lead us through the process.

Taking a Fifth Step with an untrained person or someone who is not a good guide can be a negative experience. I did one Fifth Step with a clergyman who wanted to shame and convert me to his religion. I left the session feeling guilty and insecure. That doesn't mean that taking my Fifth Step was negative; it means I didn't find the best possible person to take it with.

Jack is a minister who has been in Al-Anon for six years. He is an adult child of an alcoholic; so is his wife. She has been in Al-Anon for eight years.

"I've done Step Four in bite-size pieces," said Jack. "My goal for the next year is to do a formal Step Four and Five. But as a minister, I will not hear a Fifth Step until I've done one of my own."

Sometimes it's helpful to use word-of-mouth references to locate our Fifth Step person. If we're having trouble locating someone, if we feel stuck, we can ask around for references at our groups. We can also contact the local Intergroup office (the Twelve Step headquarters) for the Twelve Step group we attend. If our group doesn't have a local Intergroup, we can contact Al-Anon.

We can call churches and see if anyone is trained in Fifth Steps. Or we can contact a local treatment center and see if they know of anyone. Whoever we choose to bare our soul to, the most helpful person will be someone trained, someone nurturing, someone who can assist us in getting to the heart of the matter, someone who will lead us into forgiveness, compassion for self, and self-acceptance.

We also need to make certain that the person with whom we share our deepest secrets will hold our confessions in confidence.

Most agree that it is better not to do a formal Fifth Step with a neighbor, friend, spouse, or other family member: It may backfire and hurt us. We're learning to be vulnerable and honest, but part of taking care of ourselves means we choose carefully who we do that with, so that our information can't be turned on us and used to hurt us.

It's also helpful to find someone who can see the good and the worthwhile in us, especially if we're not yet able to do that ourselves.

It's frightening to do the kind of soul-searching called for in Step Four. And it's scary to waltz into someone's office and tell the most troublesome things about ourselves, the things we have worked so hard to deny. It isn't easy. But it's possible.

Sometimes we find that the most troublesome things—for many of us, stealing something when we were younger; for others our flaws about ourselves and our lives—don't seem so bad once we get them into the light. We learn that nobody is perfect and nobody needs to be. But when something bothers us, we need to get it out into the light to be healed from it. If it's bothering us, we need to talk about it. And the more it bothers us, the more shame and self-hatred it causes, the more it controls us and our lives, the more important it is to bring it out.

One guiding rule for all my Fifth Steps has been this: Whatever it is I most don't want to discuss is what I most need to talk honestly about. To be healed, whatever I am most afraid and ashamed to share is probably what I most need to share at the time.

The first time I did this, the first time I opened up about the secrets, guilt, fear, anger, and pain that had been plaguing me for years—especially the wrongs I had done—I thought the walls would come tumbling down. You know what? They did.

"The Fifth Step helped me pull down the walls I had built," said Jane. "And I don't ever want to put them back up again. I died behind those walls—I died of character defects. I couldn't remove them, but God showed me when I was ready to let them go."

DAILY HONESTY

Another part of this Step, besides making an appointment and taking a formal Fifth Step, is learning to be appropriately vulnerable and honest with others about ourselves. Earlier in this chapter, I talked about my formal Fifth Steps, where I told someone what I had done wrong. Those were difficult, frightening. But something even more difficult and frightening for me was learning to be honest with others and myself, on a regular basis, about who I am.

It's easy to show my strengths. It's easy to talk to others when I'm feeling good, when I'm in control, when things are going well. In my recovery from codependency, I've learned I must do something else. To stay healthy, I need to talk to others and show that side of myself I'd rather not show: the part that's weak, feels frightened, and has needs, including needs for people. I need to show the part of myself that gets angry, has feelings, and isn't all "together" and perfect.

So much of my codependency centered around feeling that I had to be perfect. When I feel this way, I make myself crazy. And I hide the imperfect side of myself from myself and others. When I feel like it's wrong to have feelings, I dodge my feelings, and I certainly don't share them with others. So much of my codependency revolved around not being able to identify my needs and take responsibility for them. So much of my recovery meant learning to recognize these needs and bring them to people.

One need I have learned I have is to bring myself—the real me—to people, openly and honestly. This isn't easy, but I'm learning. It is much easier to be the one people reach out to than the one reaching out.

It is good for the soul to learn to reach out when we need to do that. We aren't a bother. We aren't a burden.

I've learned that the more I can allow myself to recognize my true needs, the less "needy" (in the negative sense) I am. When I take responsibility for my needs, they stop controlling me. When I respect myself enough to listen to myself about what I need, then take responsibility for that—whether that means calling a friend and talking about what I'm feeling, taking a break and going for a walk, taking a vacation, staying in bed on Saturday morning to watch cartoons, or taking a long hot bath— the more functional I become.

Since I've taken my formal Fifth Steps, I've learned slowly to open up to others. I'm learning that my real strength lies in vulnerability.

I've also learned something else. Until I'm entirely ready to accept who I am, what I feel, what I want, and what myself is telling me, I cannot achieve intimacy. When I am ready to take that same risk with people that I took when I walked into that Fifth Step room, I will have the kind of relationships I'm seeking.

I'm not talking about confessing my sins to people. I'm talking about sharing my deepest secret—who I am.

Not revealing myself in my relationships is turning out to be the ultimate way I try to control them. If I don't tell you how I feel, what I want, what I think, then maybe you'll like me. If I become who you want me to be, if I don't rock the boat, if I don't own my power, then you'll like me. Then I can control the course of the relationship. That is an illusion. When I don't reveal who I am, my relationships become superficial, and my real self will ultimately emerge, anyway. By the time it does, I will feel resentful, angry, and needy. It doesn't work to put our lives on hold for anyone.

"I've done a formal Fifth Step, but I do mini Fifth Steps now with my friends," said Judy. "I do this by letting them know who I really am. I try to keep current."

If we want to take down the walls in our relationships, we need to take down *our walls*. That is an effective and appropriate use of our power.

ADMITTED TO GOD AND TO OURSELVES

We've talked about telling another person about our shortcomings, wrongs, mistakes, failures, secrets. We've talked about sharing ourselves with others—who we are, what we feel, want, need, think, and desire. There are two more parts to this Step.

We need to tell God about ourselves. Quietly, loudly, silently, during our morning meditation, our afternoon break, or our evening walk, we need to say, God, this is who I am. This is what I did. This is what I think. This is what I want. This is what I need. This is what I'm feeling. This is what I'm going through. This is what I'm worried about. These are my fears, my hopes. These are my old beliefs. This is what I think I can't deal with, what I can't do. This is what I need help with. Hey, God, this is me.

We need to be honest, open, and vulnerable with our Higher Power. When we can do that, we will achieve the highest form of spirituality.

We are not burdening God by bringing ourselves to God. That's what God wants. And God cares, that much.

Besides telling God, we need to tell *ourselves* who we are, what we want, what we have done, our wrongs, our secrets, our good points, our beliefs. We need to admit to ourselves what we are really feeling, what we fear, and who we are. We need to break through our own denial.

We need to be honest with ourselves.

SETTING OURSELVES FREE

There is a place I get to with myself, about my relationships, that is dark and scary. In that place, I give myself many reasons why I cannot say what I most need to say, why I can't express my feelings, why I can't put my needs out, why I can't be who I am, why I can't take care of myself or be happy. When I am in that place, I have many reasons why I cannot reach out to others, why they're not interested, and why I can't reach out to God because God isn't interested, either. I don't like being in that place, so I don't understand why I go there. But I do. And when I do, the things I need to do to get out are often the behaviors I try to talk myself out of: reaching out, being vulnerable, saying whatever it is I need to say, and admitting to myself whatever it is I need to accept.

I trap myself in myself. The answer is owning my power to set myself free.

There is another place I go to with shame about my mistakes that is equally frightening. It is a place of terror, fear, guilt about what I have done, and guilt about having made a mistake. It is a place of fear about admitting and accepting who I am. When I get there, I convince myself that the only thing to do is to hide me and my mistake from myself and others.

I can do this with little mistakes and big mistakes.

The solution to this problem is the same. Whatever I most don't want to talk about, whatever it is I most don't want to admit, is what I immediately need to tell someone, someone safe, someone I trust. I need to get it out of me and into the light, so I can be set free.

Even after we take formal Fourth and Fifth Steps, even after we take several, even when we are working hard at recovery and trying to stay honest, we have fears, limiting beliefs, and resentments. We make mistakes. Sometimes these are judgment calls we make during certain periods of our lives when we are afraid and trying to survive. Sometimes these are manipulations. Sometimes they cross the line into dishonesty. We do a thing we really are not comfortable with; we violate our own moral code;

and we tuck away the guilty thing, and all the feelings that go with it, right down inside ourselves.

We may live with this for a period of time, barely noticing, until one day it emerges. There it stands, right before our eyes. We've got a new list of fears, or shame. We did something wrong, and we've been denying, justifying, and rationalizing it for a time—sometimes a long time. Then panic may strike. What do we do? Do we run and hide? Do we keep denying it? Or do we use these wonderful Steps as a tool to free ourselves from the darker side of being human?

This happened to me not long ago. Something I had done, and tucked away deeply inside me, emerged. It just came right out one day, while I was going about the business of living. I felt terrible. Awful. What do I do? I thought. I can't tell anyone. What would they think? After all, I've authored books on recovery. I stood there in my dilemma for a while.

Then what I needed to do came to me like a gift: inventory myself. Search out my fears, my beliefs, and what it is I did wrong. Clearly take responsibility for my part. Then tell someone. Pick up the phone and immediately tell someone.

I called two sponsors and told them both. Then I asked for, and quickly received, guidance as to the appropriate amend. As soon as I made that amend, I was set free from the incident.

And I immediately took a leap forward in my growth. I benefited from the experience, within myself. I felt stronger, clearer. And so did my belief in this way of life, these Twelve Steps.

Thank God for these Steps. Thank God we no longer have to live in guilt and shame. Thank God we no longer have to try to be perfect. Thank God we no longer have to hide from ourselves and others. Thank God the gift of this program is healing, self-acceptance, and a bond—a deep connection with others, ourselves, and our Higher Power.

We are finally free to be who we are. We can trust that when and if we are to become more, that will happen by taking the simple actions called for in these Steps.

THE CLEANSING STEPS

Made a searching and fearless moral inventory of ourselves. Admitted to God, to ourselves, and to another human being the exact nature of our wrongs. Many people pair Steps Four and Five together because they are integrally connected. That's how we work them. That's how they find us.

Learn to allow Step Five to follow Step Four quickly in our lives. Learn to open up quickly, admit to God, a person, and ourselves, what it is we need to admit—a feeling, a belief, a discovery about ourselves, or some hidden wrongdoing from which we need relief, release, and healing.

These are cleansing Steps, freeing Steps.

Think of the Fourth and Fifth Steps as handy housecleaning tools that work and get the job done. In this case, the job is restoring ourselves to sanity, peace, self-esteem, healthy relationships, and intimacy—with ourselves, others, and our Higher Power.

Often in life, we're faced with a task that we cannot perform with our bare hands. It might take us hours to loosen a tight screw with our fingernail, but the right screwdriver can accomplish that same task in seconds. The act of healing ourselves from the damage and pain of our pasts could be an overwhelming task, if we didn't have tools.

The Fourth and Fifth Steps are our tools for releasing and healing ourselves. We write an inventory of what's bothering us, then we verbalize our part and our responsibility to another person, ourselves, and our Higher Power. We take responsibility for ourselves. We accept situations and ourselves the way we are.

The Fourth and Fifth Steps can be used as needed. We can do them formally, by writing an inventory and making an appointment to discuss it, or informally, whenever things arise in the course of our lives that need attention. These two Steps give us the formula for healing from our pasts, from our old negative beliefs, from repressed feelings, from mistakes, from all that we are striving to be healed from.

Look inside with an attitude of compassion and self-responsibility.

Search within and strive to do this without fear. This kind of soul-searching requires responsible thought, thinking led by healthy boundaries and guided by Divine Wisdom.

Writing can be helpful, especially concerning incidents that are confusing to us. Writing gets it out of us. Then, get it out more by sharing who we are with another person. Tell God. And tell ourselves.

Admit what happened to another person and to God. God is safe and trustworthy. And we can choose people to talk to who are safe and trustworthy. If we ask ourselves and listen, we will know who it is safe to talk to.

Learn to open up regularly to people. One of our protective devices has been to hide. That has robbed us of the joy of intimacy in relationships.

We don't have to share ourselves with everyone. It's not healthy to be indiscriminately open. But we do need to be vulnerable and open with a few people in our lives. And we need to make honesty, including emotional honesty, a habit. Learn to connect with people on an intimate, sharing level—whenever it is appropriate and timely to do so.

Learn to tell people who we are.

Learn to connect with ourselves honestly and emotionally, so we can do the same with others.

Be open to using the process, the tools defined in the Fourth and Fifth Steps. Do this to initiate change and healing in ourselves, trusting that it will bring positive results: harmony with others and good feelings about ourselves. When we are confused about our part in an incident or who to talk to about it, wait for guidance, but do not wait too long.

These Steps give us permission to be who we are, to forgive and love ourselves, and to forgive and love others. These Steps give us a formula for self-care in relationships: looking within, and honesty with self, God, and others.

The Fifth Step gives us permission to be human, vulnerable, and honest. It gives us permission to have emotions.

Ask God to reveal to us the issues—the wrongs we have done to others and ourselves, the old feelings, the current feelings, the old beliefs, the behaviors—that we need to address in the Fourth and Fifth Steps. I promise, we won't be confused for long.

Whomever we talk to—a trained Fifth Step person, a friend, God, or ourselves—strive for self-responsibility in our communication. Strive to take responsibility for our feelings, needs, and wants. Strive to take responsibility for our part, even when our part means removing ourselves from the victimizing behaviors of another. Strive also to have compassion for ourselves when we speak, and for the other person as much as possible. But remember, it is easier to have compassion for the other person after we have removed ourselves as victims. Until we do, we will often feel angry, not compassionate.

Taking responsibility for what we need to say, for speaking our truth, is one way we remove ourselves as victims.

This is the telling-the-truth Step. Use it as often as necessary. This is the Step that will set us free.

ACTIVITIES

1. Have you taken a formal Fifth Step? What was the impact of that on your life and your feelings about yourself?
2. Are you in the habit of sharing yourself—who you are—with other people? When was the last time you called someone because you needed to talk about something? Do you talk to people about what you're going through when you're going through it, or do you wait until you've resolved the incident yourself, then report it after the fact?
3. Is there someone in your life now that you need to talk to? Is there something going on—a feeling, need, or an issue—that you don't want to talk about, but need to? Is there someone you're avoiding because you have something difficult to say?
4. In the past week, have you treated yourself or another person badly? You may want to choose someone safe and trusted and tell that person what you have done. Then tell God.
5. Each morning for the next week, when you wake up, take a moment to notice what you're feeling. Often, we're at our most vulnerable in those quiet moments before we begin the activity of the day. Check in with yourself emotionally. Take

a moment to tell God what you're feeling. Tell yourself. Within the next four hours, sooner if possible, tell someone else what you were feeling. You don't have to make a "feelings group" out of it; just disclose honestly what you were feeling. Do this same activity once more during the day—either at the end of the workday, after supper, or during a quiet time in the evening.

6. The next time a big feeling strikes—hurt, fear, anger, joy, blessedness, pleasure—call another person and talk about what you're feeling while you're feeling it.

*"I always learn the hard way. But
come to think of it, so do most
people. Rarely have I heard a
person say, 'I learn the easy way.' "*
—Gary E.

STEP SIX

"WERE ENTIRELY READY TO HAVE GOD REMOVE ALL
THESE DEFECTS OF CHARACTER."
—Step Six of CoDA

"Last night was terrible," Sandy said. "I was around a woman
who's been gossiping about me, and I couldn't say anything to
her. I stood there and listened to her go on and on to me, and I
couldn't bring myself to say a word to her directly. So I got into
my passive stuff, and let my anger come out that way.

"Then I ran into the guy I was dating a while back. I stopped
dating him because he wasn't treating me very well. Now, he
was with another woman. They looked happy. They were a
couple. I'm alone, as usual, feeling unlovable.

"Then I got home, and my mother called. She started shaming me about something, and all I could do was slink away.

"I fell right back into my old despair. For just a moment, I
started wishing I was dead again. I've learned to believe I can be
successful at work. But I don't believe I'm going to be happy in
love. I don't believe God cares about that part of my life. I don't
feel lovable. All around me, daily, I see evidence of how I don't
own my power.

"Then, when I tried talking to God about it, all I could say
was 'Sorry. I'm sorry God, that I'm such a disappointment to
you, and everyone around me.'

"It's morning now, and I feel better," Sandy said. "But I'm so
aware of myself, my codependent self. I don't believe good
things are coming to me in my love life. And I'm aware that one
of my bottom-line beliefs about myself is that I'm a disappointment to people, and God. I also see—I'm acutely aware of—
how I don't own my power with people and don't trust myself.

I've been walking around each day just noticing how I don't speak up and don't take care of myself with people the way I'd like to. Now, what do I do with all this? How do I change it?"

I thought about what my friend said for a moment. Without being flippant, and trying desperately to avoid throwing out recovery clichés, I said, "Why don't you try the Sixth and Seventh Steps?"

"I've been working those Steps," she said. "And it seems to get worse. The more I work them, the more I notice what I'm doing!"

"Good," I replied. "Then you can just relax and trust the process. Because it's working."

I believe in the Steps. I love the Steps. But I have a particular fondness for the Sixth and Seventh. (As you may have noticed, they seem to come in groups. One, Two, and Three go together. Four and Five are a pair. So are Six and Seven.)

Six and Seven are perhaps the most unnoticed, unused, mistrusted Steps in the Twelve. They are also some of the most powerful. These are the Steps whereby we become transformed. These are the Steps that actually change us.

OUR PROTECTIVE DEVICES

"I hate the language 'defects of character,' " said Beth. "I choose to look at this Step this way: became entirely ready to have God heal us. I don't believe that we act out because we're defective or bad. I believe we act codependently because we're wounded. And telling someone who's wounded that he or she is defective or that they've sinned or that they fall short of the mark is abusive. Now this philosophy doesn't give anyone permission to continue to harm themselves or another person, but it seems more compassionate."

Whether we call them defects of character or our protective devices, what are we looking at in this Step? What are we becoming ready to ask God to heal us from? What are we becoming willing to let go of?

Our tight grasp on people
Controlling
Manipulation
Our need to control and manipulate
Desperation
Our fears
Old feelings that may be clogging us up
Negative, limiting beliefs
Worry
The need to blame our pain on others
Waiting to be happy

We become ready to let go of our fear of being controlled—which for many of us is as great, or greater than, our desire to control or manipulate another. We let go of allowing others to control us, our lives, or our happiness.

We become ready to let go of our caretaking—our tendency to focus on the problems, issues, feelings, needs, choices, and lives of another; the underlying belief that we are responsible for others.

We become willing to be healed from the issues underlying caretaking: weak or inappropriate boundaries or limits; an unclear sense of self, self-responsibility, and the responsibilities of others.

We become willing to be healed from the belief that others, or ourselves, are incompetent and cannot take care of us.

We become ready to let go of:

Low self-esteem
Our self-neglect, and the belief that we aren't responsible for ourselves and cannot take care of ourselves
Our desire to have others take care of, or be responsible for, us
Self-rejection
Self-hatred
Lack of self-trust
Lack of trust in God, life, and the process of recovery
Our trust issues with people—inappropriately placed trust, and not trusting when it is appropriate

Our addictions
Guilt
Shame—that pervading sense that who we are is not okay

We become ready to let go of our inability to own our power, to think, feel, be who we are, take care of ourselves, and enjoy life. We become ready to let go of our difficulty with setting appropriate boundaries and limits with people.

We become ready to let go of our reluctance to feel and deal with our feelings:

Our difficulty dealing with and expressing anger
Our inability to experience joy and love
Our negativity, hopelessness, and despair
Our fear of joy and love
Our fear of commitment
A closed mind, or a closed heart
Our attraction to unavailable people and dysfunctional systems
Our need to be in dysfunctional relationships and systems
Our need to be perfect
Our abuse from childhood
Our need to be victims and our participation in our own victimization

We become ready to let go of our fear of intimacy and closeness, and our relationship-sabotaging behaviors. We become willing to let go of our problems and fears with sexuality.

We become ready to let go of our blocks and barriers to joy and love, even when we cannot name those blocks and barriers. We ask God to take away everything that stands in the way of us having all we deserve in our lives. We ask God to show us the blocks or defects we need to be willing to let go of, and help us become willing to let go of them all.

We become ready to be healed from our pasts, from unresolved feelings of guilt, anger, hurt, and grief over the many losses we've endured. We become ready to let go of the negative beliefs that we latched onto as a result of our pasts: that we're unlovable, a disappointment, a burden, not good enough, stupid, unworthy, a problem, and a bother.

We become ready to let go of all of our "don't deserves": don't deserve love, happiness, success. Don't deserve a new hat, a new coat, a new car. Don't deserve to be heard, cared for, have fun, or enjoy life.

We get ready to let go of the entire codependent package. Whatever we uncovered in our work on our Fourth and Fifth Steps, whatever we become aware of during the daily course of our recoveries, whatever we don't like, don't want, can't stand, feel helpless about, and want to be done with, we become willing to let go of.

Anything that is no longer useful; any behavior or belief that gets in our way—these are what we become ready to release.

The deeper we're willing to go, the deeper the healing we will receive.

Do not limit the use of this Step to defects. This Step works on feelings, and feelings aren't defects. If we get stuck in a particular feeling, especially fear, anger, resentment, grief, or sadness, we can become willing to let go of that.

A friend once asked me how much we needed to let go of.

"Just about everything," I told her. "Even the good we want."

We are on a journey, but we are not meant to carry heavy baggage. We are to travel lightly.

I've learned that letting go is the key: letting go of what I want, don't want, need, want to change, feel; my plans, agenda, hopes, dreams, goals, and timing. I need to let go of people, relationships, projects. If I don't, I find myself trying to control them, and controlling doesn't work. Letting go is the opposite of fear.

What a waste of time, some might say. First we have to identify a need, want, or feeling—then we have to let go of it? Wouldn't it be easier to ignore it, to deny our feelings about it, if we eventually let go of it anyway?

Perhaps, but that's not how this process works. The victory, the healing, the joy, is in the overcoming. It is in the letting go and then in the receiving.

There is no behavior too large or too small to be worked on in this Step. When we take this Step, when we become entirely ready to have God remove our protective devices, we are on the way to becoming changed.

BECOMING READY TO LET GO

If there is any struggle to recovery, if there is a difficult, frustrating, grueling part, it can be when we become aware of the devices that once protected us but have now become self-defeating. It is when we become ready to let go.

"I go through my day, and I see over and again how controlling I am," said Jan. "I'm not stopping controlling. I'm just seeing over and again how controlling I am."

I understand the feeling.

We may have spent years behaving in a certain way without having any awareness of, or experiencing noticeable consequences from, this behavior. Then, suddenly, it becomes time to change. We begin to notice that behavior. We bump into it, over and over again. We begin to feel the pain from that behavior, the helplessness, the hopelessness, our own inability to change. And we wonder how things will or can ever be any different.

That's when it's time to remind ourselves that we are changing. Right now, we are in the process of becoming changed. That's how this program of recovery works.

Sometimes I get so sick of a certain behavior that I think I'm going to explode if I do it one more time. Then I usually engage in it one more time, and often several more.

That's how we become ready. We get pelleted, sometimes bombed, by awareness. That's how life gets our attention. Awareness. Acceptance. And change. Our part in this process is becoming ready to let go, becoming ready to have God take it from us.

Some of us get ready the hard way.

I've noticed that the closer I come to being healed of a certain defect or issue, the harder it becomes to live with myself and that issue. It glares. It bites. It stands right there in my way. I despair of ever changing, of ever being any different. I'm slowly learning that that is a time to say thank you. Thank you for who

I am. Thank you, God, for who You are. Thank you for this program that says I don't have to do it alone. Thank you that I am right where I am supposed to be.

Thank you for this defect. Thank you that I can't change it. Thank you that You can.

Thank you that all I have to do is become ready to let go.

Thank you that right now I'm becoming changed.

We do not have to struggle too hard to become ready. Just as change is a gift, so is the readiness to let go.

We can start where we are and with who we are, and that is good enough for this program to work. We can ask for help getting ready to let go.

I used to work so hard at change. I used to call recovery an effort, hard work. The reality was that most of what I did that I called hard work was simply worrying and fussing about what I was or wasn't doing. I used to roll my sleeves up, start perspiring, and then go nowhere.

One day a friend called me. I was whining and complaining about some particular defect I was facing. I believe it was my fear about love and intimacy.

"What do I do?" I asked. "How hard do I have to work on this issue, now that I've discovered I have it?"

"Melody, why don't you lighten up and go with the flow?" she said. "All you need to do is get ready to let go of it, move on to the next Step, and let God do the rest. Why don't you stop working so hard on yourself and spend more time enjoying life?"

I followed her advice and this is what I saw: I don't have to work nearly as hard. I can go through my day and let old feelings arise naturally. Then I can let them be taken from me. I can do the same with behaviors, too—the most minute and the most troublesome ones. I don't have to obsess and worry about my recovery.

I've used this Step on a multitude of behaviors, such as learning how to be intimate, learning to feel and express feelings, and learning to take better care of myself in all circumstances. I've used it on learning to own my power, learning to set boundaries, and figuring out how in the dickens to initiate a relationship. I've used it on negative beliefs, such as I'm not good enough, I'm unlovable, and it's not okay to feel.

Since then, I do not work nearly as hard by worrying and fretting about how I will change myself. I'm learning that I can identify what I want to let go of, work toward readiness to let it go, then allow myself to become changed.

I'm learning to accept with more grace and dignity those times when I'm being prepared to become ready.

So can you.

Becoming ready to let go is not something that can be taught. But it is something that each of us can learn, through practice. Don't worry. If we stay in recovery circles long enough, we will.

The readiness will be worked out in us.

Sometimes, despite the pain, we may still be reluctant to have our protective devices or character defects removed. We may be afraid of what will be left, and whether we will have enough within us to take care of ourselves. This is a normal reaction. Our protective devices may have saved our lives. At one time they may have been all we had that kept us from being crushed.

"I wanted to hold onto my defects," said Patty. "It was such a joy to realize that I didn't have to be such a wonderful and giving person all the time. I could finally be nasty and mean and sometimes not care. It took a while to differentiate which defects needed attention and which were just a part of my personality."

Don't worry. Nothing will be taken from us that we need. And whatever is taken from us will be replaced by something better.

I understand how dear our defects can become. They've been with us a long time. They got us through. Not feeling feelings helped us cope with unbearable situations. Negativity protected us from disappointment. Caretaking gave us some esteem and a purpose in life. Controlling felt like our survival and our job.

Running from our pasts may seem as imperative to us as it did to Lot, in biblical times, when he saw his wife turn into a pillar of salt after she looked behind her. Not looking back, not facing our pasts, may seem as frightening and forbidden to us. We relied on these behaviors, our codependent behaviors, as trusted friends. But they may have turned on us. What once protected us may now be our undoing.

We can learn a better way. We can rely on this Step. We can trust what happens when we take this Step. If we aren't ready or willing to let go of our defects or any person or *anything*, we can ask our Higher Power to help us become willing and ready.

THE LETTING GO STEP

One morning I woke up enmeshed in fear and pain. I had done a bit of grieving over the holidays about a piece of unresolved historical work from my past. My father had called, and for the first time, we talked openly about the day he told me he was going away.

Even though I was only three years old at the time, I still remembered the incident. Talking about it, the feelings I had suppressed when it happened now surfaced. More than thirty years later, I was feeling the way I needed to when I was three.

Waking up in emotional pain triggered my codependent behaviors, as it often does. I was afraid. I feared that I would stay stuck in my feelings forever. I panicked.

I began to think of ways I could look outside of myself to stop the pain. I wanted to start manipulating people and events to my liking, hoping that that would make me feel better.

Then I lay still for a moment and quietly worked the Sixth Step. "Help me become ready to let go of the fear, the pain, the panic, the lack of trust, and all the rest I've become enmeshed in," I said. "Help me become ready to let go of this pain, instead of trying to make other people stop it or change how I feel."

Then I got up and started my day, trusting that my prayer was heard, trusting I'd feel better, trusting I would become changed in a natural way.

My trust was not misplaced.

This is not a do-it-ourselves program. We are not abdicating self-responsibility. But we are learning to trust God, trust this process, and trust ourselves. When it is time to change, we will become changed. We will receive the power, help, and ability to do that. For now, our part is becoming ready to let go.

Even that, I'm learning, will be worked out in us if we are open to it.

Lessons don't go away. They keep repeating themselves until we learn. In fact, when it's time to change, it becomes harder to stay the same than it does to change.

This Step gives us permission to relax, trust, and become willing. It gives us permission to be who we are and let this process of change happen to us.

Alcoholics Anonymous (the Big Book) suggests that after doing our Fifth Step, we seclude ourselves and ask God to remove our defects of character, our shortcomings. It's important to take this Step, and take it big, after doing a Fourth and Fifth Step.

This is the letting-go Step. It is the beginning of transformation. It begins the process of receiving what we want and need from our Higher Power. Become ready to let go of all that stands in our way, of all that bothers, troubles, defeats, or perplexes us, of all that we cannot control. Become ready to let go of what we don't want any more and what we truly desire. Then, move on to the Seventh Step and watch what happens.

ACTIVITIES

1. What are the hard-to-handle beliefs, behaviors, feelings, wants, or needs that you're struggling with right now? You may want to begin affirming that you are becoming ready to let go of these issues.

2. How would it make your life different if you believed that you could just relax and let this process called recovery happen to you?

3. Make a list of everything you would like changed about yourself. Include on it the things you would like to stop doing, things you would like to start doing, any family-of-origin work you'd like to accomplish, things you'd like to get and have. Put everything you can think of on the list, everything you'd like to be part of your future. Then put the list away and let go of everything on it.

4. Do you believe it's safe to trust God and this process called recovery?

*"There are things about ourselves
that we need to get rid of; there are
things we need to change. But
at the same time, we do not need
to be too desperate, too ruthless,
too combative. Along the way to
usefulness and happiness, many
of those things will change
themselves, and the others can be
worked on as we go. The first
thing we need to do is recognize
and trust our own Inner Nature,
and not lose sight of it. For within
the Ugly Duckling is the Swan,
inside the Bouncy Tigger is the Res-
cuer who knows the Way, and
in each of us is something Special,
and that we need to keep."*
—The Tao of Pooh

STEP SEVEN

"HUMBLY ASKED GOD TO REMOVE OUR SHORTCOMINGS."
—Step Seven of CoDA

Fear was a large part of my life and my codependency: fear of
people, fear of life, fear of my past, fear of God, fear of recovery,
fear of myself.

One thing I feared about recovery was taking this Step. On
the one hand, I wanted God to remove my shortcomings. On
the other, I wasn't certain there would be anything left if God
did that.

Would God come down, and in one fell swoop remove everything of me that resembled me? Would I turn into a saint? A
shell? I wasn't certain I had much to lose because I didn't think
there was much of me. I felt like a shell. And to have my defects
taken, the ones I've come to call codependency, sounded a bit
like annihilation.

What would happen to me? Who would I become? Would I

have a personality? Would I become a recovery robot, chanting jargon, smiling sweetly? Would I lose the things that made me uniquely me? Would I lose my passion?

The quote at the beginning of this chapter is longer than most and it is long intentionally. It needed to be because it has something important to say.

Yes, there are some things about us—about you and me—that we need to get rid of. But we need to keep who we are, ourselves, our inherent personalities, and the traits and qualities and idiosyncrasies that make us special and unique.

When we specifically take this Step, God doesn't come down with a vacuum cleaner and suck out all that is inside us. God doesn't take my personality. God doesn't remove *me*.

God takes only those traits that restrict and stop me from being myself.

Some of the more defeating traits will be removed. Many will be turned upside down. There is a negative aspect to a trait like obsessiveness, and often there is a positive side to that same trait. Obsessiveness turned upside down becomes determination.

Some of my defects needed to be refined or tempered. For instance, caretaking—focusing on others to the detriment and neglect of myself—can become love for self and love for others. That love can be manifested in a nurturing, life-giving way that holds me and the other people in esteem.

Fear, I've learned, is one thing that can just plain go, unless it is telling me not to walk in front of an oncoming truck.

I've learned that letting go of my defects does not eliminate my personality. It allows it to come through and shine for the first time since I was a very young child.

HUMBLY ASK GOD

Aside from our fear about what will happen to us if we are without our defects and what it means to have our defects removed, there is really only one idea in this Step to discuss. We humbly ask God to remove our shortcomings. That does not mean we holler at God to change us. It does not mean we demand. It does not mean we have to whimper, grovel, beg, plead, or incessantly ask.

What this Step means is that we acknowledge that God is the power. We acknowledge the difference between God and ourselves: God is all-powerful; we aren't and don't have to be. Some things we just can't do ourselves. Changing ourselves is one of those things.

So we ask God to do for us what we cannot do for ourselves. We humbly ask God to remove our shortcomings.

It helps to say "please."

TRUSTING THE PROCESS

The first time I took this Step, I did exactly as the Big Book said. I went away by myself into a room and closed the door. I asked my Creator to take from me all my defects of character. Despite my fears, I meant it. I was ready to have those things taken from me that I had become aware of and had discussed in my Fourth and Fifth Steps. I was even willing to have those things taken from me that needed to be removed, things I had missed in my Fourth and Fifth Steps. So I said that, too.

I meditated for a while, then prepared to leave the room, wondering what was going to happen. Was a bolt of lightning going to strike me? Would I go to sleep that night and wake up a different person the next morning? Would I recognize myself?

And how much of this changing did I need to do? Did this mean I had to try to be perfect from this moment on? I didn't understand the process I had begun. I still don't fully understand it, but I've learned to trust it.

It is a gradual process, a healing process, and a spiritual process. It doesn't hurt, at least not any more than necessary to heal us from past hurts or to get our attention. It is a palatable process, and even the pain becomes palatable, once we become willing to feel instead of resist, once we become willing to surrender.

It is not, I learned, an instantaneous process.

And there is nothing to fear.

Over the years, we become changed. I did not have to change

myself. I was not instantly revolutionized when I took this Step. But taking it set in motion the process.

Slowly I began to notice things about myself, like caretaking, controlling, fear, and unresolved grief from my past. Not in a chunk. I first became aware of how controlling I was with one person. I didn't stop. I just became aware of it. Then I became aware of how controlling I was with another person. Again, I didn't stop. I became aware of it.

Then I struggled for a while—with myself. I'd try to stop but find myself unable to. Or, I'd stop the behavior but I'd still want to do it. I'd try harder. Fail. Then finally surrender. I'd stop flailing about and let myself be.

That's when gifts came. Gifts like detachment. Letting go. Realizing deep within me that I couldn't control another. That doesn't mean I did it perfectly or that the gifts all came at once. But over the years, letting go gradually replaced the need to control.

It doesn't mean the need and desire to control doesn't come back. In my life, and in the lives of the many people who volunteered their stories for this book, control stands out as a number-one issue well into recovery.

Some of that we accept. Stay alert. Become more aware. Catch ourselves. But let ourselves learn and grow. Develop a certain gentleness and compassion with ourselves, for our humanness. Let the transformation happen.

I've found that some of my most problematic issues are sometimes transformed into helpful issues. For instance, when I was a child, I was alone a lot. I didn't connect with people and had few friends. For several years, while others were attending school and socializing, I was ill and had to stay home alone, studying by myself, isolated from people. I had many feelings about this part of my life.

Once I accepted this part of my life and was able to say thank you for it (even though I didn't mean it), I was able to see the gift I had gotten from it. Learning to be alone, learning to study alone, learning to be an independent thinker, became one of the traits that qualified me for my present occupation, that of being a writer. A negative became an important positive in my life.

I am in awe of the many ways gratitude, acceptance, and working this program can transform us, and transform some of our most troublesome traits.

For years, I deprived myself—out of martyrdom or sometimes for no reason at all. Once I was able to channel this ability, I learned how to deprive myself temporarily in the course of working toward goals.

I have seen many people recovering from codependency go without, struggle, and deprive themselves for no reason or in the hopes that doing so would salvage a particular relationship. Once their recovery was underway, I have seen these same people take that ability to endure, push forward, and go without to help themselves get through college, or start their own business, or do something else that benefits them.

A character trait was rechanneled.

The desire to control can be tempered with appropriate boundaries and respect and then channeled into management and leadership abilities.

All the energy we put into despising and disliking ourselves can be turned positive, can be used to love ourselves.

Some of the endless caretaking and care giving we gave away to the world can be turned toward us, until we truly learn to love and take care of ourselves.

And on it goes.

Yes, some things we are better off without. Some things will be turned upside down. Some things we will work on, with God's help, over time. Some things we will learn to accept.

Perhaps I will never be a good cook, and I'm not certain I care. I accept that about myself. If ever it is to change, it will. But for now, I am not interested in changing that particular trait.

Some things I do well. Some with mediocrity. Some not at all. That is okay.

The longer we work these Steps, the better perspective on ourselves and our pasts we'll gain. The more fully we allow healing to take place concerning our pasts, the more we will see and be open to receiving the gifts from our past.

Once we work through our bitterness, we will be able to receive the gift from each relationship, even the most painful ones.

We will be healed. Self-love and love for others will come to us. Perhaps the most healing gift of all is self-acceptance, an immediate, ever-present acceptance of self, of all we are and have been, and of all we have been through. The more we can accept ourselves, the more we will naturally evolve into who we are destined to become.

This Step does not absolve us of self-responsibility. But we don't have to worry and fret. We don't have to force our recoveries. We don't have to abase or criticize ourselves further because we are unable to change something about ourselves. Our primary task is acceptance and self-love. From that place, all good things will happen and come to us.

We will be led into the healing we need. Situations will arise. People will come into our lives. We will hear a phrase at a meeting. Someone will call and begin talking about something that strikes a chord. We will be handed a book. A thought, an inspiration, will come to us.

We may be led to a private therapist or a specialized recovery group. We may be led into awareness of another addiction or problem within us—and into recovery for that. We may find ourselves in a relationship that begins to trigger deep healing from our pasts.

We may find ourselves in an employment situation challenging us in new ways to own our power. We may discover new parts of ourselves we can explore and work on.

The process will work, and it will work its magic on us, if we allow that to happen. Sometimes it works even when we resist. We will find ourselves being changed, right down to the core of ourselves, in ways that we could not do for ourselves.

And it happens naturally, if we let it.

This Step gives us permission to be who we are. We say please help me. Please change me. From that moment on, we can be who we are and let the changes happen.

We don't have to work so hard. We don't have to struggle so. Our task is to accept ourselves, at any given moment. Ask God to do the rest. Ask, knowing that what we want and need done for us is greater than what we could accomplish. Ask, knowing that we are not expected to do it ourselves.

Then, be open to and trust what happens next.

Yes, we do have a part in this process. That part is applying ourselves to the Steps. There are tasks at hand, and we will be shown and helped to do whatever it is we are to do, when we are to do it. But the task in this Step is simple. This is the "humbly asking God for what we need" Step. It gives us permission to come as we are and bring our needs and desires to our Higher Power. We say please, then trust that we have been heard.

THE TRANSFORMATION STEPS

Steps Six and Seven are the transformation Steps. When people ask me how I've changed, or how they can change, I do not have an elaborate reply. I never have. Yet, I have been through major transformations in my lifetime.

I began, as we all do, as an innocent child. By the time I was twelve, I was a full-blown practicing alcoholic. By the time I was eighteen, I was shooting drugs. By the time I was twenty-three, I was in a methadone program. By the time I was twenty-six, I was in treatment, initially against my wishes, for drug addiction. I became transformed into a sober person and began my connection with these Steps and a Power greater than myself.

I was transformed from a person obsessed with chemicals to a person dedicated to sobriety and a new way of life.

From there, I discovered yet another obsession—my obsession with people and my neglect of myself. I discovered a deeper part of me, a part full of pain and longing—the black hole in my soul.

Over the years, I went through another transformation. I was gradually changed into a person who was less fearful, less controlling, and more focused on personal accountability and responsibility. I was transformed from the original martyr into someone dedicated to being good to herself.

I learned to deal with feelings. I began to be healed from the backlog of feelings from my past. I even saw my past transformed and began to understand the gifts from all of it, even the most painful moments.

Daily, transformation takes place. And I am finding that the longer I live, the closer I come to that wonderful, innocent child within; the closer I come to the way I started. Yet there is another person with me, the person who has traveled with me through all the years, who has learned to survive, learned to stand alone, learned to lean, learned to care, and is learning to allow herself to be cared about.

With me is that person who has experienced much of life, often the hard way, and I'm learning to treasure and value that person too, and all her experiences. For they are what has made me *me*.

When people ask me how to change, I cannot give a long intellectual lecture. I cannot preach. I cannot even boast. What I can offer them, and you, are the core tools for change and transformation in our lives—the Sixth and Seventh Steps.

Become willing. Become open. Say please. And cherish who you are now, in this moment.

Nothing, nothing, can interfere with the good that is coming your way in life, and in this program called recovery.

This Step does not eliminate us. It embraces and brings together the beauty of that innocent, natural child in each of us and combines it with the wisdom of our experiences. It enables us to realize our potential fully.

Our gifts will become enhanced and accentuated. Our idiosyncrasies will become acceptable, at times laughable. Our negatives will be illuminated, lightened, eliminated, or made bearable.

Ask God to help us. Ask God to change us. Ask God to heal us. Become entirely ready to have God heal us, then humbly ask God to do that. That is the essence of the Sixth and Seventh Steps.

And they are the core of our healing.

ACTIVITIES

1. What are your fears about becoming changed? Write about them. Or talk about them with another person.
2. How have you already seen yourself changed? How much of this did you actually have to do? How much were you em-

powered to do? Reflect on the gradual, natural nature of change in your life.

3. Writing letters is a favorite tool of mine. Write a letter to God, as you understand God. In that letter, talk about what bothers you and what you would like to see changed about you. Ask God to help you change those things in yourself and your life that need changing.

4. If in doubt about what character defects to work on now, ask God to show you clearly what issues in your life would be improved if you would work the Sixth and Seventh Steps on them.

5. Do a creative visualization about yourself. Visualize in your mind yourself as you would like to become. See yourself doing and being all that you would like to do and be. Then let it go. Come back to now. Affirm that who you are is good. Affirm self-acceptance and self-love for yourself in the present moment.

STEP EIGHT

"MADE A LIST OF ALL PERSONS WE HAD HARMED, AND
BECAME WILLING TO MAKE AMENDS TO THEM ALL."
—Step Eight of CoDA

"When I first read Step Eight, I really misread it," said
Jason. "I thought it said, 'Make a list of all the people who have
harmed you.' "

I know the feeling. When I began recovery from addictions
and got to this Step in my recovery, my inappropriate behavior
toward others was clear. The list of people I had harmed and the
behaviors with which I had harmed them were glaring. There
was no justifying, rationalizing, or explaining them away. I had
done wrong.

When I began recovery from codependency and got to this
same place—this place of taking responsibility for myself and
my behavior in my relationships—my list was foggy, vague, and
littered with my own sense of victimization and powerlessness.

Exactly who had I harmed with my codependent antics—my
controlling and my caretaking? What was the wrong I had done?
What was my part? To whom did I owe amends? Why? And
what about the wrongs that had been done to me, my feelings of
being used, abused, mistreated, and victimized?

And, I wondered, wouldn't making amends to these people
who had victimized me put me further into their hands, leave
me more at their mercy, and render me totally defenseless?

How could I apply this Step to my codependency and come
out intact? How could I use this Step to further my health and
not my codependency? After all, a symptom of my codependency
had been running around the world apologizing and making
amends for everyone else's behavior, taking on the guilt of the

119

world, and achieving a high-level, but unnecessary, sense of martyrdom.

In this chapter we're going to explore how to use this Step to further our health and growth, as this Step applies to our codependency. There are two pertinent ideas in this Step: making a list, and becoming willing to make amends to everyone on it.

MAKING OUR LISTS

As we work this Step the first list we may want to make is a list of those who have harmed or wronged us. I understand this is a controversial idea and not what the Step says. But I have a plan for this list and some ideas about helpful amends that I'll discuss in the next chapter.

We have been wronged. We have allowed ourselves to be harmed. Sometimes, as children, we had no choice and no way to protect ourselves. Sometimes we feel wronged by many, and not just as children. Who hurt us? Who do we feel victimized, mistreated, used, or abused us? Who has rejected us, spurned us, caused us pain? Who do we resent, fear, or avoid because they have hurt us? Who are we rejecting because of what the other person has done and because of our inability to take care of ourselves with that person?

Make a list. Put every name you can think of on that list. If you have done your inventory work thoroughly, you should have gotten most of the details and grievances out of yourself. If you find new thoughts emerging and need time to write about them, do so.

Nobody is immune. Neighbors, friends, relatives, Mom, Dad, sisters, spouses, boyfriends, girlfriends, lovers, employees, employers, co-workers, schoolmates. Think back. Who hurt you? Who disappointed you? What relationships leave you with a wrenched or bitter feeling?

This is an important list, and it is your chance to get it all out. Get every name on that list you can think of—everyone who owes *you* an amend. Remember, we have started on a deep healing process, so take the time you need to be as thorough as possible. You are the person that will benefit by your thoroughness.

Once you have finished that list, put it aside. Take out another sheet of paper and make your second list. This list is just as important as the first one. This is the list of people you have harmed.

Now we are entering into some exacting, focused work. Often, it is helpful to pray for Divine Guidance and wisdom as we embark on this project. Who, exactly, have we harmed with our codependent behaviors? Do not suppress yourself by worrying now if you are going to have to apologize to these people or what you are going to say, or whether you will look foolish. It is not yet time to address those issues. For now, we are focusing on making a detailed list of those we have harmed.

Who are the people we feel most defensive and protective around? Who received most of our controlling and caretaking gestures? Was there an addict or another out-of-control person that we became obsessed with controlling?

Who was the recipient of our rage and anger? Are there people we have shamed and blamed? Remember, we are not justifying right now.

Who are the people we most fear encountering, because we have unfinished business with them? Who are the people we feel most uncomfortable around? Who, exactly, have we harmed on this journey, as we've struggled to survive? With whom have we behaved in a way that we don't feel good about?

With what people, in what relationships, would we like peace and healing restored?

Many of us find that immediate family members go on this list. Most of us find that our children are number one. It is hard to be nurturing, loving, nonshaming, and present to meet our children's needs in appropriate ways if we have never been nurtured or loved, if all we know is control and shame, and if we ourselves are doubled over in pain. Being without boundaries, not being able to set appropriate limits with our children, is doing them harm.

As we make this list, be firm but compassionate with ourselves. Avoid wallowing in guilt. Feeling guilty and ashamed is not the purpose of this list. Being done with guilt and shame is our goal here.

Think about love relationships, but don't dwell on the other person's behavior. What were your inappropriate behaviors in these relationships? If you're uncertain, ask God to show you. Ask God to bring to mind any behaviors or incidents you need to address in this list.

How about extended family members? Where is there discord and disharmony with family?

Many put in-laws high on their list, too.

Consider your work history. Is there an employer or an employee to whom you did not give what you contracted to give, because of your codependency?

Do not be obsessive. Do not become unduly entangled in irrelevancies or imagined shortcomings. Look at your behavior in a quiet frame of mind and allow the names to emerge that need to be on your list.

Now, let's move on to finances. To whom do you owe money as a result of your codependency? Put their names on the list. Perhaps we have borrowed and not repaid. We may have lied or manipulated to get money that was not legitimately ours out of fear or a need to survive.

Perhaps we got so enmeshed in our codependency that we neglected our fiscal responsibilities. Put the names of the people we—not someone else—owe money to.

As we consider and make this list, strive for a peaceful, balanced frame of mind. If guilt or anxiety overtakes us, put pencil or pen down, stop, and retreat into a peaceful place. When our balance has been restored and we are making our lists from peace, acceptance, and compassion for ourselves, return to work.

Review friendships and our conduct in those. Have we neglected someone important? Are there people we rescued over and over again out of our own codependency, then became resentful toward them because we were tired of taking responsibility for their behavior?

This Step requires soul-searching. It is not a Step to punish us nor is it a Step to remind us of our need to feel guilty. It is a Step to set us free from guilt, anxiety, and discord.

We need to be open to guidance as we work this Step. Often,

our tendency is to feel guilty about everything we've ever done and anyone we've come in contact with. Much of what we're feeling that we call codependency is unearned guilt. If we find ourselves getting enmeshed in unearned guilt, it may help to make a separate list: people we haven't harmed but feel guilty about anyway. Sometimes if we have an abundance of unearned guilt with a particular person, we may want to look behind the unearned guilt and see if there is some hurt or anger lurking there, anger disguising itself as guilt.

Make a list. Get it down, and get it out. Who have we harmed?

It helps to be specific about the harm we have caused. For instance, "Jake was the recipient of my unbridled rage." "I made Sue crazy trying to control her." "I borrowed money from Angela that I haven't paid back." "I forgot to be true to myself and got caught up in Harvey's resentments about Don, then completely abandoned Don even though I still liked him."

This is the Step where we forget about what the other person did or didn't do and focus on taking responsibility for our own behaviors. Who did we manipulate? Lie to?

The most important consideration in this Step is this: Toward whom do we not feel peace in our hearts? In what relationships are there discord and disharmony? Whether we intend ever to relate to these people again or not, what relationships need peace and love and good feelings?

In what relationships do we need to be able to hold our heads up and allow our hearts to be open and filled with love—even if that love comes from a distance and with detachment?

Now we are approaching our third list. It is as important as the other two we have made; maybe this one is the most important. For years I have heard this idea bandied about in recovery circles, but we need to take action on it, particularly as it relates to recovery from codependency. The name that goes on the third list is our own name.

We are usually the people we have harmed the most with our codependency. We are the people we most need to become willing to make amends to. By repressing our feelings and thoughts, neglecting ourselves, criticizing ourselves, shaming ourselves, denying reality, being so frightened, holding ourselves down, pushing ourselves back, believing absolutely untrue things about ourselves, being too harsh, too critical, or too demanding, we have certainly done ourselves wrong.

Denying and depriving ourselves is wrong. Not trusting ourselves or listening to ourselves is wrong. Not loving ourselves is wrong.

Allowing ourselves to be lied to and deceived to the point that we no longer listen to or heed our instincts is wrong. Thinking we're crazy and bad for surviving is wrong. Holding other people's issues or inappropriate behaviors against ourselves is wrong.

Allowing ourselves to be abused or mistreated is wrong—regardless of the degree of abuse. It is not okay to let ourselves be talked to or touched inappropriately.

It is simply not okay to allow ourselves to be victimized.

Neglecting ourselves is wrong. Ignoring what we want and need, sometimes to the point that our minds, bodies, and souls rebel by getting sick, is wrong.

Neglecting or diminishing our gifts and talents is wrong.

Being ashamed of ourselves is wrong.

Harboring anger and resentment toward ourselves is devastating. We can spend a lifetime punishing ourselves and allowing others to hurt us, too. I am learning that I was as angry at myself as I was toward others. For years, both sets of anger were denied.

Every behavior we list as codependent is in truth a wrong done toward ourselves. Sometimes it involves a wrong done to someone else, too. We need to be absolutely honest about both. Until we do, we will not have the map for the rest of our recovery.

In many of the relationships we feel uneasy about, it is not how we treated the other person that is cause for the name to go on our list—it is how we treated ourselves or allowed ourselves to be treated. Allowing others to treat us badly inevitably leads to resentment toward the other person. We need to deal with this resentment, but we also need to be willing to make amends to ourselves for not treating ourselves with the respect we deserve.

Listen, friends. Not nurturing ourselves, not listening to ourselves, not taking loving care of that delightful child inside us, is wrong. That child, unless we have totally abandoned it—and that is wrong—will be with us all our lives. Not listening and responding in a loving way to that child inside us is wrong.

It is bad enough that many of us were abused and neglected as children. For some, that abuse stemmed from growing up in an alcoholic home; others were the victims of physical, sexual, or emotional abuse. But once we understand, once we are lead into the light, there is no rationalizing or redeeming the idea that many of us continue to neglect and abuse ourselves and that child within us.

This is the Step where we come to terms with that idea. This is the Step where we list *all persons* we have harmed. Until our name goes, in ink, on that list, our lists and our recoveries will be incomplete.

This is a grueling task. But it is a good place to put our energy if we want to accomplish healing for ourselves. Do not allow it to overwhelm you. If reading this far feels overwhelming, stop until you become peaceful. If making a list becomes overwhelming, stop until you become peaceful.

It may be helpful to take this Step in small spurts. Guilt and anxiety are our weak points, anyway. Let your list be an ongoing project, adding to it as names and incidents enter your awareness. Work on it a little each day. Then do something peaceful and relaxing immediately afterward. Read a meditation book. Call a friend. Do something to uplift your spirits.

Caution: There is no reason to feel guilty or prepare to make an amend, if what we have done is to take care of ourselves. Saying no, setting a limit, not allowing ourselves to be used or abused, saying how we feel, taking care of ourselves, and beginning or continuing on a recovery course are not wrongs we have done. Often, we tend to feel guilty about these behaviors because that is part of changing ourselves and because we are breaking old dysfunctional rules that tell us not to do that. We do not have to apologize for appropriately taking care of ourselves.

Seek discernment and wisdom as we make our list. If confused, talk to God, a sponsor, or someone who has solid recovery wisdom.

We also do not have to apologize to people for not allowing them to control our lives or for beginning to live our own lives. Do not worry about perfection. As you approach and complete this part of the Step, ask for guidance and help. Ask to be shown all the names that need to go on this list. If your list is small, that's fine. That's what it needs to be. If your list is long, that's fine, too.

We can open ourselves to an honest understanding of the people that need to be on our list. We can ask God to bring to mind and heart the people's names for our list. Ask to let go of defenses, pride, unearned guilt, shame, and anxiety as we do this task.

The goal of this Step is to be honest with ourselves, not unduly hard on ourselves. For many of us, being too hard on ourselves, too critical, is a problem we associate with codependency. Often, making this list can be a relief. After thinking through and taking this Step, many of us find that much of our guilt has been unearned. Often, we come up with a few behaviors we truly do not feel good about. Sometimes more. But this Step is here to help us. It helps us clarify exactly what we have or have not done and sets us on the path to taking care of ourselves. The point of doing this Step is not to make ourselves feel guilty. It is to uncover any guilt we're already feeling or running from, then remove it.

The purpose of this Step is to restore us to right relationships—with ourselves and other people. By the time we've completed this portion of this Step, we may have three lists: people who have harmed us; people we have harmed; and the list with our names on it. Now it is time to put our pencils or pens down and do the spiritual work required by this Step: achieve willingness to make amends.

BECAME WILLING

What does it mean to "become willing to make amends to them all?" This Step calls for a change of heart. It asks us to drop our defenses, our protective devices, and to begin to seek peace and healing in all our relationships.

It does not mean we go back into dysfunctional relationships or systems. It does not mean we stop taking care of ourselves, even if others claim that our self-care has harmed them. It means we search out our indiscretions toward self and others. It means we become willing to seek peace and reparation in all our relationships, past and present.

It was so easy for me to stay justified in my hostility and resentments toward people. I had a long list of all those who had harmed me. There were the relationships with addicts and alcoholics where I had been abused. There were important people and caregivers from my past who I felt had harmed me. There were even family members who I felt had hurt or disappointed me.

I would be entirely justified, I thought, if I withdrew into a cave, became a recluse, and never spoke to any of them again.

That place, however justified, is not pleasant. It is not a place of feeling connected with myself or others. It's a place constructed of and decorated with fear.

This program offered me a better way. It offers us a better way. That way is an open heart, a connection to people, ourselves, and our Higher Power—and healing in relationships, past and present.

It begins with willingness, willingness that can begin only within us. It's a willingness to be at peace with the people in our lives, including ourselves—free of guilt, fear, resentment, and ill feelings because of what has transpired in our pasts.

Our pasts have not been a mistake. All that has happened has not been incidental or accidental. Some say we participated in choosing our destinies; others say our destinies and all the people and incidents involved were charted for us from the moment we were born. Either way, the understanding is similar: no accidents, no mistakes.

All that has come into our lives was designed to prepare us to become who we are and to help us learn the lessons we came here to learn. There is a purpose for and a gift from each relationship, even the most painful relationships. The longer I work at recovery and the less I view myself as a victim, the more receptive I am to these gifts.

Sometimes, the gift has been showing me what areas of myself I have not dealt with. Some relationships have come into my life to make me strong, teach me how to own my power, and show me how to set boundaries. Some have come into my life to bring healing. Some have come in to bring and inspire gifts of creativity, spontaneity, nurturing, femininity, and support, or to help me believe I deserve the best that life and love have to offer.

Some have come to show me what I don't want. Some are here to show me what I do want.

Our relationships, many say, are a mirror of our issues and our goals, a reflection of us. Each has a gift. Letting go of resentment and bitterness is the key to unlocking that gift.

We can say thank you for each gift.

There is a place in our hearts that will put us on the right course with people and ourselves. That place is willingness to make amends, willingness to achieve healing in our relationships with people, and willingness to find the gift.

When we achieve that place, when the idea of willingness begins to enter our minds, even before it has worked its way down into our hearts, it's already beginning to happen. We are beginning to open ourselves to the reparation, healing, and love available to us in our relationships. We are ready to begin to love ourselves, and others, unconditionally.

This attitude doesn't mean we stay in relationships that have reached their time to end. It doesn't mean we have to go back to relationships that aren't good for us. It doesn't mean we surrender to any treatment from any person who isn't good for us. If someone treated us badly, our lesson from that relationship was learning to own our power and find our own liberation. What we do in recovery is what one woman, Beth, calls "realigning myself with my relationships."

But to begin that realignment, to find that place of peace with self and others, we need to be willing.

Becoming willing does not mean we deny what is or has happened. It does not mean we forfeit ourselves or give away our power with people. It means we become ready to open our hearts to people, despite what has happened. We become ready to go lovingly to people and take care of ourselves with them.

We become willing to love and take care of ourselves.

This Step asks us for a change of heart, so that our hearts can be healed and opened to love. Do not fear the amend. For now, do not think about the amend. Contemplate willingness, a willingness to do what we are directed by our Higher Power to do, a willingness to take care of ourselves with people.

We will not be asked or required to do anything foolhardy or inappropriate. All we are becoming willing to do is make appropriate amends, to take responsibility for our inappropriate behaviors toward others and toward ourselves.

How can we learn to love until we become ready to take responsibility for our part?

Healing begins within us. It begins with a thought, a vision, a feeling of willingness. A great chain of healing and love begins when we make the decision to take care of ourselves with people and to come to a place of peace about our relationships. We take ourselves out from under the control and influence of others and their addictions; we align ourselves with recovery, ourselves, and our Higher Power.

We are beginning to own our power in new ways, ways that we have not known before. We are taking ourselves out of anxiety, shame, and guilt, and stepping into peace.

We have stopped fussing over others. We have taken the risk to look within. Now, we are asked to take an even greater risk—that of quietly, but clearly, accepting responsibility for ourselves and our behaviors.

This Step, and the next, heals our relationships with ourselves and others.

We are on our way to learning to own our power in any circumstance and in any situation. We are learning how to stop allowing others to victimize us and to stop victimizing ourselves. We are giving up our victim role.

We are part of a new consciousness. It is this recovery work that each of us is doing that will stop the chain of victimization and abuse—not just in our lives, but in those around us. Many of us have wanted to change the world. Well, we are—simply and quietly, by doing our own work and our own healing.

VICTIMS NO MORE

When I began recovery from codependency, all I could see were the wrongs and the harm others had done to me. I hurt so much. I had lost so much.

And I felt so victimized.

Looking at my own part in my relationships, even the most painful aspects of myself that needed working on, was beyond my ability. The thought of apologizing to anyone was out of the question. It felt like I would be apologizing to people for them hurting me. The good news is, I didn't need to make my amends then. I wasn't ready yet. I needed to focus on my pain, my grief, and some basic recovery behaviors I could do to stop my pain. I needed to nurse my wounds and even indulge in a little self-pity; this was part of my journey toward removing myself as a victim of other people, their addictions, and their problems.

There came a time, and that time was slow in coming, when I was ready to begin this process of looking inward. It came time to become willing to face and accept my part in my relationships. I saw how I had a part in even the most painful relationship I had been in. When I stopped complaining so long and hard about the behavior of others, I began to see them as mirrors of who I was. And the truth was that whenever I no longer needed a particular relationship anymore, I got out. I wasn't held captive. I was, all along, responsible for myself.

My relationships reflected my unresolved issues and my fears. My relationships reflected my beliefs about what I deserved from love, what I was willing to tolerate.

When I looked carefully at those I had accused of not being willing to be intimate with me, I began to see my own blocks to intimacy—my own unwillingness to be emotionally honest and vulnerable. I saw my own inability to sustain closeness or to let someone in for more than a moment.

Those I had bellowed about because "they were too dependent on me" were the same ones I found myself overly dependent on.

When I looked at those who outraged me because they were trying to control me or unduly interfering with my business, I saw a like response to them on my part—an unwillingness to accept them as they were and let them be.

I saw that I had needed and attracted all the relationships in my life for one or another purpose of growth. If I didn't learn the lesson, if I didn't face and deal with what was inside me, I found myself in a similar circumstance, repeating. When I became willing to face my part, own my part, admit to my part, and make amends for my part, I had won half the battle. Maybe the victory was already mine.

There is a quiet, honest place that this Step takes us to, a place of dropping defenses and pride, a place where we shed victimization. We become willing to clean our slate, in peace and honesty.

Take this Step as soon as possible after making your list. Take it whenever bitterness, resentment, victimization, or fear enter in. Take it whenever you seek and desire peace and healing with yourself and with others. We do not have to do this Step too soon. We do not have to do it until we are ready. But when it is time, we do not want to procrastinate.

The Step gives us permission to stop fighting with others and with ourselves. We can learn about ourselves and then grow and move forward from that lesson. We can love, forgive, and be forgiven, and accept all that has happened.

Many of us are carrying around residue from relationships that are decades old! We have not yet reconciled and made our peace with our pasts. Making a list and becoming willing—making three lists, if necessary—is how we set ourselves free.

Not only will our hearts be opened further, so will our eyes. We will learn what we need to learn—about ourselves. We will be free to let go of our pasts and move into a better future.

Some say that the past cannot be changed. This Step proves differently. This Step can transform our pasts into a necessary, acceptable, and nonregrettable part of our lives.

Many people in recovery have not made a formal list. But if we stick around long enough, we will have a list. The names will come to us, will come into our minds and hearts. Our unfinished business will become clear.

We will be aware of the people and the relationships that we need to deal with. It may be an ex-spouse, a parent, an old friend. It may be a relative. But they will come to us, mentally or in actual, physical presence. The opportunity to become willing will make itself available.

The chance to heal will come.

So will our ideas about the wrongs we have done to ourselves. Slowly, these issues will present themselves. We will see how we have neglected and harmed ourselves. Life will ask us if we are willing to change how we treat and respond to ourselves.

That's what recovery is about.

Do not worry about doing this Step well enough. Do not use it to make yourself feel guilty. Use the list you have in your heart or on paper. Then open yourself to willingness.

Ask to be shown who needs to be on your list. Ask for insight into the wrongs you have done to yourself and others. Ask for help in becoming willing.

Forgiveness, right relationships, and peace begin inside us. They begin with this Step.

All this Step asks us to do is make a list, then become willing to honestly take care of ourselves and our behaviors with people. Regardless of the part played by another, we are now free to identify, own, and take responsibility for ourselves.

ACTIVITIES

1. Have you started your list yet? Have you made a mental list of the people you believe you have harmed?
2. Would you like peace and healing in your relationships, even in those you don't wish to maintain? What are the barriers to healing that are still within you?
3. What are the relationships, past or present, that bother you the most?

STEP NINE

"MADE DIRECT AMENDS TO SUCH PEOPLE WHEREVER POSSIBLE, EXCEPT WHEN TO DO SO WOULD INJURE THEM OR OTHERS."
—Step Nine of CoDA

Beth first found the Twelve Steps through Overeaters Anonymous thirteen years ago. She weighed more than 250 pounds and was a practicing bulimic. She ate constantly and forced herself to vomit ten to fifteen times daily. Despite working the Steps, she didn't lose her weight for three years.

She was married to a newly recovering alcoholic who attended Alcoholics Anonymous meetings. At age twenty-five, this was her second marriage. Her first husband was a quadriplegic, paralyzed from the neck down, who was eleven years her senior.

"I didn't lose my weight with him," she said. "I was bitchy, rageful, bitter, mean, cruel, nasty, isolated, intolerant, depressed, and suicidal. I was also terrified, lonely, and sad, but I didn't know it then. I went from one marriage immediately into the next and decided it was time to get serious about my recovery."

During her second marriage, Beth lost her weight and also began attending Al-Anon. Life was improving, because Beth became committed to taking care of herself. But something was still wrong. Something was still not working.

"My second marriage was on the rocks," she said. "I went to four or five meetings of Al-Anon a week. I worked my program. But I didn't know what was wrong. I had such a difficult time with my husband when he was around other women. He denied any wrongdoing and told me I was insecure. Ultimately, I

133

left him. When I did, five of my women friends came to me and told me my husband had approached them sexually while we were together."

Beth spent the next five years staying "abstinent" from relationships. She attended Al-Anon, worked on herself, explored her spirituality, and learned how to be alone.

Then she met the man who was to become her third husband. She chose him carefully—a man who was comfortable to be around when other women were present, a man who professed to be committed to the same values as Beth. The minute they said "I do," something changed.

"Peter withdrew from me emotionally. He became as cold as a stone. He changed. We had been close and had fun together before the wedding. After we married, we spent very little time together, and when we did, we fought. Before we married, Peter was everything I wanted in a partner: warm, caring, sensitive, and consistent. I didn't understand this.

"And I knew it wasn't just about him," Beth said. "Here I was, by this time a highly successful woman in the business world. I was competent. I could do anything alone. I traveled alone. I didn't need a man. I had a wonderful support system. Yet something inside me was awfully wrong, and I couldn't avoid it any more."

Beth started going to private therapy, besides her Al-Anon meetings. She began confronting Peter more consistently; in fact, according to Beth, she "confronted the hell out of him." He continued to deny anything was wrong with him until one day he casually mentioned that he was going to begin attending S.A.A. (Sex Addicts Anonymous) meetings. He refused to tell her anything more. He refused to discuss why he was attending S.A.A.

"I plummeted into denial," said Beth. "I didn't want to believe he was a sex addict. I couldn't imagine the nature of his addiction. But I did begin to notice something about myself. I realized there was something about sexual addiction that made me crazy. I had acted codependently around sex addicts for years, but I didn't know that I was doing it. I didn't know that it was the addicts' behavior triggering me. I thought I was just possessive, jealous, and mistrustful."

About six months later, Peter revealed the nature of his addiction to Beth. It was simultaneously not as bad as she feared and worse than she had dreamt. Much of his addiction was covert and not acted upon. But he was obsessed with his fantasies, had acted out once, and felt ashamed by it all.

That's when Beth began attending Co-SA (Codependents of Sex Addicts.) That's when Beth began to "get" codependency recovery.

"I could feel my codependency for the first time," Beth said. "I could feel how I had belittled myself because of what some addict might do, could do, and was probably doing, and I had no control over any of it. Soon, I stopped thinking about the addict's behavior. I asked when things looked fishy. I set boundaries for myself, and one was that under no circumstances would I live with a using addict."

It was at this time that Peter found his sexual sobriety, and both he and Beth uncovered a core issue in their problems. With the help of a therapist, Beth realized she had been sexually abused by her father when she was a child. Peter also became aware of the sexual abuse in his background.

"This rocketed me into memory lane," said Beth. "I began to have all kinds of flashbacks about my father sexually abusing me—something I had run from and denied all my life. I also remembered that he had sexually abused my sister, and she, at the same time, began dealing with her incest issues, too. For as horrifying as it's been, I believe that I finally got to the 'thing' that's been gnawing at me my entire life."

When Peter began dealing with his abuse issues, he asked Beth for a separation. She didn't want the separation; she didn't want to lose her husband, but she agreed. She had no choice. Since that time, Beth has continued to work on herself, including the amends part of her recovery program. She talked to her family; she made amends to her estranged husband.

She made amends to herself.

"Life isn't all roses," Beth said. "But I have myself. I don't cry for weeks at a time. I don't want to kill myself. I cry when I need to, and then I go about my day. Thirteen years ago, I didn't know that I could cry. The only emotion I was aware of was rage. A friend used to say that I reminded him of a six-foot nun with a three-pound cross.

"Now, when I feel rage coming on, I can be certain that I am really terrified, and I'm learning how to deal with that. I have hope for my life: hope that if my marriage ends, I won't choose another sex addict as a partner. I have hope that if my husband comes out of his withdrawal syndrome, I'll know how to live with him in a manner that is respectful to both of us. I have hope that I can now have the kind of relationship that I deserve and have children of my own and not destroy them with some unknown curse that runs my life.

"I have no doubt that I will never lose myself again. I believe that everything inside, right down to the fluid in my cells, has changed as the result of my dealing with this issue."

Recently Beth was invited to be the speaker at a conference dealing with sexual addiction and sexual-addiction codependency issues. She was frightened, but she thoughtfully agreed to do it. It was a powerful event for Beth and for those who heard her speak.

Quietly, without blaming the addict, she was able to speak of her part in the process. She talked about how she was living out her unresolved issues through her marriage. She talked about her rage, her shaming, and the behaviors she engaged in to control the addict's behavior.

She talked about making amends for her part. She talked about how she had dealt with her family, as part of her amends to herself.

"Without being rageful, I was able to talk to each person in the family openly about my issues, and my recovery. I invited each to either choose to be in a relationship with me or discontinue the relationship. But I set the boundary: I would not be in a relationship with them and deny, any longer, the abuse that had taken place. I would not go back to the way I was and be part of the system on that basis."

When Beth finished her speech, the room resounded with emotions and feelings. What had happened inside Beth was even more significant. Her estranged husband was there. They talked for a moment. She still hoped they would be reunited, but she knew she would go on with her life, regardless of what took place with the marriage. And when she looked at Peter, she felt at peace.

"By talking about myself, by focusing clearly on my part—even down to needing to be married to a sex addict to work through my issues—I made my peace," Beth said. "I made my peace with Peter. I made peace with my family. I made my peace with myself. I made peace with the sex addicts of the world."

That's what this Step is about: making peace with ourselves and others. That is the purpose of amends.

TAKING OUT THE LISTS

This Step takes us a major leap forward in establishing boundaries—the difference between us and another person, the difference between our behavior and another's. It also grounds us in what will become a new way of life: allowing other people to have their paths and issues and learning to have our own. In this Step, we learn to own our power to take responsibility for ourselves and our conduct in relationships.

A fringe benefit of this Step is that we can now feel good about our conduct in relationships and can set ourselves free from conduct we feel uncomfortable with.

If you have done your work in the other Steps, you have a list of people. If you have done the work as suggested in Step Eight of this book, you have three lists: people who have harmed you, people you have harmed, and the person you may have harmed most—yourself.

You may not have a written list, but if you have been relating to people, you have a list. Any relationship, past or present, you don't feel good about; any person, including yourself, you're harboring troubled, unresolved feelings about; any relationship that brings discord to mind or heart; all are on this list. These relationships are blocking your heart and your ability to love.

Denial does not count here. If you have strife or unresolved issues, even if you are denying the feelings, they are on the list. Let's take a look, now, at what can be done to shred the lists.

DEALING WITH THOSE WHO HAVE HARMED US

The first category of amends we'll discuss is amends to people who have harmed us. I know, I know. This sounds peculiar and a bit codependent. Bear with me.

If someone has harmed us and we have not dealt with the incident, we have discord in our hearts. So how do we approach this list? Not, my friends, with denial.

This list contains the bulk of our recovery tasks. Our goal in this list is to forgive each person who has harmed us, but first we must do something important. We must work through, and experience fully, our feelings. We must clearly identify and accept the abuse. We need to figure out what our new behaviors and responses to others need to be, so the abuse or mistreatment doesn't continue. And then we will be led into forgiveness.

This is a grieving process done in stages that begins with denial and moves us into anger and sadness.

Many of us in this process find we also need to work through rage.

Once we have worked through our feelings, we are ready to forgive, but not until then. Forgiveness done too soon, done before we have stuck with and ridden out our feelings, will be premature and ineffective and will require redoing.

The goal of recovery is not to perpetuate denial. The goal in recovery is acceptance, including acceptance of our feelings.

Depending on the type of abuse we suffered, our feelings may range from mild to intense. If the abuse was severe, some of us stay stuck in the anger for years. That's okay. That's where we need to be. Understand that by feeling our feelings, we are on the way to healing and on the way to forgiveness and acceptance.

An important part of this process is figuring out what we need to do to take care of ourselves in the future with this person or anyone else who would inflict similar abuse or mistreatment on us. We cannot avoid all loss or all mistreatment in recovery, despite our intentions. But most often, when I look back over incidents where I have been mistreated, there is an important lesson there for me. The process isn't complete until I open myself to that lesson and resolve to practice it in the future. Often, the lesson is learning to own my power to take care of myself with people.

Sometimes the lesson is establishing boundaries. Sometimes the lesson is learning to say no. Sometimes the lesson is learning to own our power and respect and trust our feelings, wants, and needs. Sometimes the lesson isn't clear, and all we can do is accept that the incident happened.

Sometimes, as part of this process, we may want to confront a person on a particular issue—not to blame, shame, or extract an apology from them, but to state clearly our new boundaries with them and to let them know we've been violated. Sometimes we're wasting our time by opening our mouths. We may want to ask for guidance here. Our friends, our sponsor, and our Higher Power can help us determine what course of conduct is right in each situation.

Once the feelings have been fully felt and our lesson becomes clear, the next stage is forgiveness of each name on the list. This is not an easy task. But we will forgive when we are ready.

There are some recovery "tricks" that help me when I'm trying to achieve forgiveness and don't feel very forgiving. Asking God to bless the person and shower happiness on him or her helps. Affirming that I forgive the person helps. Forcing myself to think good, positive thoughts about the person helps. Asking God to give me the gift of forgiveness and restore the relationship to right feelings helps.

Forgiveness will come when we open ourselves to it. Forgiveness will find us when we are ready. Do not seek it too soon, before the feelings are felt. Do not avoid it too long, for it brings peace and freedom for us.

Forgiving a person does not give them permission to continue treating us poorly. If we are trying to forgive someone, and instead we feel angry and mistrustful, we may not have explored our feelings sufficiently or done the lesson work necessary for forgiveness. Occasionally, when we do this kind of work, ideas about our part in the incident may become clearer. If that happens and we realize we have had a part in an incident for which we need to make an amend, we can add that name to our second list.

Our goal is to forgive and forget the incident, when we have accepted and healed from it. We strive to remember only *our* lesson from the experience. We learn we can be grateful, for many have come into our lives to help us learn and grow— sometimes through opposition, sometimes through love, sometimes by reflecting to us what we need to work on in ourselves.

MAKING AMENDS TO THOSE WE HAVE HARMED

It is time to take out the list of people we have harmed by our behaviors. Now we are approaching some direct amends. We are getting ready to say, "This is what I did, and I'm sorry," in word and behavior. These are the people to whom we did something inappropriate, people we need to take care of ourselves with because we did something wrong. We may have lied, manipulated, used, abused, controlled, or inappropriately expressed anger to these people. In some way, these people suffered from our codependent behaviors, and now we are trying to make things right. We are on our way to freeing ourselves from guilt, taking responsibility for ourselves, removing ourselves as victims, and restoring these relationships.

As we said earlier, our children and those closest to us are often high on this list. Those around us suffered most because we were suffering. Sometimes employers, employees, or co-workers are on this list. Sometimes we owe money to people. Sometimes we owe an apology to someone from our past—maybe an ex-boyfriend or ex-girlfriend, an ex-spouse, even an ex–in-law.

Sometimes friends or neighbors are on this list.

We become ready to go directly to this person, and without defenses, own our behavior, then apologize or make any appropriate restitution—except when to do so would cause more harm *to other people*. We want to be honest; we want to take care of ourselves with people; but we do not ever want to make a bigger mess than the one we are cleaning up.

Sometimes an amend requires direct contact with the person. We say what *we* did and then apologize for our conduct. We do not talk about what the other person did. We do not justify or rationalize what we did. If we need to explain briefly, we may. The fewer words we use, the better. The most important ones are, "This is what I did, and I'm sorry."

For example: "I did really crazy things trying to control you or your addiction. I'm sorry."

"I drove you nuts obsessing about Harvey, and I'm sorry."

"I was angry at you, and instead of dealing directly with my anger, I've been taking potshots at you and treating you unfairly. I'm sorry."

Sometimes our amends are to people we do not intend to maintain a relationship with. This may be true in the case of making an amend to an ex-employer or an ex-spouse. We simply want to "clear our side of the fence."

Some of these amends are immediate amends. They are amends that can and should be made right now.

Sometimes these amends are "future" amends. For a variety of reasons, it may be better to let some time pass before going to that person. Maybe feelings are at an all-time high; maybe we are not yet clear on exactly what our part was; maybe we are not yet entirely ready. For whatever reason, the timing is not right. So we wait, but we have a reasonable deadline in mind.

Often, in this process of making amends, I ask for God's guidance. I become willing. I know I need to take care of myself with someone. Then I ask God to help me. Sometimes it feels right to wait for a while, to let that particular issue go. Sometimes, soon after I ask for guidance in making a particular amend, I either become aware that it is time to take action or I run into that person. The opportunity arises, and it feels right. That doesn't mean it isn't scary. Each time I prepare to make an amend, I feel a flutter in my stomach. It scares me to go to people, admit I did something wrong, and say I'm sorry.

But each time I do, I feel good. One of the most profound natural highs I've discovered in recovery is the feeling that comes from being honest with people, no matter how afraid I am, then saying I'm sorry when that's appropriate.

Sometimes saying "I'm sorry" isn't enough. We need to make restitution by changing how we behave toward someone.

Of course, we cannot and do not need to promise perfection, but a sincere desire to handle ourselves differently helps. We may decide we need to change behaviors with children, a spouse, a loved one, or a friend.

When I began recovery from codependency, my capacity to nurture my children was low; my ability to set and stick to limits with them was even lower. I did apologize to them for not being a good parent. But they needed more from me. They needed a mother who could combine discipline with nurturing. They needed a mother who would set consistent, reliable boundaries—limits they could count on.

An interesting event took place recently. My two children, Nichole and Shane, myself, and their friend were sitting at the kitchen table, chatting. The friend was talking about how she had recently been "grounded" for something she had done, but forty-five minutes later, her mother forgot about the grounding.

"Oh, yeah," Nicole said, "my mom used to be like that. Now, she's changed."

Then my daughter smiled, a comfortable smile. I could see she felt safe. The struggles I had gone through to own my power with the children had been worthwhile. The energy I had put into learning to set and stick to reasonable limits with my children had paid off.

They liked the security of knowing I meant what I said.

"My mom's just not so codependent anymore," Nichole said.

The purpose of amends is not to change others or expect anything different from them. The purpose of amends is to take responsibility for our own behavior, clean up any messes we've made, and feel good about our conduct in relationships.

Often I've found that even when an amend involves changing our behavior, a brief explanation and an amend for past conduct are helpful, too. The words "I'm sorry" are potent, healing words. How often have we wished someone would say them to us? Not the "I'm sorry" we hear from addicted people in the throes of remorse, but a straightforward apology. Apologies can have a healing impact on our relationships. We cannot control whether we ever hear an apology from anyone else, but we can do our part to bring healing to our relationships.

Sometimes our amends are financial amends. We need to make restitution in more than words or changed behavior. We need to pay back money. Many of us begin recovery from codependency strapped with huge financial burdens. I've talked to many people who have owed $30,000, $50,000, or more when they began recovery.

The debts are usually the result of our participating in a dysfunctional relationship, getting in over our heads, then finding ourselves—not our partner—strapped with the financial burden when the relationship ends. Sometimes we borrow to help the other person out. Sometimes financial unmanageability becomes part and parcel of the codependent package.

The willingness to take responsibility for our current financial problems is critical to recovery. Many of us have allowed ourselves to be terribly financially victimized by another. That's a hard blow to take, but if we are going to recover, we must begin now to bring reparation and healing to that area of our lives.

We do whatever we can to bring fairness and equity to the situation. If there is any way to relieve ourselves of financial responsibility that belongs to someone else, we take steps to do that. That is part of making amends to ourselves. As much as possible, we take steps to insure that each one of us is financially responsible only for himself or herself. We no longer allow ourselves to be further victimized or martyred.

Sometimes, in order to take financial responsibility for ourselves, we do end up biting the proverbial bullet. Sometimes our credit is shot. Sometimes we are stuck with another's debt whether we like it or not.

I believe we can and should take assertive steps to protect ourselves as much as possible. But if we have done what we can, yet still find ourselves responsible for someone else's debt, we often need to face and accept that fact. Sometimes the attitude of willingness alone begins to bring healing and manageability to that area of our lives. Sometimes taking even the smallest steps to make financial amends sets in motion a powerful force.

Miracles began to happen when I took financial responsibility for myself and began to make amends for the money mess I was in. Yes, I felt victimized. Yes, I had allowed myself to be victimized. Yes, I had a lot of feelings about that. But to move forward, I needed to work through the feelings and begin to work toward a solution.

I stopped blaming the financial mess on the other person and began to take financial responsibility for myself.

I stopped allowing myself to be victimized. I protected myself legally.

Then I set a goal to make financial restitution. I called creditors and sent letters. I began faithfully to make the payments I could afford. At the time, that usually amounted to $5.00 a month, sometimes on bills of $5,000. The creditors wanted more, of course, but that wasn't possible. To give more would have hurt the people I had to support monthly. I thoughtfully and carefully did what I could.

That's when miracles began to happen. That's all I can say. Things just started to happen. One hospital bill that I had incurred during the height of my codependency, when I had viral meningitis, amounted to thousands of dollars. I had no insurance. I began to make small monthly payments. Six months later, I received a letter from the hospital describing a special, one-time program to wipe away certain outstanding debts. I qualified, and my debt was wiped clean.

Other debts slowly began to be paid off. Money to help came from unexpected sources.

Fiscal responsibility is an important part of recovery. We can faithfully and responsibly do what we can as we are able.

Sometimes we aren't certain what to do about a particular amend. We may be willing to make the amend but unclear as to how to do so. Maybe the nature of our part is hazy. Maybe making the amend would bring harm to others—either to someone in our family or to the person to whom we are making the amend. Always, always, I've found that if I ask myself and my Higher Power what I need to do to make an amend, the answer comes. I'm guided into taking the best steps.

Sometimes the person to whom we owe an amend is not available; perhaps that person is deceased. Sometimes an even greater mess would result if we were to contact a particular person. We need to use discretion in our amends.

Patiently wait for guidance and direction in this process of making amends. We need to take care of ourselves with people. We want the self-esteem, peace, harmony, and relief from guilt that making amends brings about. But we do not want to run around in haste, creating more problems with our amends than we are solving.

We need to be clear about what we're apologizing for and the best way to say that. Our apology needs to count—to us. What we're doing with amends is taking responsibility for our behavior. We need to figure out the best way to do that. We need to understand clearly what we are taking responsibility for. We need to ascertain that in this process of making amends, we aren't engaging in another behavior that will be self-defeating or damaging to others. If in doubt, ask our Higher Power. Talk to people in recovery. Listen to what they have to say. Wait until we have found a course of action that feels right to us.

There is guidance and a clear path available for the amends we need to make. At times, that path leads to a direct contact and a direct apology for our behavior. There are times when what we most need to do to make amends is change our behavior with someone. There are times when restitution is appropriate.

But there are times when bringing up what we have done and then apologizing for it would make matters worse. If we have allowed ourselves to become hooked into a particular person, allowed them to control us, or if we have been rescuing them, then feeling victimized by it, we may make the relationship worse by mentioning this.

"Hey! I've been letting you control me, and I'm mad. I've been rescuing you because I really didn't believe you could take care of yourself. Now I'm going to stop!"

That may make things worse because it sounds more like a confrontation than an amend. Understand that it is sometimes important to state these kinds of intentions. Sometimes it can be clarifying and healthy to state our new behavioral goals clearly. But sometimes the best possible course we can take is to seek the path of our own self-care quietly.

We become willing to make amends. Once we do that, we can let go and tackle our amends in a peaceful, consistent, harmonious way. If we are seeking to work this Step, seeking to clear up our relationships with people, we will be led. We will know what we need to do and when and how to do it. If nothing feels right or appropriate, if it feels like what we are about to do will cause crisis or havoc, if we feel it is ill timed, we can trust that, too.

If there are amends we cannot make now, we can make plans to do so later. This may be true with financial issues or with other kinds of amends. We may want to pay someone back, but we may not be able to do that responsibly now without depriving our family. But we can be willing to make that amend a goal. There may be someone we want to apologize to, but we cannot locate that person. We can still be willing. If we are willing, if we have done our work, we will be led to the right circumstances at the right time.

There are some amends we cannot make. The person may be deceased or simply unavailable. We can discuss those amends with our Higher Power, then let go of them.

Attitude, honesty, openness, and willingness count here. In peace and harmony, we can strive to clear up our discord in relationships. We can let go of our fears about facing people and taking responsibility for our behaviors—understanding that we are not diminishing our self-esteem by making amends but improving it.

We don't have to grovel to make amends. We don't have to let someone abuse, manipulate, or mistreat us in the process of making amends. We quietly go about the task of taking care of ourselves with people in an attitude of self-respect. This is a program of forgiveness, not penance.

We can make our amends clearly, directly, and cleanly. Making an amend to someone doesn't mean we have to allow ourselves to become hooked into them again. It doesn't mean we surrender and submit to mistreatment from them.

Often, the shorter the amend, the better. The cleaner and clearer, the better. The more direct, the better. The more it comes from the heart, the better. The more it is led by Divine Guidance, the better.

Once we make an amend, the other person isn't responsible for clearing away our residue of fear, guilt, or shame. It is our job to let go of the incident, not theirs. On the other hand, we are not responsible for feelings the other person may have about the incident. That isn't our job. Our part is to make a direct amend, then do whatever work we need to do on ourselves to be done with our shame and guilt.

We can forgive ourselves and let go of the incident.

We can be gentle with ourselves.

After taking this Step, we can consider the issue resolved and let it go. If the process involves changing our behavior, we do not need to punish ourselves by feeling guilty until we have changed completely or "perfectly." We can identify what we have done, make an amend, and be finished with our guilt.

After we have made an amend, if the other person is unwilling to let the incident go, or if the other person wants us to stew in the problem for a while with them, that is their issue. We don't have to react (and do something that might require another amend), and we do not have to dwell on the issue.

We also don't have to apologize when we haven't done anything wrong. For many reasons, we may get into the habit of apologizing when it isn't necessary. A sense of shame can keep us apologizing for being alive, being here, and being who we are. Some of us may feel like a bother and apologize for nearly every interaction we have. This is not the purpose of this Step.

We may have gotten into the habit of apologizing for another person's behavior or automatically apologizing when the other person gets angry.

We can learn to examine our behaviors and figure out what we did or didn't do. We can learn to discern when we have done something we legitimately need to apologize for and when our codependency is prompting us to say we're sorry.

Sometimes, general apologies are helpful. Not all issues are clear—especially codependency issues. At times, it can clear the air simply to say, "I'm sorry for the fuss we had. I'm sorry for the way I handled that incident. Other issues got in the way, and I'm sorry it happened."

Sometimes I've said, "I'm sorry if what I need to do to take care of myself hurt you. It was not intended or designed to do that."

But we do not have to get "codependent" about our apologies. We don't have to apologize for our anger—only the inappropriate behaviors surrounding our anger. We don't have to apologize for taking care of ourselves, dealing with feelings, setting boundaries, having fun, feeling good, or becoming healthy. We don't have to apologize because people are trying to control us and induce guilt in us. We don't have to apologize for being, for being here, and for being who we are.

We don't have to apologize for not wanting to be abused or mistreated. If we're doing all the apologizing for other people's behavior, it doesn't leave room for the people who truly need to apologize to do that.

We don't have to repeat our apologies. That's annoying. If someone wants to keep extracting an apology from us for the same incident, that's their issue, and we don't have to get hooked. If we feel like we need to continue apologizing, we may want to go back to the drawing board and figure out what's really going on.

Sometimes, we don't live up to our own expectations. That's human. That's why we have the words, "I'm sorry." They heal, and bridge the gap.

But we don't have to say we are sorry if we didn't do anything wrong.

MAKING AMENDS TO OURSELVES

We've talked about our amends on the first two lists. Now let's move on to the last list—the amends we owe ourselves. It can be difficult to approach others and apologize. It can be quite a task to forgive others for what they have done wrong to us. But making amends to ourselves, forgiving ourselves, can be the hardest part of our program.

All of recovery—all of what we are going through—has to do with making an amend to ourselves. Giving ourselves permission to have our feelings is an amend. Giving ourselves permission to be alive and be happy is an amend. Taking gentle, compassionate, loving care of ourselves is an amend.

Learning to set boundaries, be direct, and stop defeating and victimizing ourselves is an amend. Learning to stop allowing others to mistreat and control us is an amend. Learning to stop expecting perfection of ourselves, own our power, and be who we are is an amend to ourselves.

Learning to listen to and trust ourselves is an important amend. Learning to trust our instincts and value our feelings and needs is an amend.

We may have many amends to make to that frightened, abused, or neglected child within us—amends for being so critical, negligent, and shameful. We owe ourselves an apology and changed behavior for not allowing ourselves to receive the love and nurturing we need, especially from ourselves.

We owe ourselves an apology and changed behavior for the sometimes terrible ideas we have maintained, dwelled on, and believed about ourselves. That we aren't lovable, aren't good enough, can't think, don't deserve success, don't deserve to have fun, or don't deserve to recover are untrue beliefs we have assumed, beliefs that need correcting as part of this program of making amends to ourselves.

"I just don't love myself," said Karen. "I don't believe I deserve love. I don't believe I deserve good things from life."

"Most of us don't," I replied. "That's why we're in recovery. That's an important part of what recovery is: changing those beliefs."

Jason, who has been recovering from codependency for six years now, writes letters to himself as part of making amends. When something is bothering him, when guilt and fear return, when he wonders what he deserves, he sits down and comforts himself in a letter. He tells himself all the good, comforting, nurturing things he and the child inside him need to hear to feel better.

"I've gotten pretty nuts-and-bolts about making amends to myself," he said. "My amends to myself look like writing letters to myself. I had my dad in for therapy. I had my mother in for two sessions. And in between the sessions, I went and bought myself a Teddy bear."

I learn more every day about taking care of the child within. I neglected and belittled her for years and years. I tried to ignore her; I hoped she would go away. What happened was that she screamed louder and louder until I began to listen.

I spent years looking to other people, looking to relationships, to take care of the child within me. I looked to relationships to comfort my fear and to nurture, support, and protect that child within. I looked for relationships to be there for me because I wasn't willing to be there for myself. I didn't know how.

Now, slowly, I'm learning a better way. I'm learning how to listen to that child I abandoned most of my life. I'm learning ways to get in touch with her, hear her, and give her the comfort, nurturing, protection, guidance, and discipline she needs.

Sometimes, she needs the simple warm care a three-month-old child needs. Sometimes, she needs to run, play, or sing, the way a four-year-old child would. Sometimes, she needs to listen to "When You Wish Upon a Star," and cry, or dream, or wish. Sometimes, she needs to say how sad or afraid she is, and simply be acknowledged and validated.

This behavior of nurturing the child within is not foolish, as I once believed. It is healing. A few moments a day of caring for that child frees my adult to be rejuvenated and responsible, and lets my child feel warm, safe, and cared for. It also enables me to be a nurturing effective parent to my children. They have taught me much about my inner child and what she needs; my inner child helps teach me about what my children need.

I've learned, finally, to release the anger and resentment I've felt toward myself for all that has happened to me, for other people's inappropriate behavior toward me, for my mistakes, and for being me. I have harbored anger and resentment toward others in my lifetime, but the silent, denied rage I felt toward myself was the most profound and the most difficult to let go.

I had no idea, until years into recovery from codependency, how angry I was at myself. It took me a long time to uncover my rage, anger, and resentments toward others, but a much longer time to detect those buried feelings toward myself. To love, nourish, and nurture myself freely, to stop the path of destructive relationships, to release my blocks to love and intimacy, I had to let go of this anger. I needed to forgive myself and develop a better relationship with myself. I needed to talk better to and about myself; I needed to forgive and forget; I needed to stop punishing myself for the wrongs I had done and for what others had done to me.

My anger and rage toward myself were quietly killing me, and I didn't even know it until one day they surfaced. I exploded in a tirade toward myself that astonished me with its ferocity and loathing. I saw the great part my self-resentment had played in my fears, in my need to be perfect, even in my need to control. If I made another mistake, if something or someone disappointed me again, I would become even angrier at myself. I saw how my self-rage had continued to attract experiences to me that would help draw it out so I could deal with it. Sometimes when I am angry with another and don't deal with my feelings, I keep seeing things to reinforce my anger. In the same way, I kept doing and seeing things about myself that reinforced my self-resentment. I kept picking on myself and wouldn't let myself live or be fully alive. My anger wouldn't let me love or be loved. It wouldn't let me love myself until I released it.

It became time truly to make amends to myself.

Recovery helped me do that. It assisted me in finding the child within. It also helped me discover the healer within, a concept discussed by many in recovery.

There is a frightened, vulnerable child within each of us, but there is also a powerful healer, protector, and nurturer within that can take care of that child and help it and ourselves heal.

We need to begin addressing ourselves in a loving way, a way that will enable us to heal, a way that is self-respecting, self-trusting, nourishing, and nurturing—and a way that is respectful of others.

As with our other amends, the process begins with willingness, with doing what is obvious, and with asking for and receiving Divine Guidance in the process.

We will be shown all we need to do to take care of ourselves with others and to begin taking loving care of ourselves, if we are open to that. We will be set free from our anger and resent-

ments toward others and ourselves. We will be healed. That is
the miracle of this process. Everything we need will come to us
when we are ready for it.

LOVING AND FORGIVING OURSELVES

This is the Step where we apologize to ourselves and others, but
we do more than apologize. We clearly own and take responsibility for our behaviors toward ourselves and others. This Step
gives us permission to be who we are now and to be who we
once were. It gives us permission to forgive ourselves and feel
good about being who we are—regardless of what we have
done.

It wipes the slate clean and gives us an alternative to feeling
guilty and ashamed. We can now experience self-awareness,
self-esteem, and self-acceptance—based on self-responsibility.

We have been given a gift in all of the Steps, but we've been
given a special gift in Steps Four through Nine. The gift is a
clear process for freeing ourselves from guilt and shame, for
forgiving ourselves, and for correcting those behaviors that need
correcting.

These Steps mean we no longer have to punish ourselves. We
no longer have to feel terrified or ashamed about our behavior—
whether it is a minute slip or a major indiscretion. We have a
specific formula, now, for freeing ourselves from mistakes and
imperfections and for creating harmony in our relationships.

We cannot control the other person and how he or she feels
about us. But a powerful chain of healing is set in motion when
we take responsibility for ourselves. When guilt hits, when
shame hits, when an old belief or an old behavior we visited on
ourselves arises, we now know we have a choice.

We can repress or deny, which for many of us is our old way
of reacting. We can become defensive, we can run, we can hide.
Or we can embrace this formula of looking within, identifying
our part, talking to another person and God about the incident,
admitting it to ourselves, becoming willing to make an amend,
then actively making that amend.

Then, we can let it go. We can let go of the largest and

smallest guilts we have. We can forgive ourselves and we can forgive others.

These Steps tell us we don't have to be perfect. There is safety and comfort in this formula for self-care—these Steps. They tell us we can love and accept all of ourselves and accept our pasts—as long as we are willing to take responsibility for ourselves.

When I first began working this Step, I was terrified. The thought of making appointments with people, then opening my mouth and admitting I had done something wrong, was frightening. I had a strong inner rule that demanded that I be perfect, and the act of admitting my wrongs and apologizing for them was difficult. I felt threatened by admitting my wrongs. I already had so much guilt, and if I acknowledged and admitted wrongdoing, I was afraid I would have more. I was so defensive about my behaviors because I felt so badly about myself.

What I was about to learn was that making amends gave me a self and self-esteem.

I reached a point where it became easier to go to people and admit to my wrongs, but I still had another place to journey. That place was a place of compassion for myself, a place where I was able and willing to notice the wrongs and harms I had done to me. These are still harder to see and care about than the wrongs I have done to others. As with other behaviors, it gets easier with time. The more I practice loving myself, the more habitual it becomes.

The more open I am to taking responsibility for my behavior and making amends, the less guilt I feel. Denying a wrongdoing toward ourselves or others doesn't make the wrongdoing or the guilt go away.

This Step does.

Take it. Trust it. And let guilt go. When we have taken the actions called for in these Steps, we are free to do that. It is not a punitive Step. It is not a Step to be feared. Like the other Steps, when we make a human effort to work it, we will be rewarded with a spiritual bonus. As one recovering man said, "We will receive the grace we need to live comfortably with ourselves, others, and our pasts."

THE NUTS-AND-BOLTS STEPS

Now we have finished with what many in recovery call the nuts-and-bolts Steps. Often we will find ourselves instinctively returning to the Step we need. Go there freely as often as necessary.

Go there whenever you need the healing that this, or any Step, has to offer. There are many things in life that can't be trusted. But we can trust these Steps, and they are always there for us. Do not worry about working this Step too soon: It will find you when you are ready. You will find yourself in places, with people, in circumstances, and it will be time to begin taking care of yourself with people.

We will begin to see how we have been treating ourselves inappropriately, too. Often these insights are gradual. We receive the insights, the direction for change, and the opportunity to make amends, as we are ready to handle them. Trust timing. Trust the process. Trust the Steps. Trust what will happen if we work them.

Listen to what it says in the Big Book (pages 83–84):

> We should be sensible, tactful, considerate and humble without being servile or scraping. As God's people we stand on our feet; we don't crawl before anyone.
>
> If we are painstaking about this phase of our development, we will be amazed before we are halfway through. We are going to know a new freedom and a new happiness. We will not regret the past nor wish to shut the door on it. We will comprehend the word serenity and we will know peace. No matter how far down the scale we have gone, we will see how our experience can benefit others. That feeling of uselessness and self-pity will disappear. We will lose interest in selfish things and gain interest in our fellows. Self-seeking will slip away. Our whole attitude and outlook upon life will change. Fear of people and of economic insecurity will leave us. We will intuitively know how to handle situations which used to baffle us. We will suddenly realize that God is doing for us what we could not do for ourselves.
>
> Are these extravagant promises? We think not. They are being fulfilled among us—sometimes quickly, sometimes slowly. They will always materialize if we work for them.

Recovering alcoholics were the first to receive these promises in return for working these Steps. Some believe that alcoholics are more bent than others on working these Steps, because their lives depend on it. We too can be committed to working these Steps and receiving the benefits in our lives—because our lives, the quality of our lives, the quality of our relationships, and the quality of love in our lives, *do* depend on it.

ACTIVITIES

1. Have you made any amends to other people yet? How did this feel?
2. If you are ready, set some amends goals. For instance, name the people to whom you would like to make amends. Set a reasonable deadline and a goal for apologizing, wherever that is appropriate. Be as specific or as general as you want. You may want to make your goal "to become aware of the people I owe apologies to, then make those amends." Or you may have a list of names and incidents and want to set a deadline for talking to these people.
3. What is the relationship that is bothering you the most right now? What do you need to do to take care of yourself in that relationship? What would you say if you were free to be entirely honest with that person about your behaviors, your feelings, and what you wanted and needed? How have you discounted yourself or not owned your power in that relationship? How have you discounted or devalued the other person?
4. What is the biggest guilt you have right now? Using the Steps as a formula, how can you deal with that, so you can be done with the guilt?
5. For any amends you have made, write a self-forgiveness affirmation that helps you let go of guilt. A sample affirmation might read: "I love and accept myself. I have taken responsibility for my behavior with _____, and I am now free to let the past go." We can also write a similar affirmation about forgiving others: "I have dealt with my feelings toward _____, and I have forgiven

him or her. I have let go of my feelings toward him or her, and I allow peace and love to settle into our relationship."

6. Explore the concept of your inner child and your inner healer. Use letter writing to get in touch with both.

Author and lecturer Lucia Capacchione has devised a simple method for doing this. She suggests drawing pictures with your nondominant hand to allow the inner child to express itself. You can also write a letter with your nondominant hand. Ask the inner child what it is really feeling, fearing, wanting, needing, or worrying about, then let it draw a picture or write a letter to you.

Now, respond with the dominant hand. Draw a picture showing how you would like the problem to be resolved or how you would like to be feeling. Write a letter to that child, supporting, comforting, and protecting the child. In your picture and letter, assure the child within that all will be well.

If you hear some things that the child within needs, take action. Respond. If it wants to go for a walk, dance, sing, be held, hold, be alone, listen to music, or rest, give it what it needs. These efforts do not have to be complicated or complex; the simpler, the better. (Capacchione's books on this process are included in the bibliography at the back of the book.)

"I do Step Ten all the time. Too much, I think. Admitting I was wrong was very, very difficult for me in the beginning. Now, I still don't like to have to do it, but I do it anyway."
—Beth M.

STEP TEN

"CONTINUED TO TAKE PERSONAL INVENTORY AND WHEN WE WERE WRONG, PROMPTLY ADMITTED IT."
—Step Ten of CoDA

My daughter and I have a fight. I react and say something inappropriate.

This Step gives me permission to walk away, cool down, apologize for my part, and let go of the incident. It also gives my daughter permission, as she watches me, to understand that I'm not perfect, parents aren't perfect, and she doesn't need to be perfect. It has given me a tool to allow for my humanness and to nurture and love myself despite it—and sometimes because of it. It has given both my daughter and me a tool to deal with our humanity: the words "I'm sorry."

I wake up and notice I haven't been feeling my emotions for a while. My body aches. I feel weighted down and troubled. I have gotten out of touch with myself. I've gone on automatic pilot again.

This Step gives me permission to accept my current state and move forward without blaming or shaming myself. It gives me permission to stop rushing about, and ask myself what I need and what would feel good.

As December moves into January, and I'm cleaning the slate for the year past, I notice I've allowed some discord and anger in a particular relationship to harden into resentment. I feel used. I am feeling uncomfortable about the status of that relationship, and I am going out of my way to avoid that person.

This Step gives me permission to accept who I am and learn my lesson from the relationship. I can ask for guidance, then trust the direction I receive and allow healing feelings to smooth the discord. By February, the relationship is back on track. I am participating in it again, this time with new boundaries. I've let the past go, not in a codependent way, but in a recovery way: I've allowed it to teach me what I needed to learn about myself and how I deal with people.

I find myself feeling trapped in a relationship—justifying not taking care of myself and not saying what I want and need. I fear losing the relationship, fear that I cannot be trusted, fear that what I want and need isn't okay. I fear hurting the other person's feelings. I fear the future.

This Step gives me permission to notice and accept that I am not owning my power. It gives me permission to begin doing that, without casting judgment on myself or another.

When I stop allowing myself to feel, when I stop owning my power, when I behave inappropriately, when I've moved into denial, when I try to control another or start letting him or her control me, when anger hardens into resentment, when I'm afraid to look honestly at my fears, when I become too harsh and critical of others or myself, this Step tells me it's okay, I'm okay, and I can move forward into a better way, nurturing myself all the while, instead of shaming and chastising myself.

This Step challenges my greatest, most predominant, and sometimes most troublesome belief about myself: that I have to be perfect—especially now that I'm recovering.

I used to be frightened of this Step. I thought it meant I had to perform a critical, judgmental inventory of myself every day, fearlessly searching out and focusing on my bad points, my defects, and what I was doing wrong.

I was good at that. I didn't need a Step to help me do that.

Now, I have a different vision of this Step. It is a tool that allows me to continue to be aware of myself, instead of focusing on others. It is also a tool that helps me treat myself in a nurturing, accepting way. Part of nurturing and respecting myself means I am free to take care of myself in a healthy way with others—admitting I did wrong and apologizing, or owning my power when I have forfeited it.

This Step gives me permission to identify when I have become angry at myself again or begun to neglect myself—my feelings and needs. It allows me to release my anger and move forward into nurturing self-love.

This Step gives me the freedom to admit promptly when I have gotten off course, so that I can get back on track with my program of self-care.

This Step also means that I am free to take a few moments each day and focus on and enjoy what I have done right—then feel good about that.

CONTINUED TO TAKE PERSONAL INVENTORY

"With an outward focus like you've got, it's a wonder you've ever had a bad day," my ex-husband once remarked to me.

His remark was intended to be funny; it was also profound in its insight. Before recovery from codependency, I had an uncanny ability to stay intensely focused on externals: what others were doing; what they weren't doing; what they were trying to do to me; what they had done to me; and how much better I'd feel if they would do something differently.

This thinking—that others were somehow in control of my life path and that they could make me feel better or different— was an illusion. And I learned it was an illusion the hard way: by bottoming out on my codependency.

If we have done our work on the Steps, we have progressed through that kind of thinking. We may fall back into it on occasion, but at least now we know what we're doing, and we know that it is an illusion. Many of us began our recovery journey because of what someone we loved was or wasn't doing. We came into this program because of that kind of thinking. Then, the First Step grounded us in a new way of thinking, a new way of approaching life, others, and ourselves.

By the time we made it to the Fourth Step, we were ready to begin focusing inwardly. We were ready to begin soul-searching. We started to take a look at ourselves and what was going on with us. We began to look at how we habitually responded to life, instead of focusing on what was going on with others.

The process we went through in Steps Four and Five took us

on a housecleaning tour of ourselves. We turned our will and our lives over to the care of God, as we understood God. Then we cleared out the package we had turned over.

Now we have been given this Step, a maintenance Step, to help us continue this process of looking within. This Step doesn't ask us to go after ourselves continually with a hammer and chisel. It doesn't tell us we have to walk through life holding ourselves under a microscope, hypervigilantly watching all that we say and do, waiting with bated breath to criticize and punish ourselves.

It *does* give us permission to continue to be aware of ourselves— and, when we are wrong, to admit and deal with that promptly.

What are the "wrongs" we look for and promptly admit?

We want to look for the wrongs we do to others, the wrongs that are so easy to rationalize and justify. We want to watch for any personal course of conduct that is less than what we reasonably can expect of ourselves.

This may include inappropriate expressions of anger and rage, inappropriate conduct when we're angry, harboring resentment, controlling, manipulating, and using people, lying, expecting others to fill up the "hole in the soul," or any other behavior that does not meet with *our own approval.*

How will we know when we have behaved inappropriately? If we have done our work, if we have cleared away the wreckage of earned and unearned guilt from the past, if we have worked these Steps to the best of our ability, we'll know.

The matter will get our attention.

We will have experienced enough peace to be able to recognize unrest, and enough guidance to know how to find our way out of any predicament we may find ourselves in. We will know and trust that we can let go and allow ourselves to be guided into a right course of conduct, whether that means saying we're sorry or attempting a course of changed behavior with another person.

I have learned I can't rely on feelings alone to do this Step. I may feel guilty when I haven't done anything wrong. Or I may feel guilty about doing things that are good for me: like playing, having fun, expressing my feelings, and saying what I want and need. Sometimes I don't feel guilty about behaviors I legitimately need to correct: I feel defensive and protective.

This Step asks us to continue the process of using our intellect, our wisdom, and recovery wisdom to review and inventory ourselves. We want to trust our feelings, but we must also call our intellect into play, so we don't get lost in the swell of unearned guilt and defensiveness.

We can think. With our new insights we can take a look at ourselves each day and lovingly figure out what it is we need to do to take care of ourselves.

ADMITTING WHEN WE'RE WRONG

Often, I've found that simply taking responsibility, then apologizing for my conduct, is sufficient to clear away issues that arise. The words, "I was wrong and I'm sorry" are so healing. To be able to give or receive those words, then let go of an incident, is one of the many gifts I've been given in this process called recovery.

Growing up, I spent most of my life with punishing people. If an indiscretion occurred, it would be filed away and used against that person over and again—sometimes for years and years. Nothing was ever let go of.

I became a punishing person. If someone disappointed me or didn't do what I believed they should have, I didn't just get angry. I hung onto it and punished. And punished.

That's also how I treated myself when I did something wrong.

I kept myself away from the love and joy available to me in relationships and life. I didn't know how to accept, forgive, and nurture myself. I didn't know how or when to accept and forgive others.

I kept trying to forgive alcoholics for drinking when I was still allowing myself to be victimized by their drinking. I kept substituting forgiveness and denial for acceptance of reality. I had concepts confused.

Now I'm learning how to accept and give apologies, then let things go. I also understand that this always, always means dealing with—feeling—my feelings and accepting reality. I'm learning that my feelings are an important part of reality.

For years, when I would feel hurt or angry, I'd run to God and ask God to forgive me. I would feel ashamed and contrite for feeling angry, for feeling hurt—for *feeling*. "Father, forgive me, for I have sinned," was my motto each time I had any kind of disruptive feeling toward another. I looked at myself and my feelings as something outside and apart from my Higher Power.

Then I would feel confused and guilty when the feelings didn't go away. When the other person's behavior continued, so did my feelings.

It took me a long time—I'm still learning this lesson—to realize that my feelings are often how my Higher Power speaks to me and tries to get my attention about a lesson I need to learn. That lesson may be setting boundaries, owning my power, or learning something about myself and relationships. My feelings are not incidentals. They are an important part of me, my life, and what I need to be paying attention to.

At the least, they are to be fully experienced before I move forward. Life, and my Higher Power, will often pellet me successively with similar circumstances—designed to provoke a certain emotion. I used to think that not feeling the emotion was what was expected of me. Now, I'm learning to surrender with more ease and dignity to the emotion as a necessary and important part of the experience.

CONTINUING TO LOVE OURSELVES

There is another area of our lives where our inventory may lead to the discovery of a wrongdoing that requires prompt admission. This area is one of wrongdoings toward ourselves. Not acknowledging and feeling our feelings, not setting the boundaries we need to set, not paying attention to ourselves, not trusting ourselves, not respecting ourselves, not listening to ourselves—these are wrongdoings that need prompt attention.

Being angry at ourselves, and punishing ourselves, is a wrongdoing.

Self-neglect is wrong.

Self-neglect can become habitual for those of us who have spent many years practicing codependency. It is much easier for me, in any given situation, to shut down my emotions and neglect myself than it is for me to value and trust myself and my emotions. This is something we need to watch for in our inventories.

Getting hooked into caretaking, focusing on another, and neglecting our own emotions and needs can be another instinctive response we might want to watch for.

Trying to control the course of our relationships, rather than allowing them to unfold and taking care of ourselves in the process, is another behavior to be on the lookout for.

Not being emotionally honest about our needs and wants— with ourselves or others—is a wrongdoing.

Forgetting or neglecting to treat ourselves with a nurturing attitude is an area that we may want to watch for. Often, our initial response to any given situation is to be harsh, demanding, critical, and shaming of ourselves. That, my friend, is doing wrong.

We may anticipate rejection when it is not forthcoming. We may fall into the trap of our old beliefs: that we are unlovable, incompetent, and undeserving. Those old beliefs are wrongs against ourselves, and they can do harm in our relationships.

We may fall into our fears and forget how to let peace and trust control our lives. That is wrongdoing.

Any time we get off course from the way of living we have discovered, it is time to take this Step and allow it to put us back on track.

Not nurturing and taking care of the child within is a wrongdoing. Looking to others, rather than ourselves, to take care of, to protect, to nurture that frightened, needy child is a wrongdoing that can lead us into desperate and codependent gestures in our relationships and our lives.

Falling back into a deprived and martyred way of living is a wrongdoing. Allowing others to control us or our lives is a wrongdoing.

Are we worrying again? Are we once again trying to control

what we cannot? Are we substituting control for owning our own power to take care of ourselves in any circumstance? Have we become fearful or ashamed again? Have our reactions to people become fear-based or shame-based? Are we fussing too much over others and over that which we cannot control? Have we gotten into a power play with someone, reacting and trying to force our hand? Are we holding on too tightly?

Are we allowing ourselves to feel? To feel our anger?

Are we doing those things for ourselves that feel good?

Are we being honest with others and setting the boundaries we need to set? Are we in touch with ourselves? Are we being true to ourselves? Are we trusting ourselves and our Higher Power? Are we clear about what we want and need?

These are areas we want to watch for in our inventory. If we uncover wrongdoings, we admit them promptly—to ourselves. Often, it helps to talk to someone else, too, and share what's going on. It doesn't hurt to tell God either. Exposing ourselves, being vulnerable, is a behavior we learned in the Fifth Step.

Any time in our recoveries the old, helpless, victim feelings return, we are doing ourselves wrong. We need to admit it promptly, take responsibility for ourselves, and own our power with people.

We are not victims, not anymore, and this Step guarantees that we do not ever have to be again.

Many of us lived lives filled with judgment and attempts at perfection. We judged ourselves and others. If we did wrong, our defenses flew up, and we tried to deny our part, afraid that we would not be worthwhile people if we weren't perfect. We used our mistakes to reinforce our anger and resentment toward ourselves, the same way we may have done with others.

This Step tells us that making mistakes is expected and anticipated. My finest and most important lessons have all come from my less-than-perfect behaviors.

I am slowly learning that perfection is allowing myself, without judgment, to be who and where I am today, and then responding to myself in a responsible, but nurturing and nonshaming way: self-acceptance rendered with a huge dose of self-love.

We need not be nearly as fearful of getting off track, I've learned, as of not loving and accepting ourselves. No matter what predicament I find myself in, by taking this Step with a loving and nurturing attitude toward myself, I can get out. Shaming myself, not accepting, and not trusting myself don't work.

By taking this Step, I usually find that the circumstance works for good. It benefits me. It teaches me something. It helps me grow and learn.

One way I work this Step is by using it to affirm myself. For instance, if I am afraid of a particular circumstance, I accept my fear, then write an affirmation that counters that fear. As I become aware of old beliefs that I'm hanging onto—old negative, self-defeating beliefs—I write affirmations, as needed, to counter those beliefs.

I also use this Step as a reminder to nurture myself.

A TIME TO INVENTORY

Some people in recovery prefer to take this Step nightly. When they retire for the evening, they review their day and their conduct. If something arises during that review, they make a mental note to deal with it. That may mean dealing with feelings, being honest with someone, telling someone they're sorry, or making an amend to themselves. We may need to go back to another Step to help us in our inventories. If we are open, we will know what to do. We have begun a process that we can trust, a process that will continually support us in our growth. This program and these Steps will not abandon us.

Some of us like to take this Step in the morning, during those quiet moments before the busyness of the day sets in. During that time, we are open and receptive to our feelings. We may want to ask, What's going on with me? What do I need to do to take care of myself lovingly and responsibly? Then we *listen* to ourselves and respond.

Others work this Step in a more relaxed fashion, trusting that if they are working their program, staying connected to other recovering people, and trying to stay on track, this Step will find them when it needs to.

"I try to be aware," said Joan. "I can't say I take a Tenth Step every day, but I talk to my sponsor three times a week and keep her up-to-date on all the stuff in my life. I admit to her when I'm wrong, even if I admit it to nobody else. I still don't remember to check things out with my Higher Power, but I know that that peace can be had. I look for the little answers. I accept things. I let things be that aren't in my plan."

I've learned this about myself and my recovery: When it's time for something to get my attention, I don't have to worry. The lesson won't go away. It will continue presenting itself until I deal with it. In a natural way, insights about ourselves will reveal themselves to us.

LOOK FOR WHAT'S GOOD, TOO

While we're busy inventorying ourselves, we may want to pay attention to what we're doing right. Step Ten says, "Continued to take personal inventory and *when* (italics mine) we were wrong, promptly admitted it." It doesn't say that we ignore what we do that is right or what's right in our lives. It says we continue to inventory ourselves.

When we inventory, we can look for many things. We can search out feelings that we may be running from. We can look for low self-esteem or inadequacy creeping back in. We can look for reversions to old ways of thinking, feeling, and behaving. We can look for those behaviors that we truly are uncomfortable with, that we have directed toward others, and we can make prompt amends.

But an important part of our inventory can also focus on what we're doing right and on all that is happening within us and around us that's good.

This is not busy work. It's an important part of our recovery. Part of our codependency is this obsessive focus on what's wrong, what's going wrong, and what we might be doing wrong. The recovery behavior we replace that with is learning to focus on and pay attention to what's right: what's going right and the positive vision of how things are working out well in our lives.

We may have to work as hard, or harder, at focusing on what's right as at uncovering what we're doing wrong.

Look fearlessly, with a loving, positive eye. What did we do right today? Did we stand still and deal with a feeling? We may have done it awkwardly, but did we do it? Did we think about a Step once, during a crisis? Did we do something differently today than we would done have a year or two ago? Even a little differently? Did we reach out to someone and allow ourselves to be vulnerable?

Did we start to get into shame or negativity, then become aware of it and get ourselves out? Did we do something nice, gentle, and loving for ourselves? Did we do something for someone else that felt good?

Did we do our work well? Did we deal positively with a bad day? Did we practice gratitude or acceptance? Did we take a risk, own our power, set a boundary, enforce a boundary? Did we talk honestly and openly to someone and feel we got a little closer, bonding the connection between ourselves and another? Did we own our power in a way that was good for us? Did we take responsibility for ourselves in a way that we might not have before?

Did we take time for prayer or meditation? Did we trust God? Did we talk to God and turn things over to God?

Did we let someone do something for us? Did we start to get caught up in someone else's issues, then practice detachment? Did we go on with our daily routine, when what we wanted to do was sit and obsess?

Did we listen to ourselves, trust ourselves, and see how well that worked out? Did we hold our own with someone who tried to manipulate or control us? Did we affirm ourselves? Did we nurture ourselves, instead of criticizing ourselves? Did we practice self-love in any way? Did we go to a meeting, read a meditation, or think about a recovery concept, even for a short while?

Look at what we did right. Look at what we did well. Strive for self-awareness, without becoming hypervigilant about it. If we did something wrong, accept and deal with that. But also look for what we did right.

No matter where we are, who we are, or what we're doing, even on our worst days—especially on our worst days—we can find one thing we did right, something good about ourselves and our lives to dwell on. We can find something to feel hopeful about, something to look forward to. We can focus realistically on a vision of what is and what can be good in our lives.

There's room in reality and recovery for "what's right." Identifying the negatives and the problems will help us solve them. Empowering the good will help that to grow, too. We can tell ourselves, others, and God what we appreciate about the other person, ourselves, and life.

We can let go of our need to be so critical of ourselves and others. We can look for what's right.

MAINTAINING SELF-ESTEEM

This is the Step of continued self-awareness and self-responsibility. In the other Steps, we began the process of looking within, rather than focusing on others. This Step encourages us to continue on that path. We don't have to use it as a rigid tool to control ourselves and keep ourselves behaving perfectly. We can use it, instead, as an anchor, to keep us grounded in ourselves and our own growth processes.

We can allow ourselves to live and trust the lessons to reveal themselves to us, when it is time, when we're ready, when our Higher Power is ready. Sometimes that lesson is a new behavior we need to work through. Sometimes the lesson is an old behavior that has crept back in.

Sometimes I need to deal with an incident, a person, or myself and clean up my act. Sometimes I have forgotten to practice a simple principle like gratitude or detachment—principles that can determine the quality of my day-to-day life.

Some of us discover that taking this Step reveals new issues and areas we need to work on—such as insights or addictions we may need to start addressing within ourselves. Sometimes this Step gives us new insight about a current or past relationship, or our history.

A prayer that helps me is this: *Show me, God, what it is I'm learning. Guide my growth, and me.*

This is the Step that encompasses our imperfections and the imperfections and humanity of others. It is a vehicle for learning to love ourselves and others unconditionally. Take it not in fear, but in trust that we are right where we need to be in our lives, our recoveries, and our relationships.

Our desire to admit our wrongs promptly will increase— whether those wrongs are toward ourselves or others—because we will learn that doing so brings peace. Unrest and discord are often signs that we need to take this Step and look within. Trust that the answer will come.

Be patient with yourself and others as you struggle forward in this process of growth, change, life, and recovery. Be patient as you struggle to identify issues and what your part is or was in those issues. Be open to the answers because they will come.

Welcome the insights. We can trust where this process is taking us. We can trust what's happening and where we're at in this process. Something is being worked out in us, something important—whether we are at a plateau or a dramatic and intense time of change.

We don't have to control this process. We can let go and allow it to happen. By working this Step, all we need to know about taking care of ourselves will be revealed to us.

Once we have worked our way up to Step Ten, we can maintain and increase our self-esteem by regularly working this Step. It incorporates the process we've gone through in Steps Four through Nine. It means we go through this process again, as needed, to keep on track.

We don't work this Step to punish or demean ourselves. We do it to maintain harmony in our relationships with ourselves and others. We do it to stay on track. We don't project this Step on others: We inventory ourselves—our own thoughts, feelings, behaviors, and paths.

When we get off track, when an issue emerges that we need to address, we now know how. We identify the issue. We talk to someone about it. We're honest, rather than defensive, fearful, or ashamed. We accept what happened and take responsibility for our part in it. Then we become willing to make any appropriate amends, and we let it go.

This process for keeping ourselves on track can become as habitual as our survival behaviors once were. The next time we do something that bothers us, we don't have to waste our energy diving into shame. The next time we get caught up in an old behavior, even when we know better, we don't have to punish ourselves. We can take a Tenth Step: identify it, talk about it, then promptly make an amend, whether that means correcting our course with ourselves or others. Let the process happen. And move on with our lives, in love for self and others.

Admitting I was wrong in how I was treating myself or others used to be difficult for me. I felt that my entire self-esteem rested on my being right—all the time. That attitude didn't leave room for much growth—or self-esteem.

Now, as I'm learning to be more comfortable with myself, I find it somewhat easier to admit my wrongs. I am more open, vulnerable, and humble about this process of growth and recovery.

It's still difficult for me to go to people and admit my wrongs. It's difficult for me to become aware of a new behavior I need to work on. I still gulp and think twice before I apologize. I have to fight with my defenses and my pride. My need to be perfect, my need to be right, is still there in the background, trying to be heard.

This Step, this program, is teaching me that I don't have to listen to that old message. My peace, my joy, my love for self and others comes when I accept myself. It comes when I allow myself to be honest, open, and responsible with those I love, work with, and relate to. It comes when I'm responsible to myself and my own needs.

My self-esteem and self-love come back when I promptly address the wrongs I do to others and myself.

This Step gives me permission to be me and to be imperfect. It gives me permission to love and nurture myself and focus on what's right with my life. It allows me to be a vulnerable human being in relationships with other vulnerable human beings. It allows me to forgive myself. And it has taught me much about forgiving others, too.

It weaves the concept of forgiveness and acceptance into my daily life. This Step is teaching me to love others and myself unconditionally—and still take responsibility for me.

We don't have to be perfect and right. Now we can say, "I was wrong, and I'm sorry" to ourselves as well as to others.

This Step gives us permission to be honest about who we are. We can deal with things as they come up. Use it regularly to grow and maintain the good feelings we have discovered.

ACTIVITIES

1. How do you continue your process of self-awareness and inventorying? Do you spend time each morning or evening reviewing your day? Or do you allow your insights to happen naturally, as you go through life and recovery? Do you combine tactics? What works best for you?
2. When was the last time you caught yourself doing something you didn't feel good about? Did you take care of the issue promptly?
3. Either daily or weekly, force yourself to find one thing in your life and one idea about yourself that is good. Affirm that good until it sinks in and feels real. Strive to find one thing that you like about someone who is important to you, then take the risk of telling that person.
4. Watch for ways that fear, anger, and resentment arise in your life. Watch for beliefs underlying these feelings. Watch for ways that your anger toward yourself influences your anger and behavior toward others and yourself.
5. What is the affirmation you and your inner child most need in your life today? Do you need to tell yourself that all is well, that you can slow down and take your time? Do you need to promise yourself that you will protect and take care of yourself in a particular relationship? Do you need to affirm that the love you want and need is coming to you and that you deserve a loving relationship? What is the fear or idea that is bothering you most today about yourself and your life? Are you facing a stressful or fear-producing circumstance? Are you feeling inadequate about something? Create a loving, nurturing affirmation that helps you and your inner child know that your life will be fine.

"Whatever satellite goals may be found in life, the singular intent is always the soul's process of becoming one with the Self and God. Be comforted and walk your life in Light and trust, for nothing will come to you that is not meant to be."
—Emmanuel's Book

STEP ELEVEN

"SOUGHT THROUGH PRAYER AND MEDITATION TO IMPROVE OUR CONSCIOUS CONTACT WITH GOD AS WE UNDERSTOOD GOD, PRAYING ONLY FOR KNOWLEDGE OF GOD'S WILL FOR US AND THE POWER TO CARRY THAT OUT."
—Step Eleven of CoDA

"Go with the flow, Melody. Go with the flow."

How many times have I heard those words from my sponsor? How many times have I gotten angry about hearing those words? Many times.

How can I go with the flow? How can I stop believing in loss and deprivation and begin believing in fulfillment?

I am slowly learning that not only can I go with the flow, I can trust it. I am part of it. If I am plugged into my Higher Power and God's will for me, I will know what I'm supposed to do and when I'm supposed to do it. Taking care of myself, owning my power, will be—and is—a natural part of the flow. I will grow and change as I am meant to, as I am ready to, as I want to.

Step Eleven is my favorite Step. It has taken me from addictions to sobriety. It has taken me through poverty, pain, and despair. It has led me through the pain of bottoming out on my codependency. It has given me all I need to begin recovery and continue healing. It continually leads me from confusion to clarity, from being victimized to owning my power. This Step has led me into a real life—a life of my own, a full life that works.

172

It takes me from where I am to where I'm going; it helps me trust both places. It takes me through each day. If we stare at the maze of our lives, we can easily become confused with all the pathways, hallways, doors, and choices. This Step helps us to focus on the details of our present path and allows us to walk confidently through the maze.

Going with the flow doesn't mean we don't rock the boat. It means we finally can. By listening to ourselves and God, we'll know when it's time to do that, and we'll be empowered to do that. The debate we have about whether we can take care of ourselves is not with God; it's with ourselves. Our next course of action is deciding the best way to do that and asking God for help.

There are times to surrender, times to let go, times to give in. There are times to wait and times to take action. There are times to be gentle and nurturing, times to give, and times to receive. There are times to speak up, own our power, and take care of ourselves. By working this Step, we'll know what time it is.

IMPROVING CONSCIOUS CONTACT

My recovery from chemical addictions began with a prayer. I was in treatment for chemical dependency. I didn't want to be there. I didn't want to get sober. But I had nowhere else to go. I can remember staring at the ceiling in the tiny cubicle that was my room and saying, "God, if you're there and if you care and if there's a program—a way for me to recover—please help me do that."

I thought my prayer bounced off the ceiling and landed on the floor. I was wrong. Within weeks, my sobriety began. Someone told me to ask God each morning to help me and thank God at night for doing that. I did. Someone else handed me a copy of a daily meditation book and told me to read it each morning. I did that, too.

I had stopped talking to God when I was eleven. I can still remember that day. I was walking down the street on my way to church one Sunday morning, filled with despair and confusion. I couldn't figure out my family. I couldn't figure out myself.

And I hurt. I looked up at the sky and shook my head. If there was a God, this God didn't care about me. How could a loving God let me be in so much pain and misery? I decided to forget God, forget the church, and find my own way to cope with my pain.

Within a year, I was an alcoholic. Within several years, I was addicted to narcotics. Now, fourteen years later, I was in a state hospital for addiction, praying to a God I wasn't certain was listening. God did hear me. In spite of myself, I got sober in that state hospital. I believe it was time for that to happen in my life. I believe it happened by the grace of God and because of God. I also believe in the power of prayer. My soul finally opened up.

I asked.

Thus began my journey into prayer and meditation—my spiritual journey. My first steps were simple, faltering ones, but my actions were sufficient. This Step began to work in my life. Then I began working on another important part of this Step: learning to trust God's will and plan for my life— and learning that this plan included taking care of and loving myself.

Of all the relationships we are learning to rebuild in our recovery from codependency, our relationships with ourselves and with our Higher Power are the most important ones. They are the foundation for all the other relationships we will participate in. Our relationship with God, as we recover from codependency, will lead us into a loving, close, intimate relationship with ourselves. The opposite is also true. An intimate, loving relationship with ourselves will bring us closer to God.

As one woman said, "Then, all the other relationships become icing on the cake."

This Step tells us how to do that. We pray and we meditate, to improve our connection with God and ourselves. We ask to be shown the best possible course of action for ourselves each day and the power to do our part.

SOUGHT THROUGH PRAYER

We are each free to understand God as we choose to, according to our vision and our truth. What is specific in this Step is that we are to talk to the God of our understanding by praying, then ask God to show us God's will for us and help us carry it out.

Praying is talking to God. A prayer can be a word or a thought. It can be an expression of joy or sorrow. A prayer can be a letter to God. Or it can be a traditional prayer.

I have a computer filled with my letters to God. I love to reread them and see in retrospect how each was heard and answered. Some answers came quickly; some took longer. All were read by God, even though they were tucked away in the electronic and magnetic recesses of my hard disk.

We are free to pray any way we choose: standing, sitting, kneeling, eyes closed, eyes open, lying in bed, or walking down a dirt path through the woods.

"I try to keep a conscious contact with God at all times," said Beth. "When I'm standing in line at the bank, I'm talking to God. When I'm driving, I'm talking to God. Always . . . talking to God."

"Throughout the day, I repeat the phrase 'Thy will be done'," said Gary. "I chant it like a mantra."

Prayer doesn't need to be complicated. We can talk silently, directing our thoughts to God. Or we can talk aloud, as we would to a person. We don't have to change our language to talk to God. We don't have to be someone or something we're not. We can be who we are with God. We can say what we need to say, when we need to say it. We build a working relationship with our Higher Power and discuss what we need to keep that relationship going.

Sometimes we get a vision or a sense of what the future holds, but we get our directions from our Higher Power one day at a time. That is also how we receive the power to carry out those directives. When I reinstated my relationship with my Higher Power after a fourteen-year break, I was timid and un-certain about how to do that, and I wondered if I was even heard. I went through the discipline of praying each morning and each night, forcing myself to say something silently with my eyes closed.

I relied heavily on the Lord's Prayer. It's a prayer used by many Twelve Step groups, and it's an efficient prayer. It felt like a safe prayer. Later, as my recovery progressed, I developed my own recovery prayer, based on pages 84 through 88 of *Alcoholics Anonymous*. My prayer is this:

> Thank You for keeping me straight yesterday. Please help me stay straight today. For the next twenty-four hours, I pray for knowledge of Your will for me only, and the power to carry that through. I pray that You might free my thinking of self-will, self-seeking, dishonesty, and wrong motives. I pray that in times of doubt or indecision, You might send the right thought, word, or action. Show me what my next Step should be, and help me work through all my problems, to Your glory and honor.

Then, in between my recovery prayer and the Lord's Prayer, I've learned to talk about the things I need to say. I tell God what's bothering me. I ask God to protect my children. I ask God to heal my fears. I ask God to help me with anything specific I'm facing that day.

I talk about my feelings to God. Being open with God didn't come easily. Sometimes it's still not easy. Some days I don't feel connected—to myself, others, or God. Some days my prayers are just words with no feelings, no expression. In the beginning I barely told God anything. Now I sometimes go on and on.

Before recovery from codependency, I begged God a lot to control and change other people. I have stopped doing that, at least most of the time. I went through a long period of despair, because God didn't answer my prayers to control and change others. I began to wonder if God had gone away. I began to wonder what God's will was for me in my life because others weren't doing what I wanted and expected them to do. Things weren't working out as I had planned.

Then, slowly, I began to realize that God's will meant accepting my present circumstances, even, and especially, when God's plan was different from mine. But I learned God's will also meant learning to remove myself as a victim and take care of myself—no matter what was going on. God's will meant learning to trust God, and me.

I learned God's will means feeling and accepting my emotions instead of apologizing for having them.

God's will sometimes means setting boundaries and standing up for myself, instead of asking God to make people stop doing things that hurt me.

Sometimes God's will means I apologize. Always, I am coming to learn, it means I accept and nurture myself.

Besides the discipline of morning prayer, I pray throughout the day. Sometimes I talk about what's bothering me. Sometimes I yell for help.

I ask for guidance and direction when I'm unsure. And the more I can remember to say thank you, no matter what happens, the better things go.

Prayer transforms us. Grateful prayers transform our lives and our circumstances. Gratitude turns negative energy into positive. It breeds acceptance and brings out the best in any circumstance.

Some days, I get caught up in the busyness of the day before I have time to pray. I don't like those days, but I'm learning to trust that even on those days, God doesn't and won't abandon me.

Slowly I'm learning to bring more of myself to God. I'm learning to trust God. That trust doesn't mean I will never experience pain, stress, or situations I don't like. It does mean that I can trust what's happening to work out for the good.

I'm learning, also, that I can bring every request to God. None is too big, too small, or too unimportant. I can place it all in a prayer, then let go, asking that God's will be done.

Each of us can find our own way to pray, our own discipline for prayer, our own method of communicating. Some people like the prayers suggested by certain religions. Some enjoy a less structured approach to communicating with God.

How we approach our praying is not nearly as important as making the effort to do it. I'm learning to pray whether I want to or not. I'm learning I can trust, whether I feel trusting or not.

Many times I have begged God for something, gotten furious because I didn't get it, then felt so grateful a year later when God's agenda worked out much better than mine. Often, I end up thanking God profusely for not allowing me to have my way.

I'm learning slowly that it's safe to thank God now for all that's taking place, even if it's not what I want, even if I'm not grateful today.

Sometimes I get stubborn and refuse to ask for the help I need. Often, I am reminded that although I am strong and competent, there is a Power that will help me in miraculous, energizing, and healing ways.

Praying is how we keep ourselves—our souls—connected to God. It is where change begins.

MEDITATION

Praying is how we talk to God. Meditating is how God talks to us.

Many people in recovery practice meditation in a variety of ways. As with praying, we are each free to find a way that works for us.

Reading a meditation book is one way. There are many meditation books available in bookstores. These are little books that have a quotation, a reading, and sometimes a prayer for each day of the year. Many of these books are aimed specifically at codependency recovery. Some are more general but are still favorites of people recovering from codependency. A listing of some of them is included at the back of this book. Many people like to take time at the beginning of the day to do this little reading, to remind themselves of recovery principles, to help them feel good about themselves and get on track for the day.

I've gone through periods where I've used more than one meditation book. I keep several around. In times of stress, I may read one in the morning, at noon, in the afternoon, and in the evening—whenever I need that kind of help.

Some people listen to tapes as a way of meditating. There are many tapes available now that can help us attain a relaxed, peaceful state of mind. Some people like subliminal tapes. These are tapes with messages audible only to the subconscious mind. Sometimes the message is audible on one side of the tape; on the other side the same message is subliminal. Other tapes are all subliminal. Many include a script, so we know the message. The messages are subject-oriented, such as serenity, letting go of fear, accepting ourselves, and the like. What we hear consciously on the subliminal side of the tape is usually relaxing meditative music or nature sounds, such as ocean waves. What our subconscious hears is the positive messages.

Some people use therapeutic massage as a way to relax, meditate, and become centered.

Some people use alternative forms of meditation. "I was rageful at traditional religion," said Jake, "but I discovered that my anger at religion pushed me away from all forms of spiritual expression. Now I have found a spiritual path through some Native American practices, Zen meditation, and shamanistic practices. I am discovering, in the process, a strong sense of my spirituality."

Some people prefer traditional forms. They retreat to a quiet place and meditate. "Every night and every morning, I take time to tune in," said Sarah. "I listen for messages and direction about what to do that day. I ask for guidance all the time."

However and whenever we do it, the goal of meditation is to quiet our selves and our thoughts, relax, become centered and peaceful, and tune into God and ourselves. We rid ourselves of the chaos, tension, and fear that so often accompany living. We let go of it all and be still.

I used to think meditation was a waste of valuable time. I felt so pressured, so busy, that taking any extra moments to relax seemed like a waste of valuable energy. I have learned differently.

Meditation, I've discovered, is no more a waste of time than stopping to put gas in the car. Meditation is how I rejuvenate and renew. Meditation is one way I rid myself of negative energy and open myself to a positive flow of good.

Meditation means opening our minds and our spirits—our souls—to the God connection. Obsession, worrying, and rumination are not God connections. They are fear connections.

To connect with God, we need to relax and open our conscious and subconscious minds to a Higher Consciousness. In the busyness of our days and lives, it may seem like a waste of time to slow down, stop what we're doing, and take this kind of break. It is not a waste of time. Meditation can create more time and energy than the moments we take to do it.

We build a connection to God by building a connection to ourselves.

Once we become tuned into ourselves and trust ourselves, we will know when we need a meditation break. We can meditate regularly on a disciplined schedule. And we can listen to ourselves and know when we need to remove ourselves from the busyness of life and get centered.

Meditation and prayer are powerful recovery behaviors that work. We need to be patient. It is not reasonable to expect that the moment we meditate, we will get our answer, our insight, our inspiration, or our healing. It is not reasonable to expect on-site, instantaneous answer to prayer.

But the answer is coming. It is already on the way, if we have done our part by meditating and praying.

GOD'S WILL FOR US

Prayer and meditation are not meaningless tasks we are asked to do. Prayer is how we become transformed; meditation is how we become renewed. Both disciplines benefit us and help us stay on track.

I used to worry and fret so. I worried about what would happen, what I would do, if it would be good enough, if I could get done all that needed to be done each day. Sometimes I worried about whether or not I actually had a life to live.

Sometimes I'd enviously watch others go about the business of their lives. Their lives seemed so alive, so fun. I wasn't sure my life was real.

Fretting and stewing about the course of my day is needless. Praying for knowledge of God's will for me only and praying for the power to carry that through simplifies life. It tells me that if I pray for knowledge of God's will for me, I will receive all the power I need each day to do that which I am meant to do. If I can't do it, I don't have to. If it is mine to do, I shall be given the power I need to do it.

It means I can trust the flow. I can trust myself. I can trust God. When it is time, I shall be empowered to do that which I need to do. I shall receive the insights, the help, the ability, the growth, the guidance, when it is time. If I can't do it yet, then it's not time.

If it's time to take action, I'll know. If it's not, I can quietly go about the course of my life, making the best possible choices about how to conduct myself on any given day.

If I am unable to take any action, I can let that go. Some days are busier than others.

But always, I can trust my path.

Asking for knowledge of God's will for me and the power to carry it through is a prayer that will always be answered "yes."

This Step also assures each of us that there is a path for our lives. Sometimes it is a simple path with simple duties. Sometimes the path means waiting. Sometimes it means feeling or healing. Sometimes it means giving; sometimes receiving. We can choose. We can participate in creating our path.

Sometimes it means saying yes; sometimes saying no. But there is always a path for our lives, even when that path is not clear to us.

Something is happening. Something good is being worked out, in and around us. Something important. We are learning our lessons, and we will continue to learn them. When it is time, we will be empowered to do all that we are meant to do.

We can relax and go with the flow.

I sometimes feel like that flow is taking me over the rapids. One friend calls those times "the darkness of our soul."

In spite of our best efforts to work our program, to recover, to take care of ourselves, we may have days when we feel like our lives or our recoveries aren't working. The pain may feel unbearable. It may seem like God has gone away. God hasn't.

We don't have to punish ourselves when times are hard, and there are certainly hard times in recovery. We don't have to punish ourselves for our feelings, doubts, concerns, and mistakes.

We don't have to punish God either.

We can relax and go with the flow, even when the flow hurts, even when we're not certain where it's taking us. The hard times will not last forever. The confusion will not last forever. Clarity will come. The answer will come. The darkness of our soul will leave, and daylight will come.

The hardest part of prayer and meditation for me is dealing with my impatience. I like immediacy. I like answers now. I want change now. As one woman said, "I'm used to operating three to six months ahead of myself."

That is not how prayer and meditation work. We pray. We talk to God. Then we let go. And let go some more. The answer will come, but not by holding on and usually not instantly. The answer will come by letting go and allowing the flow of life to move us forward. The answer will come when we let go of our fear.

Sometimes meditation does not work instantly or immediately. I can meditate and feel almost as chaotic when I finish as when I started.

But we can trust these behaviors and keep practicing them anyway. Sometimes it may feel like we've asked, begged, and pleaded for knowledge of God's will for us and the power to carry it through, and nothing is happening. That's an illusion. Something, my friend, is happening.

Sometimes our part is simple. We do the dishes. We go to a meeting. We call a friend. Or we wait. Sometimes doing nothing is God's will. Sometimes that is much harder than doing something.

Sometimes it's time to take action. But we don't have to worry about that. When it is time, we will receive all the guidance, power, and assistance we need to do what we have to do, and we can let go of the rest. If we wait until it is time, our part will be clear. It will be possible. It will happen—naturally, gradually, and with ease.

That doesn't mean we won't have to overcome obstacles and face challenges. It doesn't mean we won't have to fight for what we want. But we will be given the power and help we need to face obstacles and challenges, and to break through barriers.

This is the go-with-the-flow Step. By talking and listening to

God, we can relax, let go, and allow our lives to happen. By asking for knowledge of God's will for us and the power to carry it through, we can trust what is happening, what has happened before, and what will happen tomorrow. We can trust our part in the flow.

We are safe now. We are cared for. We are protected. We are free now to live our lives and love ourselves.

This Step gives us permission to let go of our need to control and our efforts to control others and our lives. We can do our part by setting goals, using affirmations, and practicing our basic recovery behaviors. We can do our part by praying and meditating. Then we can let go and allow ourselves to be guided into truth, health, healing, happiness, joy, freedom, and love.

We can trust what is happening, even when it doesn't look like we can. Or as one man put it, "We can trust God, even when it doesn't feel like we can."

Some days our lives feel "in synch." Things fall immediately and wonderfully into place. Other days we may pray 'Thy will be done,' and all the events feel ill-timed and out of place. Nothing feels right.

All the days count.

Feel our feelings, when they arise. Love and nurture ourselves as many times each day and each hour as we need loving, nurturing, and accepting. Say thank you for everything. Ask for what we want and need.

Then complete the process by saying, "Thy will be done."

And trust what happens.

This Step can take us through the best of times and the worst of times. It can take us through difficult feelings and pleasant ones. It can take us everywhere and anywhere we need to go. Work it often. Work it as soon as possible in our recovery. If we do the other Steps—admitting and accepting powerlessness, turning our will and lives over, cleaning house—we will be a clean vessel, one that is easily guided.

Listen. Listen to ourselves. Listen to God. Trust what we hear.

I used to think that following God's will for my life meant following a rigid set of rules, instructions, and prohibitions. I used to think following God's will meant I needed to be perfect.

Now I've learned that's codependency.

Often, in my life, God's will is that still, small voice we call instinct or intuition. It is within us, not in a book of rules. But it's hard to hear it when we're noisy and scared.

Sometimes, when we begin to live this way—trusting ourselves and our Higher Power—we will find ourselves making mistakes, doing foolish things, thinking we are doing God's will.

That's okay. We can keep moving forward in this direction, anyway. Let it go, and keep working this Step. Keep listening to and trusting ourselves and God. Work this Step as many times each day as we need to stay centered, grounded, and balanced. When it's time to learn a lesson, we learn it.

Be still. Be quiet. Ask for guidance. Then allow ourselves to move forward in confidence. Learn to combine instinct with reason *and* emotion.

When in doubt, when confused, stop and ask: What do I need to do to take care of myself? Then listen, and trust what we hear.

One man said, "When I get into a sticky life situation, I now ask myself, 'What is the most life-giving thing I can do right now? Am I living out of that, or am I living out of responding to other people's needs?' "

This Step tells us that we have a path, and no one can interfere with it. We don't have to hold on so tightly. Others do not hold the key to our happiness, nor do they hold the key to our lives.

No one, not one person, can stop or interfere with the good and the love that is coming to us. Others do not hold that in their hands: It is between us and our Higher Power.

We can love ourselves unconditionally; we can love others unconditionally. We are free to own our power and do what it is we need to do to take care of ourselves, in faith and confidence that nurturing, self-care behaviors will move us forward on our journey.

All we need will come to us. All the good we desire, the love we want, the success, the friends, the healing, the meeting of needs—big and small—will come.

This is the Step where we say, "Show me what you want me to do, then help me do it." This is the Step where we talk to God and let God talk to us—by calming our souls and speaking to them. We ask God to show us what we need to do to take care of ourselves, then we ask God to help us. We ask God to help us take responsibility for ourselves.

We are in good hands now. The moment we open ourselves to spiritual consciousness, we have started a positive chain of events that will benefit us, our lives, and our relationships. Whether we pray and meditate first thing in the morning, during a coffee break, in the shower, on the wing, or in the car, is our choice.

When our conscious contact with God improves, our connection with ourselves and others will, too. We will find and maintain our connection to God—and our connection to ourselves.

Take a moment for prayer and meditation. Do not criticize ourselves for not doing it well enough. Let go of our fears about whether or not God hears and cares. God is there, and we are each able to tap into the spiritual consciousness.

This Step will carry us through the difficult times and the good times. When we don't know what to do next, God does.

We can trust that each day we are exactly where we need to be and where we are meant to be.

Trust God. Trust ourselves. And trust our lives. God never, never asks us to do anything that God does not equip and supply us to do. If we are to do it, we will be empowered. That's the easy part of this program: We never have to do more than we can. We never have to do anything we can't. We never have to do anything before it's time.

And when it's time, we will do it.

ACTIVITIES

1. Have you begun the discipline of prayer in your life? What does that consist of? What are your feelings and fears about praying, about talking to God? What time of day works best for prayer? Do you have a favorite place?
2. How do you meditate? Do you like meditation books? Which are your favorites? When is your best time for reading a

meditation? Do you like tapes? Have you experimented with any other forms of meditation?

3. What other activities help you relax and get in touch with yourself?

4. The next time you get stressed, instead of pushing harder, you might want to walk away from what you are doing and find a way to get quiet and centered. If you are at work, you may want to retreat into a private area—your office, if you have one, or even a bathroom will do. Breathe deeply, then let go of your thoughts, worries, and chaos. Allow peace and healing to enter your body. Stay with it as long as you can or as long as you need to.

"Oh, I've been a victim all my life," he said.
"No, Joe," she said. *"Your whole life is ahead of you."*
—*Joe and the Volcano*

STEP TWELVE

"HAVING HAD A SPIRITUAL AWAKENING AS A RESULT OF THESE STEPS, WE TRIED TO CARRY THIS MESSAGE TO OTHER CODEPENDENTS, AND TO PRACTICE THESE PRINCIPLES IN ALL OUR AFFAIRS."
—Step Twelve of CoDA

I was sitting on the lawn at Willmar State Hospital. It was about two weeks after I had prayed my little prayer to God, the one I thought probably bounced off the ceiling, asking God to help me find a recovery program—if indeed a real program existed, if indeed I could be helped.

I was still using drugs. I didn't know how to stop. I wasn't even sure I wanted to. A few days earlier, I had had a glimpse into my powerlessness. I had some amphetamines hidden in my radio, and I realized I could not stop using drugs, even though I was facing severe consequences for doing so. I was also slightly aware of my unmanageability, even though denial still permeated me.

I lay back on the rolling green lawn and took a hit off the marijuana cigarette I had managed to get from someone else in treatment. It wasn't my drug of choice. But it was a drug. And I was hoping it would do something to change the way I felt—keep me high and not feeling.

I inhaled, exhaled, then stared up at the sky. In a moment, the clouds seemed to open up. I felt the power of the universe speaking to me. I felt, for the first time in my life, the clear presence of God.

This Presence saturated my conscience, which up to that moment had not been operative. I became aware, and I became afraid. Right down to the core of my soul, in that moment, I knew I had no right to continue doing to myself what I was doing. I had no right to fill my body with chemicals.

187

Whether I liked it or not, God was real.

The heavens seemed to open up and turn purple. My consciousness was transformed.

I took one more hit off the marijuana cigarette, put it out, and walked back into the treatment center. I didn't tell anybody there what had happened. I was already in a nut house; I was afraid the admission of this incident might keep me there permanently. I took all the energy I had focused on being chemically dependent and now began to focus it on working the Steps and achieving sobriety.

This incident turned out to be more than a drug-induced hallucination. Except for one incident a few months later when I had a drink of alcohol, I have been chemically free ever since—by the grace of God and with the help of the Twelve Steps. That happened in 1973.

That was my spiritual awakening. It transformed me. It transformed my life. It didn't happen as a result of working these Steps: It enabled me to work these Steps and enabled the Steps to work in my life.

This was a tremendous awakening of my soul and spirit. It was a transformational experience. It was as or more real than anything else that has transpired in the material and physical realms of my life. In fact, my spiritual awakening created a new material and physical dimension in my life. But in spite of its grandness, it was not complete. There was another awakening, a completing of this process, that happened when I threw myself just as wholeheartedly into my recovery from codependency.

Let's examine the components of this Step: carrying the message, practicing these principles in all our affairs, and spiritual awakenings as a result of working these Steps.

CARRYING THE MESSAGE

The Twelfth Step says that after we have had our spiritual awakening from working these Steps, we try to carry this message to others. What is our message? One of hope, love, comfort, and health. Better relationships and a better way of life, one that works.

It is a message of self-love, self-nurturing, paying attention to our own issues, and taking responsibility for ourselves, whether that means addressing our own behaviors or owning our power to take care of ourselves. It is also a message that we can allow others to have their own issues and take responsibility for themselves.

We are free now to be done with shame and self-hatred. We can love others and allow them to love us, giving in ways that are helpful and allowing ourselves to receive.

Our message is that fear and controlling backfire. We can't control others, and we don't need to allow ourselves to be controlled by them.

We are free now, at last, to feel, to think, to make our own choices, and to take responsibility for those decisions. We are even free to change our minds. We now understand that we will be controlled by our pasts until we do our historical work and release old feelings and beliefs.

Our message is that we are lovable and deserving people, and we need to begin loving ourselves.

We are not victims. We have choices, more than we know, in any situation. We can stay, we can leave, we can take care of ourselves any way we need to, as long as it does not infringe on the rights of others.

We can trust ourselves and our Higher Power to show us how to do that.

How do we carry this message? Not by rescuing. Not by controlling. Not by obsessing. Not by becoming vigilantes or evangelists. Not by trying to force others to see the light. Not by standing in the darkness waiting for others to come with us on this journey.

We carry the message in subtle, but powerful, ways: by doing our own recovery work and becoming a living demonstration of hope, self-love, self-nurturing, and health. Learning to remove ourselves as victims, take care of ourselves, and walk our own path is a powerful message.

A general consensus among those recovering from codependency is that Twelve Step groups for codependency recovery are naturally less service-oriented than Twelve Step groups for other addictions. That is because for many of us, too much service to others and not enough self-care is part of what has harmed us in the past—harmed us and not helped others.

Many of us feel a need to back off from helping others for a while, as part of our recoveries. While our goal in recovery is to become healthy givers—giving from a sense of high self-esteem, giving because we want to, giving in a manner that is not over-extended, compulsive, or guilt-ridden—we may need to go to the extreme of not giving for a while in order to find that balance and to be able to discern healthy giving and caring.

We will know how and when it is time to begin giving again. By paying attention to ourselves, we will learn healthy ways of carrying the message.

Inviting someone to a meeting is a powerful way to help others. Going to our meetings and sharing how recovery works for us is another way to carry the message.

This is a wonderful program, a miraculous program. Part of the miracle of this program is that much healing is accomplished through storytelling. Sometimes we share bits and pieces of our story; other times we tell more. By telling our story, we help others and ourselves. By listening to others talk, we become helped. Talking about ourselves, what we are learning, what we are facing, what we are overcoming, is a powerful way to carry the message.

We can allow ourselves to be guided. When I carry the message incidentally or accidentally, it is usually more effective than when I set out to reform, convince, or coerce someone into recovering. The most powerful form of helping others comes from helping ourselves. When we do our own work, feel our own feelings, change our own beliefs, and take care of ourselves, when we are honest and open about who we are and what we are working on, we affect others more than by our best-intentioned helping gestures. We cannot change others, but when we change ourselves, we may end up changing the world.

Each time we do our own work or a piece of it, each time we take a step forward, we pull the collective consciousness of the recovery movement forward. We can relax in quiet confidence that we will help others greatly when we do our own work and allow ourselves to be guided.

However we choose to help people, we can strive to carry the message in ways that work—for them and for us. We can let go of our need to help people, change them, or show them what is best for them. Instead, we can focus on helping and changing ourselves and figuring out what is best for us. If an opportunity arises to share a piece of information or some part of our story, we can do so quietly and without a desire to control. If we must show people something, we can show them comfort, empowerment, and hope. We can show them how much we love ourselves, how we deal with our feelings, and how we are refusing to be victims anymore.

Sometimes it's hard to let go of people we love and move forward with our growth and recovery anyway. Some of us want so badly to bring those we love with us on this journey. But we cannot. That decision is not our choice. The only person we can take on this journey for certain is ourselves.

Just as we each have our own path, so do those we love.

Sometimes wonderful things happen in recovery. I have observed situations in which, after a short time, an entire family began recovering. I've also seen cases where that was not true, where people had to leave their families behind and begin a solitary journey into health.

Understand this, my friend: We do not ever help anyone or have one iota of positive influence on them by standing or staying in the darkness with them. Ignoring ourselves does not benefit us, and it does not help others.

Often, when we begin recovery—and sometimes well into recovery—we want to share our discoveries about recovery with family members. We want them to find the same health, hope, freedom, and good feelings that we're discovering.

We want to share what we've learned about caretaking, victimization, controlling, dealing with feelings, doing our family-of-origin work, and caring for ourselves. We want to share our new discoveries about relationships and how we are learning to participate differently in them. We want to talk about how certain behaviors are predictably self-defeating and how we've felt justified about them all, only to learn that this is something called codependency. We want to explain that when we changed, our relationships often did too.

We want to tell people about setting boundaries and owning power. We want to share with those we love all the ideas that are bringing us freedom and healing. We want to bring them with us on this journey.

We may find that our bubble of enthusiasm for sharing recovery with our families quickly bursts when we approach them with our new ideas. Their denial, resistance, and anger toward our recovery ideas may cause us to react with hurt and confusion. We may get caught up in trying to control them, trying to force recovery on them, and feeling victimized when they choose not to accept it. We may wonder why they do not want the marvelous, wonderful gift we've found.

We learn to let this go. We learn to let *them* go. We cannot run anyone's recovery show but our own. It doesn't matter if our ideas would help Mom or Dad, brother or sister, Grandma or Grandpa. It doesn't matter if we've found some answers that they desperately need and that would really help them change their lives for the better.

It doesn't matter one whit.

Calm yourself. Be patient. Temper your enthusiasm to help your family see the light. Ask for guidance and wisdom in approaching family members. When you talk, talk about yourself and what you're learning, not about them and what they need to be learning. The most powerful and positive impact we can have on our family is to lead a healthy, happy life.

Detach in love whenever possible. If you cannot detach in love, then detach now, deal with your feelings, and allow love to come later.

Here is an excellent piece on helping, excerpted from *A Basic Pamphlet*, Families Anonymous conference-approved literature:

HELPING

My role as helper is not to do things for the person I am trying to help but to be things; not to try to control and change his actions but, through understanding and awareness, to change my reactions. I will change my negatives to positives; fear to faith; contempt for what he does to respect for the potential within him; hostility to understanding; and manipulation or overprotectiveness to release with love, not trying to make him fit a standard of image, but giving him an opportunity to pursue his own destiny, regardless of what his choice may be.

I will change my dominance to encouragement; panic to serenity; the inertia of despair to the energy of my own personal growth; and self-justification to self-understanding.

Self-pity blocks effective action. The more I indulge in it, the more I feel that the answer to my problem is a change in others and in society, not in myself. Thus I become a hopeless case.

Exhaustion is the result when I used my energy in mulling over the past with regret, or in trying to figure ways to escape a future that has yet to arrive. Projecting an image of the future and anxiously hovering over it, for fear that it will or won't come true, uses all of my energy and leaves me unable to live today. Yet living *today* is the only way to have a life.

I will have no thought for the future actions of others, neither expecting them to be better or worse as time goes on, for in such expectations I am really trying to create. I will love and let be.

All people are always changing. If I try to judge them, I do so only on what I think I know of them, failing to realize there is much I do not know. I will give others credit for attempts at progress and for having had many victories which are unknown.

I, too, am always changing, and I can make that change a constructive one, if I am willing. I CAN CHANGE MYSELF. Others, I can only love.

PRACTICING THESE PRINCIPLES

Another part of the Twelfth Step refers to "practicing these principles in all our affairs." What that means to many of us is learning to practice our recovery behaviors and the principles of the steps in all areas of our lives.

That means we surrender to and accept healing in all parts of our lives. We turn in lives and relationships that don't work and allow these principles to give us, in return, lives and relationships that do work.

Some of us begin recovery to deal with our own addictions. Many of us enter recovery thinking it is really about our spouses and the effects of their problems on us. Or we may enter recovery thinking our problem centers around our families. We may be experiencing unmanageability in some or all areas of our lives, but it is often a serious problem in one focused area that gets our attention enough to move us into recovery. Initially, then, we limit our recovery task to meeting the challenge in that one area—either with the one person causing problems in our lives or with the one problem in our lives that is creating pain. At some time, the bliss of this shortsightedness disappears. We begin to see that we're seeking a solution for all aspects of our lives.

We have begun a journey, a spiritual journey.

We want healing and health in all areas of our lives—with friendships, love, work, recreation, family, emotions, mental health, physical health, and spirituality. Many of us find that this solution, this whole-life healing, happens in one area at a time. We work the Steps and tackle one portion of our lives at a time. We receive our healing in one area at a time.

These Steps work in all areas of our lives, however we choose to compartmentalize these areas. They will restore manageability to all areas of our lives. They will bring healing, peace, love, and freedom to all areas of our lives.

We can practice these principles and receive their benefits in all our affairs—our home lives, our businesses, our finances, our love relationships, our relationships with relatives and friends. We can practice recovery behaviors in all parts of our lives because those are the same places we practiced our codependency behaviors. At some point, we will wake up and know our new way of life has really become a new life.

A SPIRITUAL AWAKENING

Often, when we begin recovering from codependency our vision of what recovery means is narrow. We attend meetings, work the Steps, and begin taking care of ourselves primarily to ease the pain we believe has been caused in us by another person and his or her behavior. Our hopes for ourselves are that we can stop obsessing about others and stop feeling guilty or ashamed about other people's problems.

Those are good reasons to begin recovery, but they are only starters.

There comes a time to expand our vision and look for more from recovery. The time comes when our recovery—this program and our place in it—is no longer about other people but is truly about ourselves and our journey.

We need to go to meetings long enough to learn that the other person's problem isn't our fault. We need to go long enough to learn it's a "selfish" program of taking care of ourselves. But those two ideas are not the end; they are only the beginning.

If we stop working our program there, we have stopped at the starting gate.

Each one of us is on a spiritual journey. The journey is gradual, progressive, and healing. As we heal, we achieve higher levels of love for ourselves and others. We discover a life of our own and new ways of living that work. We discover the flow and choose a path for our lives. We begin to see the importance of that path. We learn to live life on a spiritual plane, a life that then becomes reflected on the physical plane.

This journey will take us places we never planned or expected to go. Experiences will come to us, experiences that help us resolve important issues. We will find ourselves experiencing a range of emotions, from joy to despair, along the way. We will be drawn to the people and circumstances we need in order to help us learn and help the other person, too. Many of the experiences that come to us will not be what we asked for or wanted, but eventually we'll learn that each holds an important lesson, one that was critical to molding and shaping who we are and who we will become.

When we learn to surrender to our present circumstances, we also learn to trust that whatever will come will work out in our best interests. Ultimately, we will see good things being worked out in our lives, better than we could have planned or imagined. This good does not always come easily or without struggle.

But it will come.

We will become aware of and healed from our pasts. To quote the Big Book, "We will not regret the past, nor wish to shut the door on it" (p. 83). This healing will include our relationship history.

Self-defeating behaviors that we have relied on most of our lives will be taken from us and replaced by new, more effective, behaviors. We will be done with self-pity, except for momentary lapses that will take us forward to healing.

The need to be perfect will be replaced by a sense of accepting and cherishing ourselves. The fears that have haunted us will be replaced by peace and trust—in ourselves, our lives, our Higher Power, and eventually in others. Despair will be replaced by joy and hope. Martyrdom will be replaced by a desire to be good to ourselves.

The guilt that has saturated us will be taken from us.

We will learn to recognize when we are dancing the dark dance of death in a relationship, and we will learn how to get ourselves out. We will learn to recognize the "codependent switch" in relationships—that moment in time when things change from what we expected and we start to feel crazy because reality has shifted.

We will also know when it is safe to open our hearts to love.

We will learn what it means to take care of ourselves.

We will know we are not alone. That sense of being disconnected will be replaced by a strong sense of connection—to ourselves, to others, and to our Higher Power. We will know we are being led and guided by a loving Power greater than ourselves.

We will learn that we can take care of ourselves, for the tools we need will be provided to us.

We will begin to trust and rely on instinct and intuition, instead of will, control, and rules. The need to control others, circumstances, and ourselves will gradually be lifted from us.

We will see our past relationships in a new light and become grateful for all of them, even the most troublesome and painful, as we see the good worked out in us from each.

Our most troublesome character defects will become illuminated in a new light. Many will be transformed into assets. The others we will come to accept as a demonstration of our humanity and uniqueness.

Some of us will discover other addictions, other problems of our own that we need to address on our journey. We will come to accept those issues as part of our journey. We will become aware of them and deal with them when the time is right.

Shame and self-hatred will be replaced by self-acceptance and self-love. That love of self will become real and will transform our relationships with ourselves and others. We will find ourselves giving and receiving love in the highest sense, and our relationships will begin to work.

We will become healed from the impact of abuse. After going through a range of emotions, including denial, rage, and sadness, we will achieve forgiveness for others. We will learn to forgive ourselves.

Our emotions and hearts will become healed and open.

We will be done with both inferiority and superiority. We will begin relating to people as equals and with compassion and understanding for them and for ourselves.

Our tolerance for being victimized will decrease.

We will learn to express anger constructively, set boundaries, say no, and walk away from abuse and from that which is not good for us. We will develop an accurate sense of our responsibilities and other people's responsibilities. The desire to take care of others will be replaced by a desire to allow each person to be responsible for himself or herself.

We will embrace our issues and allow others to have theirs.

We will learn to nurture ourselves and others without caretaking.

We will begin addressing and feeling our emotions, taking responsibility for them ourselves. We will stop letting our feelings catapult us into controlling gestures that damage our relationships with others.

We will begin to deal directly and honestly with people, without manipulation and hidden agendas.

We will no longer think or behave as victims. That deep sense of being victimized by life will disappear, and we will know what it means to own our power. We will accept our powerlessness, find our Higher Power, become empowered, and learn to share the power by participating in relationships as equals.

Our lives will begin to make sense and have value and meaning. Our needs will begin to get met.

Laughter and fun will become part of our lives. We will learn to lighten up.

We will become fully alive.

Along the way, bitterness and remorse will be replaced by gratitude.

And for once in our lives, we don't have to do it ourselves. We aren't doing it ourselves. Above all else, this program of recovery, this path opening up to us through the Twelve Steps, is a spiritual process.

We have begun a spiritual journey.

We discover *ourselves* and *God*. Then, we are ready to begin opening up to the beauty and gifts of other people in our lives. We will appreciate the validity of our path and the validity of theirs.

Although we may have started our journey because of the impact of another person, our recovery has never really been about the other person. It is about us. We are learning the lessons we need to master in this life.

There are differences in working the Twelve Steps for recovery from codependency and working them to recover from addictions. Many people agree that in recovery from addictions, people need a harder, almost harsh, focus on themselves and their behaviors if they are to stop the addictive process and learn new behaviors. Many also agree that in codependency, we need to develop a gentle attitude toward ourselves.

The shame must go. By the time we get to codependency recovery, whether or not we are recovering from other addictions, we are ready to let go of shame and low self-worth. We stop using fear and shame to control ourselves or others. We stop allowing others to control us through fear and shame.

In recovery from addictions, there is also a heavy focus on "getting out of self." This is necessary to stop the addictive process. But by the time we reach codependency recovery, it becomes time to begin paying attention to ourselves, to loving and valuing the self.

There are some common denominators between recovery from addictions and recovery from codependency. As the Big Book of Alcoholics Anonymous points out, "We have entered the world of the Spirit." These Steps, this recovery from codependency, is a spiritual experience.

I regularly encounter debate about whether codependency is a disease, a problem, an addiction, a condition, or an issue.

I don't know whether it is a disease, a condition, or an addiction. I do know that it is a problem, a painful, persistent problem that has afflicted many of us. It is a serious, ongoing problem, one that is progressive.

It can also be terminal. We may develop stress-related illnesses that can kill us. Or we may spend our lives walking around wishing we were dead.

Of the people interviewed in the research for this book, several stressed the idea of the terminal nature of codependency.

"I watched my sister die from cancer," said Jake. "We were adult children of alcoholics and lived with an abusive father. I got into recovery. She was in denial—both about her codependency and her cancer. My sister was in extreme denial, and I feel like she died from codependency. One thing that I got from her death is, 'This kills. This kills.' It is one of the things that I stress in my program. I get really mad at people that think Al-Anon and codependency are less serious than drug addiction. It is just as deadly, if not more. Because there is a way of living with it that feels like you're alive, and you aren't."

There were many stories told to us and millions more to tell. There are moderate stories of unhappy marriages and alcoholic parents, people who didn't need bizarre and dramatic experiences to "get it."

There are people who have suffered from the impact of certain religious beliefs. There are people who have been in recovery for a while and are still struggling with their guilt.

There are newcomers who go to six meetings a week and vow to attend fewer meetings when they have a real life to live.

There are people with other addictions—food, sex, alcohol, drug, and gambling addictions—who discovered codependency to be a core, underlying issue in their addictions, an issue they needed to address in order for their recoveries to work, an issue they needed to address to avoid relapses.

Some were driven to recovery by dramatic, intense, and intensely painful experiences. Others were led to recovery by boredom, loneliness, and a sense of inner irritation.

There are stories that are gentle; there are stories of bizarre lives turned holy. There are stories telling how a dating relationship can mirror unavailability and intimacy issues. There are stories of how children—even one child—can affect and torment an entire family.

There are stories of couples in recovery, separately and together, working on themselves and their "coupleship"—heartwarming stories of people deciding to stick together and work through their issues.

There are stories of men who are seeking recovery because they want it, not because women have pushed, prodded, and nagged them into it.

There are stories of overtly crazy, abusive situations. There are stories of covert abuse, equally painful but sometimes more confusing.

There are people at many different stages of recovery, and each stage is equally valid and important. What is clear from talking to people and listening to their stories of recovery is that those who are making the most progress and finding the most freedom from their codependency are those who work the Steps and allow the Steps to work in their lives.

Regardless of their progress or how much time they have spent in the program, most have begun to have a spiritual awakening. To some, this means connecting with friends and beginning to feel and express feelings. To others, it means the power to begin taking care of themselves, in spite of what another person is or isn't doing.

To some, it means the power to stay in a relationship and work on it and enjoy the love they are finding. To others, it means the power finally to exit a relationship that has been destroying them.

To most, it means an awakening to God, and an awakening to self—to who we are, to our spirits.

Certainly, we begin and continue recovery by changing behaviors, paying attention to our thoughts, and dealing with our feelings. But what we are working toward, what we are getting to, is that miraculous deep healing and change that takes place in the very core of our being.

We have a spiritual awakening as a result of working these Steps. The work may appear and feel difficult, but it is easier than we think. It has been mapped out for us. We are not on our own. We are not floundering and stumbling in the dark, even when it feels like we are. We are being guided, led, shown what to do next and how to do it.

Some of us have an immediate, overpowering spiritual awakening. Some of us awaken slowly, gradually. Some of us awaken in fits and starts. There is no one way, except the way it happens for us, as a result of working these Steps.

And yes, sometimes it hurts a little, sometimes a lot, to be healed. But codependency hurt a lot, too. Any pain we feel in the process of healing has a promise and a reward at the end of it. We are no longer suffering needlessly and endlessly. We are hurting only as much as is needed finally to heal from our pain. Then, we feel better than we ever imagined possible.

Spiritual awakening, the core healing we are seeking, is not something that *might* happen if we work these Steps. It is promised to us.

Codependency is, at the very least, a problem. Now we have a solution if we want it. We come together in community to share our problem and our solution—our experience, strength, and hope. At times we go on our private journeys—journeys we must take alone, to heal, to learn, to grow. Then we come together in community again, to share our solution and give and receive support.

Together we become healed.

We all describe our spiritual experiences and awakenings differently.

Laura described hers as follows:

"I don't know what the incident was with my husband. I did something and was complaining about him not giving to me. This caused him to get very upset, and we had an argument.

Suddenly, I realized for the first time how much he has been giving to me and how hard he has been trying to please me. I cried because I was so critical of him. I cried because I was trying to squeeze blood out of a turnip. I saw that I wanted and needed so much, and he was giving so much, and I still needed more. For as much as he was giving, I still needed more. I was sad that I was so wrapped up in myself and my own neediness and so busy looking to him to satisfy me that I couldn't see how often he bought me flowers or called me from work. The reality is that he is very giving, very willing, and very accommodating. It made me realize that he is a separate person from me, and he is who he is. That was my spiritual awakening."

Pete described his spiritual experience this way:

"Before the program, I was more organized, more focused, but totally dishonest. I didn't allow myself to feel. I was depressed, lonely, isolated, and secretive. I felt a lot of shame. Now, my heart is on the path of my life."

My experience was different still. As I said earlier, it began at Willmar State Hospital, in a sudden burst of God consciousness. In that moment, I knew God was real.

Over the next seventeen years, I have learned something else. I am real, too.

As my spiritual journey continued, I became aware that I no longer had the right to inundate my life with sabotaging, self-defeating fears and beliefs—fears that made me want to control and beliefs that destroyed my joy. It was time to let go of them so I could heal. It was time to begin truly loving myself.

I am not separate from God. I am not an outsider knocking on the door, cringing in fear, waiting to be let in. I can take God's hand, and be cocreator, allowing God to take the lead. I am not helpless. I have choices.

We have choices. One choice we have is not to be victims anymore.

This is a lesson I find myself facing again and again. Always, I must learn it before I can move forward. I must transmute my present circumstances and allow myself to be transformed by them. I cannot do this when I am a victim.

I am not outside of the Creator. I am a creation. Now, finally,

I am connected to myself. I awakened to God, and I awakened to myself.

And I am learning how to be connected to others. I can look to them to love and comfort me, but I am learning that nurturing the frightened child within is my job, and I will be in trouble when I run around the world expecting someone else to do that job for me. I am learning daily to accept myself and all my feelings as valid and important. I am learning how to take care of my feelings and myself.

I no longer have to become enmeshed in the downward spiral of trying to control others, and allowing them to control me, my life, or my happiness.

My healing has run deep—deeper than I expected it to. I had pain and negativity stored in my body, in my cells, my muscles, my organs, from the time I was born. My negative beliefs were packed away so tightly in my subconscious I wasn't aware I had them, but they were, in fact, controlling my life.

The biggest pain I have felt and faced in my life has been the pain of being me. Recovery from codependency has unmasked and healed that pain.

The journey has not been easy. It has been good, but sometimes difficult. Sometimes I believe the good parts have been harder than the pain. Despite my success, things still don't always work out the way I want.

But they happen as they are meant to happen. And I am still in awe of what happens when I let go.

And comfort is always available.

"I am trusting that God will keep directing me in this journey," said one woman, after sharing her story—a story of pain, growth, disappointments, and healing. A story of lessons learned and still learning.

I am trusting that God will direct each of us, you and me, in our journeys. Nurture ourselves. Nurture others. Learn to love, and learn how to be loved.

May our journey be a safe one.

ACTIVITIES

1. Describe your experiences in carrying the message to others. Describe an effort that backfired or didn't work. Describe one that you believed was successful.
2. How have you begun to take recovery principles to areas of your life other than your primary relationships? In what areas of your life would you like to experience healing and more growth and change? You may want to turn these wants into written goals.
3. How has your relationship with yourself changed since you began recovery? How do you treat yourself differently now? How does it feel when you treat yourself well and in a nurturing, loving manner?
4. Describe your experiences trying to share or explain your recovery to family members. Get feedback from someone else in recovery, someone you trust, about these experiences.
5. How have you grown spiritually since you began recovery? How would you describe your spiritual awakening?
6. Have you awakened to the beauty and joy of yourself?

WORKING A PROGRAM

This chapter is not a compilation of ideas about how to work a program. In this chapter, I've included some words to newcomers, including what it means to work a program, some general observations about recovery gathered as a result of researching this book.

IN THE BEGINNING

"For the first three months, I thought everything about the Twelve Step group I first attended, Adult Children of Alcoholics, was weird and couldn't possibly work," said one man. "Then, I started to see more change happen to me in those few months than I had in all my life previously."

Despite the miraculous changes that can and will take place in us and in our lives, many of us aren't happy about beginning this process of change and growth. We may find things wrong with the people and the group. We may not understand what we're doing there.

We may have a range of reactions to finding ourselves sitting in a Twelve Step group, listening to people talk about recovery. Here are some common reactions people have to their first Twelve Step meetings: "For the first six weeks I sat in Al-Anon meetings, all I could do was cry," said one woman.

"At first, I couldn't stomach all the God talk," reported several men and women.

"I sat in meetings for almost a year and didn't have the slightest idea why I was there. Then, I gradually began to understand. I'm still not entirely certain how the Steps work on me, but I do know they work."

"I resisted going to Al-Anon for years," said another woman. "After all, my husband had the problem. Why should I go to the meeting!"

"I found something wrong with everything, at first."

"For the first year, I thought I was in the group to help everyone else get better. Then, I realized I was in worse condition than they were."

We may hear people say things like, "I'm a grateful recovering codependent, [Al-Anon, ACA, etc.]" and feel bewildered and irritated.

That's okay. That's normal. Feel the resistance. Feel the irritation. But stay open. Cultivate honesty and a willingness to try. Gratitude will come later.

How do we come to these Steps for codependency recovery? Many of us come kicking, screaming, and with a great deal of resistance.

Some come angrily. Some come in fear, confusion, or desperation.

Some of us come quietly, because of a profound awareness of a hole in the soul. Some of us come again and again, having worked the Steps once, sometimes more, on other addictions, only to find ourselves still facing the journey to codependency recovery.

Some of us come to these Steps to help another person or to deal with the impact another's problem has had on our lives. We may begin attending Twelve Step groups because someone left us, or because someone in our lives is drinking, gambling, using drugs, or having affairs.

Initially, some of us are furious about having to address our own issues when someone else has the problem.

Some of us come timidly, some scoffing, some in despair.

Most of us come because we have nowhere else to go.

Most of us eventually become grateful that we had nowhere else to go and landed at the first of the Twelve Steps.

This is truly a come-as-you-are program. We come in our present circumstances, protected by anonymity.

We start where we are, with who we are at the present moment. We begin not with expertise, but with a willingness to try.

Be open to the Steps, work at the Steps, and let them work on us. We don't have to do this perfectly. We don't have to do this at once. Many of us spend much time listening, absorbing, and letting the healing powers in the groups and the Steps work on us.

WORKING AT RECOVERY

There are millions of people whose lives have been transformed by attending meetings and applying the Twelve Steps to their issues and problems. We call this recovery process "working a program."

The components to working a program include: establishing fellowship with other recovering people, attending meetings, talking about our recovery at these meetings, and listening to others talk about their recovery.

Between meetings, we often call another person in recovery, or they call us. Many of us find it helpful to read a meditation book daily to help us stay on track.

Between meetings, we try to focus on the Steps and other recovery concepts, both as a regular practice throughout the day and in times of stress.

We first use the Steps as an alternative to our previous coping behaviors: fear, control, caretaking, shame, and self-neglect. Then, we use the Steps to help us work out the issues in our lives and move forward through the problem to a solution.

We don't have to do the Steps perfectly. We don't need to wonder if we're doing them well enough. We only need to work them the best we can.

Think about the Steps. Think about them until they sink down into the core of us and transform us into who and what we want to become.

Then work them some more.

There will come a time when the Steps and other recovery concepts become more than words. The words, the ideas, move into our minds and down into our hearts. They become a truth that is manifested in our lives.

This moves us forward into a new way of life. That might be a new way of looking at our present circumstances, changed circumstances, or both.

We become changed.

We have found it not nearly as important to understand *how* the Steps work as to understand that they *do* work.

When we begin recovery, most of us are confused about the Steps and what it means to work them. We don't have to understand all at once. We don't ever have to do something we find ourselves unable to do, for this program to work.

Most of us have found that an honest, sincere, and humble effort works.

That means that we think about the Steps between meetings, when a problem arises, or as a habitual practice as we go through our day. If thinking about a Step guides us into taking a particular action, we do that.

Working a Step means we listen to how others work on the Steps.

Working the Steps requires that we become open to what these Steps can and will do for us and our lives.

"After listening to people talk about the Steps, I found them presenting themselves to me as Great Truths in my life," said one woman. "It was as though each Step took on a life of its own and worked its way into my consciousness, when I was ready for it."

The important idea here is, we begin to focus on the Steps, instead of focusing on our problem or our codependent behavior.

We try to do something each day that is a recovery behavior, whether that something is reaching out to someone, praying, meditating, attending a meeting, thinking about a Step, or doing something good and loving for ourselves.

Enjoy the benefits of fellowship that Twelve Step programs can offer you. Talk to others; listen to them. Strive to maintain healthy limits in program relationships. Understand that we need to take care of ourselves in *all* our relationships.

We will find ourselves being led, within the program, to the people and places we need, when we are ready for that. We trust that when it is time to do, know, or learn something, we will know and become empowered to do it.

Be patient with ourselves and the program as it begins to work on us and our lives.

ABOUT THE RECOVERING COMMUNITY

During the course of interviewing people for research on this book, some ideas became clear:

Each person interviewed talked about the importance of doing family-of-origin work in their recovery.

Many couples are now working at recovery both individually and together, as couples.

All but one expressed total commitment to continued recovery. The people interviewed understood that recovery is an ongoing process, one that needs to be continued if recovery is to be continued.

Most old-timers in the program were open to alternative methods of assisting recovery. They tried more things and appeared less rigid.

Old-timers go to fewer meetings than they did in the beginning but feel good about life, live full lives, and are very active.

Multiple marriages are common in people recovering from codependency.

Men use the Twelve Steps to get in touch with their feelings more than most women do.

The recovering men who felt most balanced and satisfied with life were those who had dealt with their incest issues. The men in Sex Addicts Anonymous said that unless men deal with their incest issues, they will usually relapse in their sexual addiction recovery, and they will continue to act codependently. They will continue to feel worthless, hopeless, and ashamed.

Many people have a difficult time doing a Fourth and Fifth Step around codependency issues. Fourth and Fifth Steps were easier for those who were addicted. Some were so hard on themselves when they began recovering that they needed to wait a year or so to do a Fourth and Fifth Step.

Steps One, Two, and Three were most important to the people interviewed and most likely to be discussed.

People in codependency recovery don't use service to others as a way to stay sane, unlike people in recovery from other addictions.

A codependent slip wasn't considered the same as a substance-abuse slip. Perfection is not our goal in codependency recovery.

Most agreed that there are appropriate places to bring up certain issues. For instance, in A.A. meetings, it is appropriate to talk about alcoholism, but not sex addiction; Overeaters Anonymous is the place to deal with food issues, not cocaine abuse. Some groups are more open than others to talking about recovery issues not specific to that group.

Most people thought the slogans Let Go and Let God, Easy Does It, One Day at a Time, and Live and Let Live, were corny and beneath them when they started the program but found them helpful as they progressed in recovery.

Most codependents did not want to give up control.

SPONSORS AND RECOVERY

An important part of working a program is having a sponsor. Sponsorship means a defined relationship between two people in recovery.

It is a special recovery friendship, in which the sponsor agrees to be a "mentor" and "recovery helper" to the sponsee.

Unofficial program policy, regardless of the Twelve Step program, is that one should have a sponsorship relationship with a person who is not the same gender of their sexual preference. This is done to avoid love relationships and sexual entanglements. It is suggested that people get a sponsor soon after getting into the program. Program etiquette also suggests that the sponsee ask the person of his or her choosing to be his or her sponsor. We look around, find someone we feel comfortable with who has a year or more of experience in the program, and we ask that person to sponsor us.

It is okay, if we are asked to be a sponsor, to say yes or no. It is okay to terminate a sponsorship relationship if we feel uncomfortable with it, or to set any other boundaries we believe are important.

It is important for sponsees to remember that although someone may have more recovery time than we do, it is not their role to tell us how to live our lives. We also do not have to accept any information that does not feel right to us.

We trust our sponsor, if that feels right, but we also trust ourselves. If it comes time to change sponsors, end a particular sponsorship relationship, or add someone else as a sponsor, we can do that without guilt.

It is important for sponsors to remember that it is not our role to control or take care of sponsees. Nor do we have to give anything we feel uncomfortable giving—whether that is time, listening, rides, or any other type of help.

Sponsorship relationships are important to recovery. They can be a special place to give and receive the benefits of recovery. They can be a safe place to talk about feelings and to get tidbits of information that we may not have time for in meetings.

The bonds in some of these relationships can be strong, lasting years and years. Sometimes they turn into the strongest and best relationships we will ever experience in our lives.

But they are also fine ground on which to practice recovery behaviors, such as setting boundaries, detaching, saying no, and learning to help in ways that work.

A WORD ABOUT OUR FAMILIES

In this program of recovery, we do not dwell on blaming our families or holding them accountable for our behaviors. But we do find the freedom to explore feelings we may not have had permission to feel in those families. We finally have the freedom and safety to identify abuse and take steps to heal from it. And we have the freedom to correct and change self-defeating patterns of behavior and thought that we learned in these families. We strive to do this with love for ourselves and for our families, although many of us learn to interact differently with our families as a result of our recoveries. We do this with the understanding that our parents were probably at least as victimized as we were, perhaps more so, but we temper it with the knowledge that understanding does not mean we have to continue to allow ourselves to be harmed or brainwashed.

SEEKING PROFESSIONAL HELP

Seeking professional help is an entirely different matter from attending Twelve Step meetings. During the course of our recovery through Twelve Step groups, it sometimes becomes apparent to us that we might benefit by seeking professional help in addition to attending our meetings.

We neither encourage nor discourage seeking any particular form of therapy at Twelve Step groups. We can, of course, share our experiences. We always encourage people to ask for what they need, including help. We can empower individuals to trust themselves to seek and find whatever help feels right for them.

Suicidal ideation or attempts, chronic depression, and physical or sexual abuse—whether we are the abuser, the abused, or both—may warrant outside help.

CROSSTALK AT GROUPS

People can choose to talk or not talk at any meeting they attend.

At some meetings, when people talk, others in the group respond to what was said. This may be in the form of a suggestion, advice, or simply a reflection on what was said. Sometimes the person responding shares a similar experience.

This is what we call crosstalk.

Crosstalk at groups is a matter for each individual group to decide.

Many CoDA groups frown on crosstalk. Some people have reported that there is more of a tendency to engage in crosstalk at ACoA (Adult Children of Alcoholics) meetings.

Some people like to hear responses to what they have said. Others don't. They want only to be heard, because by being heard and accepted, they will be enabled to take responsibility for themselves.

Some people occasionally want a response but will take care of themselves by asking for that, when they want it.

Some people find crosstalk confusing and irritating.

In our meetings, some of us may inadvertently get into the very behaviors we no longer want to engage in: controlling, caretaking, taking responsibility for another person, not taking responsibility for ourselves.

If we feel we need to say something to another, we can strive to keep our comments "clean"—that is, free from control and advice. Many of us find it helpful to limit our responses to relating our own experience with a similar situation.

If we feel we *have* to say something, if we feel the other person's destiny hinges on our words and what we say must be listened to or else, then we may be better off not saying it.

The other person might be better off, too.

MULTIPLE ADDICTIONS AND RECOVERY

Gone are the days of people with only one issue. Yes, there are some plain codependents, people recovering only from the issue of codependency.

But many of us are recovering from more than one problem.

We are coming to believe that while we may have several addictions or issues to resolve, we have only one recovery. As part of that recovery, we may need to attend more than one meeting on a regular basis—for instance, Alcoholics Anonymous and ACoA; Overeaters Anonymous and Al-Anon.

This process of allowing our issues to unfold is a highly personal one. Many people recovering from multiple issues have learned that a hard-line approach was necessary to recover from their addictions, such as alcoholism or sexual addiction. Later, a gentler, more loving, approach to self was appropriate. Many of us learned this gentler, more loving, approach through codependency recovery.

We have learned that if we have an addiction, we must give that issue the care, attention, and priority it needs by attending an appropriate group. We do not substitute codependency recovery for recovery from addictions. But we also address our codependency issues as we feel necessary.

If we begin recovery and our addictions begin to unfold one after another, we allow that to happen without shame or remorse. We go where our recovery path leads us, trusting that all is well. We allow others to do the same. We do what we need to do to take care of ourselves, as we learn what that is. That means we accept and address all our addictions with an appropriate plan of self-care, as those addictions present themselves in our lives.

In the chapter entitled "A Vision for You" from the Big Book, the original writing on the Steps, Bill Wilson wrote:

> We realize we know only a little. God will constantly disclose more to you and to us. Ask Him in your morning meditation what you can do each day for the man who is still sick. The answers will come, if your own house is in order. But obviously you cannot transmit something you haven't got. See to it that your relationship with Him is right, and great events will come to pass for you and countless others. This is the Great Fact for us.
>
> (p.164)

Many of us have come to believe that this vision, this prophecy of great events coming to pass, includes the expanded vision of recovery consciousness that takes into account codependency and recovery from it.

Just as individuals grow and change in their recovery, so does the wisdom and view of the collective consciousness as a whole.

I almost lost my sobriety once. It was after a fire that burned down my home just before Christmas. The insurance company had put my husband, myself, and our two children up in a small apartment. I had a pathetic one-foot-tall artificial Christmas tree. I had a car with no insurance, a child who needed to go to school across town, no money, and no hope.

I had spent years watching people around me drink whenever they felt like it. I had watched irresponsibility in others. And watched it. And watched it. All the while, I had been so strong, so brave. I had never given in. Now, I thought, it's time.

Although I had been sober for years, I deliberately drove to the liquor store, bought a bottle of Scotch and some fancy liqueur and drove home with the bottles. I stared at the bottles but decided not to drink that night. I didn't want the children to see me drunk. I had been sober well before they were born. They didn't need that. By the time they went to sleep, I was tired and put myself to bed.

The next night the same thing happened.

The third night I decided to talk to God about it. Give me one reason, I said, why I shouldn't drink. My life is in a shambles. Everything has gone wrong for years. I have nobody. I am nobody. Show me why I shouldn't get drunk. Show me why I shouldn't medicate my pain with alcohol, at least for one night.

You've got one chance, I said to God, and that's it.

I grabbed the Bible next to my nightstand, opened it, and read where my thumb had landed: "You cannot serve two masters." The words jumped out at me.

Quietly, I walked to the kitchen, poured both bottles of liquor down the drain, and slowly became ready to face the unmanageability of codependency in my life.

Many of us believe that dealing with our codependency issues is critical to recovery from other addictions as well. Codependency can contribute to relapse if it is not addressed. Although abstinence from our addictions is essential, we believe that our codependency issues are also core issues.

Our sobriety began with abstinence and recovery from our addictions. Our lives began with recovery from codependency.

Not all people recovering from addictions agree with this philosophy. If people argue with us, we do not debate the issue. It is not a matter of right or wrong. We know what we need to do to take care of ourselves.

When they tell us that if we were really working a good program of recovery from our addictions, we wouldn't need anything more, we allow them to have their belief, and we have ours.

We understand that this spiritual path, this journey, is collective but also individual. If our path has taken us on a winding road through one or more addictions, unresolved abuse issues, and finally codependency, we embrace that as our path, the journey that is intended and right for us.

HOW MANY MEETINGS A WEEK?

How many and what kinds of meetings to attend is an individual decision that will probably fluctuate and change over the years.

The number and kinds of groups we attend at any period in our recoveries will depend upon us, our issues, and our needs at the time.

Some people suggest that newcomers attend ninety meetings in ninety days. This is a matter of individual preference and will again depend on individual circumstances, such as a person's present state, background, and ability to attend that many meetings. Many people initiate recovery by attending one or two meetings a week.

Some people attend one each of different kinds of meetings a week, such as Overeaters Anonymous, Alcoholics Anonymous, and Codependents Anonymous.

Some alternate between groups, attending an Alcoholics Anonymous meeting one week and an Al-Anon meeting the next.

"I found myself led down a progressive path," said one woman. "I started in Overeaters Anonymous. I stayed there as long as I needed to, about five years. I lost my weight, but something was still missing.

"Next, I found myself led to Al-Anon. I stayed there for four years, got what I needed, and moved to Co-SA, Codependents of Sex Addicts. I usually attend one meeting a week—more when I need to and occasionally less."

Most of us, regardless of our circumstances, find we benefit by attending more meetings in the beginning of our recovery and during times of stress.

We attend as many meetings as we need, as often as we need, to get healthy and stay on track. We plan on making meeting attendance a regular part of our life. But we also plan on having a life.

The Twelve Steps and Twelve Step programs are not meant to be a substitute for life. The purpose of the Steps is to help us live our lives and develop a life to live.

"I attend five or six meetings a week," said Henry, who has been recovering from adult children of alcoholic issues and abuse issues for two months. "I feel like it's too many, but I can't decide which one to stop going to. But someday, if I get a real life, I'll have to go to less. If I went to one meeting a week, I feel like I'd be lost for a year."

We can be open to our needs and the fact that our needs change.

DISSENSION IN GROUPS

Since the beginning of Twelve Steps groups, there has been occasional dissension and difficulty within groups. Sometimes, this difficulty leads us to find another group; sometimes, it leads a particular group to disband or split into two or more groups.

We try to avoid controversy whenever possible. If we do not like the way a particular group is going, we can say something. If we continue to dislike the way a particular group is going, we can find another one.

CHOOSING THE RIGHT GROUP

We can each choose the kind of group that feels right for us and the particular group we like within that category. We even have the freedom, with the support of a particular intergroup association, to start a group, according to the traditions and procedures suggested by that intergroup.

Some groups focus on feelings. Some groups are problem-solving groups. Some groups focus on a theme or idea. Some focus on a Step. Some alternate, focusing on a Step one week and a recovery topic, such as detachment, the following week.

Some meetings are open. That means anyone can attend. Some are closed. That means only people who identify themselves with the common problem and solution of that group, as dictated by the tradition concerning membership, are invited to attend. The differences in some of the Twelve Step groups and their focuses are discussed on pages 229 to 240.

Most groups last from sixty to ninety minutes. Some larger groups begin with all members meeting together for an opening session, then breaking into smaller groups.

Some groups meet with members organizing their chairs in a circle; then each member is free to speak, or pass, as he or she chooses. Some meet around a table.

Some groups are speaker meetings, where one person has previously agreed to tell his or her story of the problem and how he or she has recovered.

Some groups allow smoking. Some are nonsmoking.

Some groups meet in the morning, some at lunch hour, some in the evening, some on weekends.

A few groups provide baby-sitting at the meeting.

It does not cost money to attend a group, although most "pass the hat." Voluntary contributions cover expenses such as rent, coffee, tea, and literature. Most people, if they want to and can afford it, throw in about a dollar per meeting, but this is not required.

Within any particular category of group, such as CoDA or Al-Anon, there are different kinds of groups. Each group seems to develop its own personality, based on the group consciousness. We might attend one particular meeting of Al-Anon and feel uncomfortable; then we might attend another meeting and find it feels just right for us.

If we have questions, we can ask. We can also ask for any literature concerning a particular group.

Find the group that feels right for us. If we go to one and don't like it, we can go to another. Most of us have found that we needed to shop around to find the group that fit.

Others of us found it helpful to attend a group at least six times before making a decision, because some of our dislike for that group was based upon our general resistance to change.

If we are beginning recovery and aren't certain where to begin, remember that it's better to begin someplace than not to begin at all. If we suspect we may be recovering from multiple addictions, we don't have to overwhelm ourselves. We can choose the problem causing the most pain and start to seek help for that.

A listing of most of the Twelve Step groups, and information on how to locate one in your community, can be found at the back of this book.

RELATIONSHIPS AND RECOVERY

A short word about relationships and recovery: When we begin our recovery, many of us are advised to avoid intimate love relationships for a time. For some of us this is not advisable because we are in a committed love relationship when we begin recovery.

Some of us may choose to abstain from relationships for a time. This is an individual decision.

Some of us may decide to terminate a particular relationship. This is also an individual decision.

Many of us crave a safe place to talk about what we are experiencing as we initiate and work on relationships. Sometimes, it is not possible to do that in groups because the members have a shaming, disdainful attitude toward relationships and the people who want to be in them.

The goal of recovery from codependency has never been permanent abstinence from relationships. The goal has been to restore us to sanity so we could participate in healthy, loving relationships—if that was our decision and choice.

There is a great deal of wisdom inherent in the policy of keeping our hands off other people's business, as it pertains to their choices about relationships. It is not our job to advise others about what their choices need to be or when they need to make those choices.

If a person is to abstain from relationships, he or she will become aware of that. If a person is to begin or end a relationship, he or she will be guided into that, too.

If a person asks for support in ending a relationship, we can gently offer encouragement. We can also offer that same kind of support to those who are building or working on relationships.

That doesn't mean we can't have boundaries. If a person is consistently whining about a particular relationship year after year and we're tired of hearing about it, we can say so. But we can also be gentle, supportive, and compassionate, remembering that many of us learned our most valuable lessons from the most painful relationships we've been in.

We can learn to value the individual and place value on relationships, though many of us have indulged in ones that haven't worked out the way we wanted.

It is entirely appropriate, valid, and necessary for individuals to work on their own issues apart from a relationship. It is equally valid for people to want to work on their relationships together. We can place value on both and trust ourselves for timing.

GOD AND RECOVERY

For once in our lives, we don't have to do it ourselves, and we aren't doing it ourselves. Above all else, this program of recovery, this path opening up to us by working the Twelve Steps, is a spiritual process.

We become open to help, loving care, and guidance from a Power greater than ourselves.

If care is exerted in studying the Steps, we notice that the first reference to God is this: a Power greater than ourselves. The second is this: God as we understood God.

This was done intentionally by those in the beginning of recovery consciousness. God was intentionally inserted into the Steps because we learned we could not recover without God and without a profound spiritual experience, whether that happened immediately and intensely or gradually and quietly.

God was inserted into this program of recovery because God is fundamental to recovery.

The decision to refer to God as a Power greater than ourselves and to allow people to develop their own understanding of this Power was just as intentional.

GLOSSARY
OF RECOVERY TERMS

Following is a directory of some recovery "jargon," words you may not find in a dictionary but will probably hear in recovery circles.

Addictive. Addictive behaviors are more dangerous than compulsive ones. "Addictive" refers to behaviors that are out of control and causing negative consequences in our lives, but that we persist in anyway. Addictive behaviors usually are engaged in to get high or get numb. We can be addicted to a substance, such as alcohol or drugs, or to a behavior, such as sex or gambling.

Being who we are. This means being true to ourselves, letting ourselves be, and loving, cherishing, accepting, and nurturing ourselves.

Boundaries. Our boundaries are our limits: how far we go with others, how far we allow them to go with us. We can define boundaries only for ourselves. Our boundaries define what we allow to come into our lives. We are seeking to allow less pain, chaos, abuse, and negative energy into our lives, and we're making room for positive experiences.

Caretaking. This is one of the most important words we learn in recovery. It means taking responsibility for others. Too often, it also means *not* taking responsibility for ourselves. We may tend to take inappropriate responsibility for the feelings, thoughts, behaviors, problems, choices, and life course of others. Now we are learning to do that for ourselves. We can tell if our caretaking is appropriate or not by the results of the behavior: Codependent caretaking makes us feel used, victimized, unappreciated, and unsuccessful in our efforts. We feel

221

controlled by the needs of others and simultaneously feel that our needs are not getting met. True helping and healthy giving are good, and different from caretaking.

The child within (inner child). This popular recovery concept refers to the fact that regardless of our age, we each have a young child within us with all the feelings, fears, complexities, simplicities, and needs we had when we were that age. We may be forty years old, brave, successful, and competent, but inside is a frightened four-year-old who needs a hug, some comforting words, and a balloon. Many of us ignore this child within. That doesn't work. This child will start acting out and defeating us until we listen. Gradually, we learn how to recognize, listen to, and nurture this part of ourselves.

Compulsive. When we act in a compulsive manner, we do things because we feel that we have to. Often, when we aren't dealing with our feelings, compulsivity sets in. That's because compulsive behaviors help us run from our feelings.

Controlling. Our behavior is controlling when we are trying to force things to happen, trying to make people do what we want them to do, and trying to make life happen the way we think it should. We learn to recognize when we are controlling because a) we feel crazy; b) our efforts don't work; and c) we alienate others. We learn that the best way to deal with controlling is not to sit on our hands, but to deal with the feelings underlying our need to control. Usually those feelings include fear.

Crisis (Chaos). Chaos is the ongoing state of unmanageability in our lives. When a critical stage is reached, crisis occurs. This is what we're trying to avoid in recovery, not through denial but by setting up lives that are peaceful and manageable. Many of us lived with a great deal of crisis before recovery. Some of us learned to enjoy the drama and found ourselves getting into chaos that was not our business or creating it when life got too peaceful. Some of us are so used to crisis that we react to everything as though it is a crisis situation. Now, we're learning to relish peace instead of chaos and stop making the proverbial mountains out of molehills.

Dealing with feelings. This can be an uncomfortable experience, initially. It means we stop running from our emotions, from what's really going on with us. We stand still and feel our feelings. Feelings are emotional energy; our feelings are our responsibility. We avoid blaming our emotions on others; letting our feelings control us; and trying to control others with our feelings. Usually, that's all that's required to make them go away. Ignoring our feelings doesn't make them go away; it makes them get bigger, or come out in strange, unpredictable, and often undesirable, ways. Many of us learned in our families that it wasn't okay to feel. Now, we're learning differently. We're learning to accept and value the emotional part of ourselves as important and closely connected to happiness and health.

Denial. Most of us are good at this. Denial refers to our ability to ignore what is happening, even when it is right before our eyes. We do this to protect ourselves until we are ready to face the truth. Part of us knows what's true; part of us knows what's real. By connecting to recovery groups and other recovering people, that part of us feels safe and strong enough to surface.

Detachment. This is often our first lesson in codependency recovery. It is the beginning of learning boundaries: the difference between us and the other person. It is the remedy for caretaking and controlling. It means we let go of others; we release them with love. If we're too angry to detach in love, we detach anyway; we work on our angry feelings and let love and compassion come later. We detach daily from others, from what we cannot control, from what we cannot change. We detach from unhealthy entanglements with the business and affairs of others. Detachment means we stop trying to make someone or something different. Instead, we try doing nothing for a while, which is usually harder for us than doing something. After we detach, we focus on taking responsibility for ourselves. Then, we learn about acceptance.

Easy Does It. Twelve Step slogan that gives us permission to relax, lighten up, and let things happen. It tells us we don't have to try so hard, when trying so hard makes us crazy.

Things work better with a light, natural touch. We need to go with the flow.

Family-of-origin work. This phrase refers to the process of looking at our pasts to learn what behaviors we brought forward to our present. This work allows us to heal from our pasts. This includes healing from the feelings, behavior patterns, beliefs, and any incidents of abuse we suffered as children. This is an important process.

Guilt. Guilt is the feeling of self-reproach we experience when we blame ourselves for things that happened or feelings we've had. Most of us feel at fault for everything when we begin recovery. Some of it is earned; some of it isn't. By working the Steps, we learn to tell the difference so we can deal with it appropriately. Amends and forgiveness of self and others is the remedy for real guilt. Unearned guilt can be banished with self-love and realistic thinking.

Hidden agenda. This refers to a secret plan or list of needs that one is not talking about but that is nevertheless controlling one's relationships with others. It means things are different than they appear. Sometimes, we may not know what other people's hidden agendas are; sometimes, we're not certain what our own are. Our goal in recovery is to avoid people with unhealthy agendas (for instance, the need to use or abuse us); and to keep in touch with our true agendas.

Insanity. This is a term we use to describe the unmanageability in our lives. It is *not* used to describe a typical psychotic state: We use it loosely to describe our crazy, self-defeating behaviors.

Issues. An issue is a point of debate or controversy, a matter to be resolved. In recovery, we let other people have their own, and we take responsibility for ours.

Let Go and Let God. This is a famous Twelve Step program slogan. It means we stop trying to control everybody and everything, and we let God do God's work. Many of us find this is a delightful concept when we practice it, because God manages things better than we do.

Letting go. This means that we stop obsessing, controlling, or engaging in any other futile, self-defeating behavior, and we let people be and things happen. We specifically try to let go to God. We deal with our feelings, take care of ourselves, live one day at a time, and trust. The rest, we let go of.

Live and Let Live. This is a Twelve Step slogan that defines our search for healthy boundaries. It means that we let others go about their business, and we put our energy into living our own lives.

Manipulation. This behavior is closely related to controlling. It means that we try to get what we want indirectly or in a dishonest fashion. We try to seduce, control, trick, or trap people into doing what we want them to do because we are afraid to ask and be direct or hear a "no." Many of us have done this so long we may not be aware we're doing it. Sometimes manipulation works, but it's usually accompanied by bad feelings.

Nurturing. Nurturing acts are those that cultivate growth and good feelings in ourselves or others. In recovery we learn to nurture ourselves, and others when we want to. We also learn to let others nurture us. Nurturing activities include: hugging, positive touch, dancing, playing, rocking, going for a walk, sleeping with a Teddy bear, picking a flower, taking a hot bath, and getting a back rub. Any treatment of ourselves that makes us feel comforted, helps us play, or is pleasurable, is nurturing. Nurturing can be a well-timed gentle word, a feeling, an activity, a touch, or a gift.

Obsessing. Obsessing is what happens when our mental energies become compulsively tied into nonproductive thought patterns, usually about another person or a situation. We find that we can't stop thinking about someone or something. That person or circumstance has gained control of our minds and sometimes our lives. The remedies for obsession are detachment, dealing with our feelings, meditation, and letting go. Obsessing is a second cousin to worry, which doesn't work either.

One Day At a Time. This is a Twelve Step slogan that defines an innovative but effective approach to life: Instead of living tomorrow today, or next week today, or reliving yesterday, we live each day as it comes.

Owning our power. Our power is our ability to take responsibility for ourselves—to think, feel, solve problems, and find our direction. Our power lies in speaking our truth, setting appropriate boundaries, refusing to tolerate abuse or mistreatment, and sometimes, being vulnerable. Our power means discerning what is real and right for us. Owning our power does not mean controlling others or having power over them. It doesn't mean allowing others to control us. It doesn't mean reacting to others out of fear or a need to manage them. It means finding that centered place within us and acting from that place.

Pain. In recovery the word *pain* refers to emotional pain, like anger, guilt, and hurt. Some of us are so used to being in emotional pain, we think it's normal. It's not. Our goal in recovery is to feel any emotional pain we have and be done with it. If painful feelings arise during the course of our recovery, which they will, we accept and feel them. We stop doing things to cause pain and begin doing things that help us feel good. Most of us find that our tolerance for pain decreases, the longer we've been recovering. We like to feel good.

Peace. Peace is a state of tranquillity and harmony. Peace feels good. It comes with the recovery package. It may make you feel uncomfortable at first, but you'll learn to like it.

People-pleasing. People-pleasing means doing things simply to make people like us. Usually, we do this because we don't believe people would like or love us otherwise. This behavior is closely connected to caretaking. In recovery, we learn to do things that please ourselves. And we trust ourselves enough to understand that this will include engaging in loving, nurturing behaviors toward others: not to make others love us, but because we love others.

Reactions. Often, we have patterned reactions to people that have been learned, reminiscent of Pavlov's dogs. They do something, and we immediately and instinctively react in a predictable manner, even though our reaction may not accomplish anything. In recovery, we learn that we can choose how we want to act. That takes the control of our lives away from others and frees us to choose a course of conduct that will work more effectively for us and our relationships.

Resentment. Resentments are angry feelings that we haven't dealt with, resolved, or let go of. They develop from anger that isn't fully felt. The remedy for resentment is fully feeling our anger, releasing our anger, taking any appropriate action (such as setting a boundary or making an amend), then topping it off with forgiveness. In recovery, we learn to talk about our feelings, including our anger and resentment, in a productive, healthy way.

Shame. This is that dark feeling of unworthiness and guilt. Most of us have so much of it that we think it's normal. In recovery we gradually learn to substitute self-love and acceptance for shame.

Sharing. This doesn't mean we let others drive our car. It means we open up about who we really are.

Spirituality. In recovery we are growing spiritually; we're on a spiritual journey. Spirituality is not the same as religion, although many recovering people go to church. It is about our spirit, our personal relationship to a Power greater than ourselves, and our relationship with ourselves.

Surrender. This means to accept, give in, give up, and let our lives happen. It's a spiritual concept. It is also ironic in that many of us fight doing this but find ourselves feeling quite good once we do.

Taking care of ourselves. This is when we give ourselves physical and emotional care and support. It means taking loving and appropriate responsibility *for* ourselves, and our responsibilities, including appropriate responsibilities *to* others. It's what many of us haven't been doing but are learning to do. (Taking care of ourselves is not to be confused with rolling over others. When what we're doing is self-care, we don't need to announce it with a bullhorn.)

Unfinished business. If we don't do our family-of-origin work, this is what we will have. Unfinished business refers to unresolved matters, feelings, and past incidents, that constitute issues that we still need to address. If we have unfinished business, we will be attracting lessons and situations into our lives that will be reminiscent of the feelings, behavior patterns, beliefs, and abuse we suffered as children and sometimes as adults. We will be controlled by our pasts. Our goal in recovery is to set ourselves free from our pasts, so that what we do today is what we choose to do.

Victim. A victim is someone who suffers—voluntarily or not—pain or harm inflicted by self or others. This is what we used to believe we were. This is what we're not.

GUIDE TO TWELVE STEP GROUPS

There was a time when the menu of Twelve Step programs was short: Alcoholics Anonymous for the alcoholic, and Al-Anon for the person affected by the alcoholic. Those times have changed.

Since the founding of Alcoholics Anonymous in 1935, 148 groups, each with a different recovery focus, have requested permission to use the Twelve Steps. Most of these requests occurred from 1985 through 1990, according to representatives from the World Service Office of Alcoholics Anonymous.

From Joyous Anonymous to Gangs Anonymous, people with a common problem have used these Steps to achieve a common solution. We call the solution "recovery."

The first group that asked for permission to use these Steps was Al-Anon.

Here is a partial listing of Twelve Step groups. I've included the groups most widely used by people recovering from codependency issues. Following that is a listing of groups focusing on recovery from addictions.

In the listing of codependency and codependency-related groups, I've included the address and phone number (if available) of each group's national headquarters (often called a World Service Office) and other information pertinent to making an inquiry. Also included is a brief description of the group, information about the focus of the group, and the "requirements" for membership. The latter is usually a description of the common problem and is taken from the traditions that guard the operations of groups.

As of the writing of this book, the phone numbers and addresses were current. Please be patient when making inquiries;

some of the World Service Offices are staffed entirely by volunteers. It may take six to eight weeks to receive a reply.

FINDING THE RIGHT GROUP FOR YOU

There are several ways to find a good group—one that is right for you.

Read over the following list. If you find a group with a focus that looks like it fits your situation, write or call the national headquarters and inquire about meetings in your area.

Check the phone book, both the white and yellow pages. Some listings use the full name of the group (Codependents Anonymous); others list by initials (CoDA).

Check with your local community agencies, treatment centers, hospitals, mental-health units, social-service agencies, or churches. They may have information about groups in your area.

Check with the primary addiction recovery groups in your area, such as Alcoholics Anonymous. They may have information about other kinds of Twelve Step meetings in the community. They will usually have information about the codependency group related to that addiction. For instance, Alcoholics Anonymous will probably be able to point you to Al-Anon; Cocaine Anonymous will probably be able to tell you where the Co-Anon groups meet.

Ask! Word of mouth is one of the best ways to locate a group. Talk to people with issues similar to yours, and find out where the good groups meet!

Another good way to find a group is by contacting the National Self Help Clearing House (25 West 43rd Street, Room 620, New York, New York 10036). This organization is connected to seventy clearing houses across the country and responds promptly, efficiently, and courteously to requests. A phone call or letter to them can direct you to available meetings in your community. The Clearing House has a paid staff but also relies heavily on volunteers to answer written requests. Some of the offices are government run. Information about this organization is included in the following listing.

If the group of your choice does not exist in your community, you can start a group. Most of the World Service Offices have start-up information packets available. And in areas where meetings are in short supply, people desiring to recover from codependency have been known to attend open meetings of Alcoholics Anonymous to begin their connection to the Twelve Steps.

Each meeting within each of the group categories will have its own personality and format. Many begin with the Serenity Prayer and end with the Lord's Prayer. Twelve Step groups are anonymous. That means you don't ever have to use your last name.

Requirements for membership center around having a common problem. Except for some of the groups concerned with incest or sexual addiction—where screening for anonymity is critical—becoming a member simply means you decide to go to the group, walk in, and sit down.

Be patient as you search out the right group for you. Experiment and attend several different groups.

GROUPS FOR CODEPENDENCY AND RELATED ISSUES

ACA
Adult Children of Alcoholics
P.O.Box 3216
2522 W. Sepulveda Boulevard, Suite 200
Torrance, California 90505
(213) 534-1815

Adult Children of Alcoholics is a Twelve Step program for adults whose parents were alcoholic. The requirement for membership is that the person "identifies with the problem." As one member said, "ACA is a gentle way to enter the Twelve Step program."

There are many different kinds of ACA meetings around the world. Some are called ACoA. There are also specialty meetings: ACA for incest survivors; gender-separated meetings; gay and lesbian meetings. Some meetings focus on the material from books such as *Women Who Love Too Much* by Robin Norwood and *Codependent No More* by Melody Beattie.

ACA is an international organization. There are approximately 1,500 groups throughout the United States and Europe, Iceland, Australia, Canada, and many other countries.

Al-Anon

Al-Anon Family Group Headquarters, Inc.
P. O. Box 862
Midtown Station, New York, New York 10018-0862
(212) 302-7240

Al-Anon, the first Twelve Step program for codependency, was founded by Lois, the wife of Bill W., the founder of Alcoholics Anonymous. Al-Anon meetings are based on the Twelve Steps and Twelve Traditions of A.A. The only requirement for membership is that there be a problem of alcoholism in a relative or friend.

Al-Anon meetings generally follow a standardized format, and there is usually a Step discussion. Some meetings offer feedback, others discourage it. You may want to try several meetings before finding one that best suits you.

Al-Anon is an international organization with approximately 30,000 groups in 100 countries.

Alateen

Al-Anon Family Group Headquarters, Inc.
P. O. Box 862
Midtown Station, New York, New York 10018-0862
(212) 302-7240

Alateen is Al-Anon for teens. The meetings are run by teenagers and guided by Al-Anon members. Contact your local Al-Anon chapter for locations.

Co-Anon

P. O. Box 64742-66
Los Angeles, California 90064
(213) 859-2206

Co-Anon is a Twelve Step group for the families and friends of cocaine addicts. The program is about seven years old. The only difference between a Co-Anon meeting and an Al-Anon meeting is the drug of choice.

Co-Anon is still small; the meetings are scattered throughout the United States. In some locations the meetings are called Coc-Anon.

CoDA
Co-Dependents Anonymous
P.O. Box 33577
Phoenix, Arizona 85067-3577
(602) 277-7991

CoDA is a Twelve Step group to help men and women maintain functional relationships. The only requirement for membership is a desire for healthy and loving relationships with oneself and others.

Members are searching for ways to overcome conflicts in relationships; many of the members belong to other Twelve Step groups. Many also find that their present issues stem from unresolved experiences in a dysfunctional family system.

This rapidly growing program was founded in 1986 and already has more than 2,000 groups in thirteen countries.

Co-SA
Codependents of Sex Addicts
Minnesota Co-SA
P. O. Box 14537
Minneapolis, Minnesota 55414
(612) 537-6904

Co-SA is a recovery program for people who are codependents of sex addicts. The only requirement for membership is that there be a problem of sexual addiction in a relative or friend. Co-SA also states a sobriety goal for members: to be sober from "our own addiction."

Both men and women can participate as members, although some meetings are gender-separated. Most of the meetings are "walk in," but some of the groups are "contact first." This means that you must meet with a group member before being given the location of the meeting. This is to protect the anonymity of the members present.

Co-SA meetings follow the Twelve Step program. Co-SA is allied with S.A.A. (Sex Addicts Anonymous). There is no World Service Office yet, but the Minneapolis Intergroup fields all requests for information.

EA

Emotions Anonymous
International Services
P. O. Box 4245
St. Paul, Minnesota 55104
(612) 647-9712

The goal of this Twelve Step group is to help people recover from a variety of emotional difficulties, from severe, chronic mental illness to anger, guilt, depression, grief, anxiety, and phobias. The only requirement for membership is a desire to become well emotionally.

EA meetings are similar to other Twelve Step meetings. They use the Twelve Step format, and the meetings are open. There are both "lifetime" and "crisis" members. Ann Landers has suggested that people seek help from EA for codependent issues.

EA was founded in 1971 in St. Paul, Minnesota. EA groups exist in 28 countries and in nearly every state in this country. There are 1,524 groups worldwide, including 100 in the United States, 150 in Canada, and 300 in Germany.

FA

Families Anonymous, Inc.
P. O. Box 528
Van Nuys, California 91408
(818) 989-7841

The only requirement for membership in Families Anonymous is a "concern about the use of mind-altering substances or related behavioral problems in a relative or friend." FA is particularly concerned with substance abuse in children.

FA members are parents and grandparents, some with children in their thirties and forties. Some FA parents are dealing with anorexia and bulimia in their children. The FA program is based on the belief that all basic acting-out behaviors follow the same patterns, regardless of the drug of choice. The meetings follow a Twelve Step format, but there are also feelings groups, speaker meetings, and open meetings.

FA is an international organization, operating since 1970. There are approximately 500 groups worldwide, including those in 41 American states, Australia, Canada, England, India, Portugal, and Trinidad.

FA
Fundamentalists Anonymous
P. O. Box 20324, Greeley Square Station
New York, New York 10001
(212) 696-0420

Fundamentalists Anonymous is the only national support system to assist people recovering from an experience with a fundamentalist religious group.

When leaving a fundamentalist organization, people may experience guilt and anxiety. It may be difficult to talk about their experiences and find understanding and support. FA offers a place to heal with others suffering from the same symptoms.

FA does not require that members believe in God. Having a "relationship" with a group can also be anxiety producing because FA members have been in abusive organizations and groups. FA meetings are not discussion groups about theology. They treat fundamentalism as a mind-set, not a religion. The mind-set is the mental-health hazard that they're recovering from.

FA uses a scaled-down version of the Twelve Steps. It is a five-step program. The Higher Power concept is not used in FA because it is what the members are trying to escape from. The Steps have been modified to accommodate the special needs of recovering fundamentalists. They include: (1) *Taking responsibility* for the fact that there is a problem and for making decisions for our own lives; (2) *One step at a time*; (3) *Association*—not doing it alone; (4) *Self-esteem*; (5) *To be brave, act brave*—letting our behavior affect our feelings. (Other groups use the phrase "act as if" to mean the same thing.)

There are 60,000 members nationwide. Unlike other Twelve

Step groups, FA is involved politically to help prevent further abuse from religious experiences.

Gam-Anon
Gam-Anon International Service Office, Inc.
P. O. Box 157
Whitestone, New York 11357
(718) 352-1671

Gam-Anon offers hope and recovery to the families of compulsive gamblers. The only requirement for membership is that there be a problem of gambling in the family.

Gam-Anon meetings are run very much like those of Al-Anon or other Twelve Step programs. Although comments might be offered in some meetings, as a general rule advice is not given.

There are approximately 320 groups active worldwide. There are chapters throughout the United States, but the major concentration of groups is on the West and East coasts.

I.S.A.
Incest Survivors Anonymous
P.O. Box 5613
Long Beach, California 90805-0613

I.S.A. deals with all kinds of childhood sexual abuse, including ritualistic abuse. I.S.A.'s definition is broad. The only requirement for membership is a desire to stop being an incest victim and to become an incest survivor. New members are screened, however, for the purpose of keeping perpetrators, victimizers, and initiators out.

I.S.A. bases their meetings on A.A.'s two main texts, *Alcoholics Anonymous* (the "Big Book") and *Twelve Steps and Twelve Traditions* ("12 and 12"). They do not endorse any outside enterprise or therapist. They stick closely to the A.A. Traditions, but they do have a lifetime head person in Erin, the founder.

I.S.A. is an international group. To obtain information about groups in your area or about starting a group, write to the above address. You must register with the main office; all incoming calls to the I.S.A. office are monitored.

Nar-Anon (Family Groups)
P. O. Box 2562
Palos Verdes, California 90274
(213) 547-5800

Nar-Anon is a Twelve Step support group similar to Al-Anon. It is for those dealing with narcotic addiction in a friend or relative. Many of the members of Nar-Anon started their Twelve Step journey in Al-Anon.

Nar-Anon has been in existence since 1967. There are meetings all over the United States. Canada also has a very strong Nar-Anon system. There are Nar-Anon groups in many other countries, including Germany, Japan, Ireland, and Argentina. Nar-Anon literature is available in English, French, and German.

O-Anon
General Service Office
P. O. Box 4350
San Pedro, California 90731

O-Anon is a Twelve Step group for the families and friends of compulsive overeaters. The only requirement for membership is that there be a problem of food abuse in a relative or friend. O-Anon helps the families and friends of compulsive overeaters to understand all aspects of the disease—including obesity, anorexia, and bulimia—and to cope with the effects of living with an active addict.

O-Anon offers hope and fellowship and encourages members to attend to their own spiritual program through the Twelve Steps. To locate a group in your area, contact the General Service Office listed above.

RCA
Recovering Couples Anonymous
P. O. Box 27617
Golden Valley, Minnesota 55442

This program, founded in 1988, is for couples in recovery together. The only requirement for membership is the desire to remain in a committed relationship. While other programs have a strong emphasis on the self, RCA is for the couple. "Nontraditional" couples are welcome, too.

At the first RCA meeting, the commitment of the two partners is defined. The idea is to have a commitment to work on the relationship, even if only for two weeks at a time. The group encourages each partner to become independent, with his or her own friends, own life, own skills, and own recovery network, but at the same suggests that the partners bring these things back to the coupleship. Mutual interdependence is the goal.

If a couple splits up, neither of the partners returns to the meeting. The goal of RCA is not to keep the couple together but to support the couple while they are together.

RCA grew out of the We Came to Believe program developed by Dr. Patrick Carnes, a leading authority on sex addiction. RCA is new, but growing rapidly. There are approximately thirty groups throughout the country.

S-Anon
S-Anon International Family Groups
P. O. Box 5117
Sherman Oaks, California 91413
(818) 990-6901

S-Anon is for the families and friends of sex addicts. The only requirement for membership is that there be a problem of sex addiction in a friend or family member.

S-Anon is allied with SA (Sexaholics Anonymous). The meetings are similar in format to those of Al-Anon and Co-SA.

S-Anon was founded in 1982. It is an international organization with groups in the United States, Canada, Australia, and Europe. Approximately seventy groups meet regularly across the United States.

SIA
Survivors of Incest Anonymous
P.O. Box 21817
Baltimore, Maryland 21222-6817
(301) 282-3400

SIA is for persons over the age of eighteen who have been

sexually abused by a family member or other trusted adult. The organization's interpretation of "abuse" is broad.

The SIA program of recovery is based on the Twelve Steps. Some meetings are gender-separated. Many people who contact SIA are in other Twelve Step programs but consider their incest or abuse a key issue in their recovery.

SIA has been in existence since 1982. It is an international organization with groups across the United States and Canada, England, Ireland, the Netherlands, and other countries. SIA has recently merged with Sexual Abuse Anonymous. (S.A.A.'s name was confusing because it implied that it was for the abuser, not the victim.) SIA is for survivors.

TWELVE STEP GROUPS FOR ADDICTS

Alcoholics Anonymous
P.O. Box 454
Grand Central Station
New York, New York 10017
(212) 686-1100

Cocaine Anonymous
World Service Office
3740 Overland Avenue, Suite G
Los Angeles, California 90034
(213) 559-5833
800-347-8998 (meeting referrals)

Debtors Anonymous
General Service Board
P. O. Box 20322
New York, New York
   10025-9992

Drugs Anonymous
P. O. Box 473
Ansonia Station
New York, New York 10023
(212) 874-0700

Gamblers Anonymous
P. O. Box 17173
Los Angeles, California 90017
(213) 386-8789

Marijuana Anonymous
1527 North Washington Avenue
Scranton, Pennsylvania 18509

Narcotics Anonymous
P. O. Box 9999
Van Nuys, California 91409
(818) 780-3951

Overeaters Anonymous
P. O. Box 92870
Los Angeles, California 90009
(213) 542-8363

Parents Anonymous
22330 Hawthorne
Torrance, California 90505

Pill Addicts Anonymous
P. O. Box 278
Reading, Pennsylvania 19603
(215) 372-1128

Sex Addicts Anonymous
P. O. Box 3038
Minneapolis, Minnesota 55403
(612) 339-0217

Sexaholics Anonymous
P. O. Box 300
Simi Valley, California 93062
(805) 581-3343

Sex and Love Addicts
   Anonymous
Augustine Fellowship
P. O. Box 119, Newtown
   Branch
Boston, Massachusetts 02258
(617) 332-1845

Smokers Anonymous
2118 Greenwich Street
San Francisco, California 94123

RECOVERY BOOK LIST

Recovery books are books that change people's lives. They may support or affirm us in the changes we're making. They may help us identify a problem or guide us toward a solution. They help us see things in a new way. They are treasures.

Many times a book has been my friend, by educating, supporting, guiding, nurturing, affirming, or uplifting me.

Here is a list of some recovery books that are popular in the recovering community. They are grouped by topic. This list isn't complete; my apologies if I've neglected any of your favorites.

ABUSIVE FAMILY SYSTEMS

Bradshaw On: The Family: A Revolutionary Way of Self Discovery
John Bradshaw
Health Communications, Inc., 1988

This is a comprehensive look at the "family system," how it affects us in adulthood, and how to heal it. Helpful to anyone doing family-of-origin work.

Dear Dad: Letters from an Adult Child
Louie Anderson
Viking Penguin, 1989

Tender and humorous, *Dear Dad* is comedian Louie Anderson's journey toward understanding, accepting, and forgiving an alcoholic parent. In trying to make peace, Anderson explains his own addictive process with food, which began at an early age— a process he used to deal with the stresses of the alcoholic family. This well-written book is a gentle exploration of family dynamics.

Soul Survivors: A New Beginning for Adults Abused as Children
J. Patrick Gannon, Ph.D.
Prentice Hall Press, 1989

This is a thorough investigation into child abuse and its effects on us as adults. It is appropriate reading for the individual who is beginning to wonder if he or she was abused as well as for the person who has been healing from abuse for a while. Gannon addresses how to determine if you were abused as a child, common problems of adult survivors, overcoming addictions, surviving on the job, and healthy parenting skills. There is also an excellent chapter for the partners of survivors. Gannon offers a twenty-one–step program of recovery for those who need to overcome child abuse.

**Toxic Parents: Overcoming Their Hurtful Legacy and
    Reclaiming Your Life**
Dr. Susan Forward with Craig Buck
Bantam Books, 1989

Toxic Parents discusses how our parents' behavior affected us as children and as adults. Forward explains what abuse is and its many forms, including emotional and physical abandonment; neglect, verbal abuse, and physical abuse; covert and overt sexual abuse; controlling parents; alcoholic parents; and more. The stories of the survivors are powerful and direct. Included are excellent sections on stopping the legacy of abuse and confronting one's own parents. Any adult child can find pieces of his or her story in this comprehensive work.

ADULT CHILDREN OF ALCOHOLICS

Adult Children of Alcoholics
Janet Geringer Woititz, Ed.D.
Health Communications, Inc., 1983

The definitive book on the characteristics of Adult Children. It includes suggestions for parents interested in breaking the cycle with their own children. This text is used in many ACA meetings.

Adult Children of Alcoholics in Treatment
Stephanie Brown, Ph.D., Susan Beletsis, Ph.D., and Timmen
Cermak, M.D.
Health Communications, Inc., 1989
A text for clinicians dealing with Adult Children. Includes
information on group therapy, understanding the adult child,
and family transference in groups of adult children.

Adult Children: Secrets of Dysfunctional Families
John Friel and Linda Friel
Health Communications, Inc., 1988
Highly recommended for its wealth of information and clarity
on the subject of adult children. The authors gently and compas-
sionately help the reader understand what happened to them
and how to begin recovery. The stories of the Bear, the Rabbit,
and the Goose are heartwarming.

It Will Never Happen To Me
Claudia Black, Ph.D., M.S.W.
Ballantine Books, 1987
A pioneer in Adult Child issues, Black offers an in-depth look
at the alcoholic family system and its effects on the children. She
explains how rules like "Don't Think, Don't Talk, Don't Feel"
are carried over and control our adult lives. The book offers
suggestions on how to change these patterns and recover. Also
included is a section that addresses violence and sexual abuse in
the alcoholic family.

A Primer on Adult Children of Alcoholics
Timmen L. Cermak, M.D.
Health Communications, Inc., 1989
This is a quick introduction to the Adult Child syndrome.
Cermak briefly defines alcoholism, codependency, the character-
istics of the child of an alcoholic as a youngster and an adult,
and the recovery process.

The Self-Sabotage Syndrome: Adult Children in the Workplace
Janet G. Woititz, Ed.D.
Health Communications, Inc., 1987
With a special emphasis on the Adult Child in the workplace, this text explains in detail the effects of the dysfunctional family on the employee and employer. Also addressed is the Adult Child as a counseling professional.

Struggle for Intimacy
Janet G. Woititz, Ed.D.
Health Communications, Inc., 1985
A guide to defining and building successful relationships. Unconditional acceptance and growth for both individuals are the goals. Included is a list of myths and fears of the Adult Child and how the ACA characteristics affect relationships.

A Time to Heal: The Road to Recovery for Adult Children of Alcoholics
Timmen L. Cermak, M.D.
Avon Books, 1989
Filled with personal stories and information, this book offers an extensive look at the causes and cures of the Adult Child syndrome. Cermak covers healing, denial, remembering childhood, feeling, post-traumatic stress, separation from family, honesty, trust, and finding the courage to heal.

The 12 Steps for Adult Children
Recovery Publications, 1987
This book focuses on the Twelve Steps as they apply to issues specific to adult children of alcoholics. Written by an anonymous group of recovering persons, it includes a situation-specific Twelve Step review and a meditation for ACAs.

CHANGING BEHAVIORS

The Angry Book
Theodore Isaac Rubin, M.D.
Collier Macmillan Publishers, 1970
Rubin discusses the barriers to healthy anger, the destructive

ways we handle anger, and how to change these. He talks about cleaning out the "slush fund" of stored anger from the past so we can be current with our feelings.

attrACTIVE WOMAN: A Physical Fitness Approach to Emotional and Spiritual Well-Being
Marvel Harrison-Davis, M.S., R.D., and Catharine Stewart-Roache, D.Min., M.A.
Parkside Publishing Corporation, 1989
For women who want a more physically active life, this book offers many helpful suggestions. The authors stress that becoming physically strong increases our psychological strength; they take a holistic look at our lives from the vantage point of physical movement. It is especially helpful and affirming for women who have been sedentary for a time and want to change.

Creating Choices: How Adult Children Can Turn Today's Dreams into Tomorrow's Reality
Sheila Bayle-Lissick and Elise Marquam Jahns
Hazelden, 1990
This is a book for people who want more from life but aren't sure how to get it. It includes sections on trusting intuition, meditation, visualization, affirmations, becoming more aware of details, and guided imagery. Also included are many helpful suggestions on how to change lives to fit dreams.

The Dance of Anger: A Woman's Guide to Changing the Patterns of Intimate Relationships
Harriet Goldhor Lerner, Ph.D.
Harper & Row, 1985
An excellent book about how to honor your anger and deal with it respectfully. Although many women deny and "stuff" their anger, this book also addresses explosive anger. Lerner believes that "anger is a signal . . . that we are being hurt, that our rights are being violated, that our needs or wants are not being adequately met, or simply that something is not right." Good reading for men and women from families where anger was not allowed or was the controlling factor.

The Dance of Intimacy: A Woman's Guide to Courageous Acts of Change in Key Relationships
Harriet Goldhor Lerner, Ph.D.
Harper & Row, 1988
Lerner gives practical examples of how to change the level of intimacy in our relationships. She addresses different kinds of primary relationships, from our biological families to our chosen ones. Recommended for couples strengthening relationships and people grappling with the parent-sibling connection.

Guilt Is the Teacher, Love Is the Lesson: A Book to Heal You, Heart and Soul
Joan Borysenko, Ph.D.
Warner Books, 1990
This book describes the difference between healthy and unhealthy guilt. The writer connects guilt and shame issues with spirituality, both in origin and healing. Several chapters are devoted to spirituality and religion in today's world. New-Agey but not inaccessible.

Raise Your Right Hand Against Fear: Extend the Other in Compassion
Sheldon Kopp
CompCare Publishers, 1988
A book to help you face fears.

Rock, Paper, Scissors: Understanding the Paradoxes of Personal Power and Taking Charge of Our Lives
Sheldon Kopp
CompCare Publishers, 1989
This is an enjoyable book about how to have power in your life, interwoven with fables, mythology, and cultural tales.

Stage Two Recovery: Life Beyond Addiction
Earnie Larsen
Harper & Row, 1985
Larsen claims that sobriety is only the first stage of recovery; what happens after is Stage Two Recovery: "making the most of

a life that has been rescued from obsession and addiction." The book addresses switching addictions, defining recovery, the dry-drunk syndrome, self-defeating learned behaviors, and change. It includes practical suggestions for changing the habits that keep us stuck. A great book for those looking for more out of recovery.

Survival Handbook for the Newly Recovering
Scott Sheperd, Ph.D.
CompCare Publishers, 1988
This guide is filled with practical suggestions on how to survive low self-esteem, boredom, loneliness, resentment, and depression. Although aimed at the recovering addict, it offers useful alternatives for the recovering codependent.

What Smart Women Know
Steven Carter and Julia Sokol
M. Evans, 1990
A must for any woman, whether in a relationship or not. Carter and Sokol's pithy, humorous text makes you laugh and think. Cutting past emotions, sentiment, and denial, this book helps the reader understand the sabotaging behaviors women get into in relationships with men. A good book to read before any romantic interlude.

CLASSICS IN RECOVERY

A.A.'s Godparents: Three Early Influences on Alcoholics Anonymous and Its Foundation—Carl Jung, Emmet Fox, Jack Alexander
Igor I. Sikorsky, Jr.
CompCare Publishers, 1990
The author explains how these three men influenced the development of A.A. Carl Jung and Emmet Fox had a great influence on the spiritual aspects of the Twelve Steps; Jack Alexander is known for writing an article in *The Saturday Evening Post* that tripled the membership of A.A. in one year. This book will help readers understand the spirituality of this program.

Al-Anon Family Groups (formerly **Living with an Alcoholic**)
Al-Anon Family Group Headquarters, Inc., 1966, 1986
The opening page states: "The purpose of this book is to help those who feel their personal lives are being or have been affected by the obsessive drinking of a family member or friend. The light which it sheds on the problem of alcoholism should also be helpful to those who come in daily contact, professionally and socially, with alcoholics." It offers a brief history of Al-Anon, information about the disease aspect of alcoholism, a review of the Twelve Steps, the Twelve Traditions, and the slogans, and an overview of the business aspects of Al-Anon.

Al-Anon's Twelve Steps and Twelve Traditions
Al-Anon Family Group Headquarters, Inc., 1986
This is the official Al-Anon interpretation of the Twelve Steps and Twelve Traditions. It addresses issues faced by the families and friends of alcoholics.

Alcoholics Anonymous
Alcoholics Anonymous World Services, Inc., 1939, 1986
Many consider the A.A. "Big Book" a divinely inspired work about the Twelve Steps of A.A. It is mandatory reading for anyone in recovery. "I've read this book one hundred times and every time I read it, I find something new and helpful that I hadn't seen before," say many.

The Courage to Change: Personal Conversations about Alcoholism
Dennis Wholey
Warner Books, 1986
Wholey has compiled the recovery stories of many well-known and some not-so-well-known members of A.A. This is a direct account of how alcoholism affects our lives and offers hope and courage.

Twelve Steps and Twelve Traditions
Alcoholics Anonymous World Services, Inc., 1953
Written by the co-founder of A.A., this book looks at each step individually. Many other books on the Twelve Steps are an

interpretation of this classic text. Another mandatory book for those working a Twelve Step program.

The Twelve Steps for Everyone . . . who really wants them.
Grateful Members
CompCare Publishers, 1975
   Helpful for people in any Twelve Step program. This is another interpretation of the Twelve Steps using nongender pronouns.

CODEPENDENCY

Beyond Codependency: And Getting Better All the Time
Melody Beattie
Harper/Hazelden, 1989
   Written for those who have been recovering from codependency issues for a while, this book explores the recovery process, shame, family-of-origin work, relationships, and the ongoing need to surrender and trust as we walk this journey called recovery.

Co-Dependence: Misunderstood, Mistreated
Anne Wilson Schaef
Harper & Row, 1986
   This compact book examines the development of the concept of codependency. It was one of the first books to propose the relevance of codependency for members of dysfunctional families where addiction is not evident.

Codependent No More: How to Stop Controlling Others and
    Start Caring for Yourself
Melody Beattie
Harper/Hazelden, 1987
   A primer on codependency and how to recover from it.

Diagnosing and Treating Co-Dependence: A Guide for Professionals Who Work with Chemical Dependents, Their Spouses and Children
Timmen L. Cermak, M.D.
Johnson Institute, 1986
A quick read, this basic manual is aimed at professionals working with addictive systems.

The Dilemma of Love: Healing Co-Dependent Relationships at Different Stages of Life
Susan Cooley Ricketson, Ph.D.
Health Communications, Inc., 1989
Ricketson explores the roots of codependent behavior in our families of origin. She explains why and how we end up being codependent, offers suggestions on what a healthy relationship looks and feels like, and includes an excellent chapter on teen issues. The book offers hope that we can indeed recover from a lifetime of unhealthy relationships.

Facing Codependence: What It Is, Where It Comes from, How It Sabotages Our Lives
Pia Mellody with Andrea Wells Miller and J. Keith Miller
Harper & Row, 1989
An overview of codependency and its effects. Mellody develops her concept of the "precious child" within who must be healed if codependency recovery is to be effective. A comprehensive view of codependency and its treatment.

Letting Go with Love: Help for Those Who Love an Alcoholic/Addict, Whether Practicing or Recovering
Julia H.
Jeremy P. Tarcher, Inc., 1976
This book is the story of an Al-Anon member and includes exercises to assist in working the Steps. It can be particularly helpful in doing Steps Four and Five. It is geared toward the codependent who is dealing with an alcoholic or drug addict.

Loving Tough, Loving Smart, Loving You: You and the Alcoholic
Arnie Wallace, Ph.D., and Adryan Russ
Challenger Press, 1990
    A down-to-earth, direct approach for the codependent facing
the reality of living with an alcoholic. This book demands that
you change, learn to say no, get tough, and love smart. A
powerful, fast read with many suggestions.

Men Who Hate Women and the Women Who Love Them:
    When Loving Hurts and You Don't Know Why
Dr. Susan Forward and Joan Torres
Bantam Books, 1987
    "He was charming, sexy, and romantic, and I had fallen in
love with him almost immediately after we met. But I soon
discovered that he had a great deal of anger inside him and that
he had the power to make me feel small, inadequate and off-
balance. He insisted on being in control of everything I did,
believed, and felt," writes Forward. If this is your story, this
book is worth reading. She describes men who hate women and
the dynamics of such relationships. She offers hope for women
who feel stuck in relationships of this type.

Painful Affairs: Looking for Love Through Addiction and
    Co-Dependency
Joseph R. Cruse, M.D.
Health Communications, Inc., 1989
    Cruse tells the story of his recovery as both a chemically
dependent and codependent physician. His recovery model draws
parallels between chemical dependency and codependency progression and recovery.

When Society Becomes an Addict
Anne Wilson Schaef
Harper & Row, 1987
    "The good news is that, like the individual alcoholic/addict,
the Addictive System can recover. Before that can happen, we
must admit that the society we care about has a disease," writes

251

Schaef. She builds a case for the underpinnings of addiction that operate in our society as a whole.

Women Who Love Too Much: When You Keep Wishing and Hoping He'll Change
Robin Norwood
Pocket Books, 1986

This book details the anatomy of an addictive relationship. It addresses the connection between our destructive and painful relationships in adulthood and abuse in our childhood. Writes Norwood, "The more difficult it is to end a relationship that is bad for you, the more elements of childhood struggle it contains." Excellent reading for women who continually find themselves doing all the work in their relationships.

HELP ALONG THE JOURNEY

How to Survive the Loss of a Love: 58 Things to Do When There Is Nothing to Be Done
Melba Colgrove, Ph.D., Harold H. Bloomfield, M.D., and
Peter McWilliams
Bantam Books, 1983

This book is designed to give you ideas about surviving the grief process. It offers suggestions for how to take care of yourself during the phases of loss, surviving, healing, and growing. Good for people grieving any kind of loss, including breakups, separation, divorce, death, job loss, or the death of a pet.

The Magic Within: Avoiding Self-Deception in Recovery
Mary Lee Zawadski
Health Communications, Inc., 1990

Written for the recovering person who still feels that life will always be painful, this book offers some helpful suggestions for changing the patterns that keep us stuck. Part of the healing, the author claims, is learning to take responsibility.

The Miracle of Recovery: Healing for Addicts, Adult Children, and Co-Dependents
Sharon Wegscheider-Cruse
Health Communications, Inc., 1989
An uplifting and affirming approach to recovery. Cruse shares her personal story to make the point that we can choose to experience the miracle of recovery. She covers many topics, including forgiveness, workaholism, self-worth, self-parenting, and divorce.

The Road Less Traveled: A New Psychology of Love, Traditional Values and Spiritual Growth
M. Scott Peck, M.D.
Simon & Schuster, 1978
A classic best seller and a positive addition to your library. Peck does a good job connecting our spiritual growth to our emotional and mental processes. The clear-cut definition of love—what it is and what it isn't—is helpful. Don't miss this one.

INCEST SURVIVORS

The Courage to Heal: A Guide for Women Survivors of Child Sexual Abuse
Ellen Bass and Laura Davis
Harper & Row, 1988
An excellent manual for those dealing with sexual abuse. The authors cover the stages of healing; dealing with the crisis from remembering to confronting the abuse; dealing with a partner who is a survivor; changing the patterns of our lives; and more. A book that any survivor, partner, or counselor will want to read. Highly recommended by many sexual-abuse survivors.

For Your Own Good: Hidden Cruelty in Child-Rearing and the Roots of Violence
Alice Miller
Farrar, Straus & Giroux, 1983
A technical book about "poisonous pedagogy" that has informed many other recovery texts.

Incest and Sexuality: A Guide to Understanding and Healing
Wendy Maltz and Beverly Holman
Lexington Books, 1987
Provides concrete help for survivors of childhood sexual abuse, rape, and other traumas. Highly recommended by recovering survivors as a guide to reclaiming one's healthy sexuality.

Thou Shalt Not Be Aware: Society's Betrayal of the Child
Alice Miller
New American Library, 1986
A powerful examination of the implications of Freud's Oedipus complex and the ways society blames the child and protects the parent. Miller is passionate and moving in her defense of the child. This is a thoughtful, healing book.

Victims No Longer: Men Recovering from Incest and Other Sexual Child Abuse
Mike Lew
Harper & Row, 1988
A survivor's manual for male victims of sexual abuse and incest, this book is a groundbreaker. Also includes a chapter for partners and family members.

REFERENCE

The Recovery Resource Book: The Best Available Information on Addictions and Codependence
Barbara Yoder
Simon & Schuster, 1990
A comprehensive guide to addiction and the resources available for dealing with it. The book covers all kinds of addictions, including alcohol, nicotine, caffeine, sugar, food, prescription drugs, street drugs, marijuana, cocaine, codependence, love and sex, money, and work. Yoder discusses the available resources for all addictions, such as anonymous programs, special concern groups, and government agencies. Packed with facts, personal stories, and quotes, this is an excellent source for the individual or professional.

INNER CHILD

The Drama of the Gifted Child: The Search for the True Self
Alice Miller
Basic Books, 1983
This is an early and still authoritative contribution to the concept of the inner child. Miller points out the damage done to children whose parents have used them, consciously or unconsciously, to meet their own needs.

Growing Up Again: Parenting Ourselves, Parenting Our Children
Jean Illsley Clark and Connie Dawson
Harper/Hazelden, 1989
This book looks at the parenting functions of structure and nurture and illustrates healthy parenting through common situations and possible responses. It is also sensitive to our need to reparent the inner child within ourselves. Full of practical, supportive suggestions.

Oneness and Separateness: From Infant to Individual
Louise J. Kaplan, Ph.D.
Simon & Schuster, 1978
The book focuses on the need for the child to separate successfully from the parent. Provides support for parents going through that process.

Recovery of Your Inner Child: Re-Parenting Yourself, Healing Your Life
Lucia Capacchione, Ph.D.
Simon & Schuster, 1990
This book gives many concrete exercises to help you get in touch with and bridge the gap between your intellect and the child within. It will help you learn how to discover the nurturing and protective parent within yourself as well. This is a book full of healing.

Self Esteem: A Family Affair
Jean Illsley Clark
Harper & Row, 1979
The author presents stories of eight families who have worked to enhance a sense of self-esteem in both parents and children. Includes work sheets and practical suggestions and is a great help for parents in recovery. A classic.

MEDITATION BOOKS

Affirmations for the Inner Child
Rokelle Learner
Health Communications, Inc., 1990
Learner wrote this to address the "child within," which gives it a different feel from meditation books written for the "adult."

Daily Affirmations for the Adult Child
Rokelle Learner
Health Communications, Inc., 1985
Many ACA meetings use this meditation book. Highly recommended by many recovering Adult Children.

Each Day a New Beginning
Hazelden, 1982
A meditation book written for women but also used by many men. Subject index included.

God Calling
Fleming H. Revell Company, 1984
A classic in meditation books, this book was the basis for *Twenty-Four Hours a Day*, (a classic A.A. meditation book). A soothing book that goes right to the spirit.

Help for Helpers: Daily Meditations for Counselors
Parkside Publishing Corporation, 1989
Written by many counselors, this meditation book addresses the concerns in the daily life of a care giver. The fifteenth and

thirtieth of each month are left blank so you can write your own meditations.

The Language of Letting Go: Daily Meditations for Codependents
Melody Beattie
Prentice Hall Press, 1990
A daily meditation book written for men and women recovering from codependency issues. Practical and personal. Subject index included.

One Day at a Time in Al-Anon
Al-Anon Family Group Headquarters, Inc., 1973
The original Al-Anon meditation book.

Our Best Days
Parkside Publishing Corporation, 1990
A meditation book for young adults.

Touchstones: A Book of Daily Meditations for Men
Hazelden, 1986
A meditation book with men's issues as a focal point, but used by women as well. Subject index included.

Twenty-Four Hours a Day
Hazelden, 1975
The classic and first daily meditation book for recovering alcoholics.

PAMPHLETS

Bittersweet: For Those in Other 12 Step Programs
Survivors of Incest Anonymous, 1986
This is an exceptional piece of literature designed to help members of other Twelve Step groups get in touch with unresolved incest issues. Highly recommended for anyone dealing with incest.

Rebuilding Trust: For Couples Committed to Recovery
Jennifer P. Schneider and Burt Schneider
Hazelden, 1989
A guide for couples dealing with sexual addiction, this pamphlet offers information that can smooth the beginning of recovery.

Transferring Obsessions
Judi Hollis, Ph.D.
Hazelden, 1986
Hollis looks at how we transfer obsessions instead of making real change. She explains how we can switch our focus to food, money, shopping, sex, smoking, caffeine, and any number of other substances and behaviors.

When A.A.s Go to OA
Judi Hollis, Ph.D.
Hazelden, 1986
Written to assist the recovering alcoholic in accepting his or her food addiction. Hollis covers the questions and concerns of an A.A. old-timer taking on a new Twelve Step program.

RELATIONSHIPS

Coupleship: How to Have a Relationship
Sharon Wegscheider-Cruse
Health Communications, Inc., 1988
An excellent, easy-to-read guide for the couple who wants to bond and commit. The author explains coupleship and intimacy and offers suggestions for dealing with "invaders" of relationships and enhancing your coupleship.

Getting the Love You Want: A Guide for Couples
Harville Hendrix, Ph.D.
Henry Holt & Co., 1988
A notable book for any couple trying to create the marriage they want. Hendrix explores the unconscious dynamics that brought them together and may be tearing them apart. He discusses the mystery of attraction and our unconscious pull

toward a mate who will reenact our childhood issues. He directs readers toward a "conscious marriage," one that helps you satisfy your unmet childhood needs in positive ways.

Stage II Relationships: Love Beyond Addiction
Earnie Larsen
Harper & Row, 1987
Larsen brings his Stage II model to relationships, offering insights into why we may not be getting what we want from our partners. The focus is on each individual working a personal program of recovery to make the relationship healthier.

SEX ADDICTION

Back from Betrayal: Recovering from His Affairs
Jennifer P. Schneider, M.D.
Hazelden, 1989
Beginning with her own story, Schneider looks at the issues and concerns of the partner of a sex addict. To heal from the pain of living with a sex addict, she claims, we must face our codependency, whether we choose to stay in the relationship or not.

Contrary to Love: Helping the Sexual Addict
Patrick Carnes, Ph.D.
CompCare Publishers, 1988
Carnes explains the origin of addictive behavior, how it grows, the patterns of the sex addict, and the components necessary for recovery. Included is an excellent chapter on the co-addict. Highly recommended for professionals as well as addicts.

Hope and Recovery: A Twelve Step Guide for Healing from Compulsive Sexual Behavior
CompCare Publishers, 1987
Used in many S.A.A. meetings, this book is a recovery resource for those dealing with sex addiction. Included is an interpretation of the Twelve Steps and a discussion of abstinence and sobriety. Hopeful stories of recovery comprise the bulk of the book.

Out of the Shadows: Understanding Sexual Addiction
Patrick Carnes, Ph.D.
CompCare Publishers, 1985
This groundbreaking book brought sex addiction into public consciousness. Carnes was the first to describe sex addiction and its deadly hold on the addict and the addict's family. Excellent, enlightening, and highly recommended.

Women, Sex, and Addiction: Search for Love and Power
Charlotte Davis Kasl, Ph.D.
Ticknor & Fields, 1989
This is the first complete work to address the woman's perspective on sex addiction and sexual codependency. It discusses the roles of society and family in our sexual development and issues and continually makes connections between sexuality and spirituality. Recommended for all, men as well as women, who want affirmation and permission to be healthy sexual and spiritual beings.

SHAME

Bradshaw On: Healing the Shame That Binds You
John Bradshaw
Health Communications, Inc., 1988
Bradshaw synthesizes a wide range of ideas to develop his concept of shame-based behavior and to indicate a path toward healing.

Facing Shame: Families in Recovery
Merle A. Fossum and Marilyn J. Mason
Norton, 1986
A classic book about how shame works and where it comes from. Based on the authors' work as family therapists.

Understanding Shame: Why It Hurts, How It Helps, How You Can Use It to Transform Your Life
Eunice Cavanaugh, M.Ed., M.S.W.
Johnson Institute, 1989

The author explores the feelings of shame and guilt, the ways we mask them, the positive and negative aspects of shame, its consequences, and how to change the influence of shame in our lives.

SPECIAL INTERESTS

Accepting Ourselves: The Twelve-Step Journey of Recovery from Addiction for Gay Men and Lesbians
Sheppard B. Kominars
Harper & Row, 1989
This book is a tender, compassionate, and honest look at the specific issues facing recovering homosexuals. It focuses on concerns relating to being a homosexual person in a homophobic society. Kominars reviews the Twelve Steps and addresses the Higher Power issue with insight and grace. Any recovering person will benefit from reading this courageous work.

Feeding the Empty Heart: Adult Children and Compulsive Eating
Barbara McFarland and Tyeis Baker-Baumann
Hazelden, 1988
The authors address the connection between being an Adult Child and compulsive eating. An excellent text for anyone struggling with food issues as well as for professionals.

Getting Free: A Handbook for Women in Abusive Relationships
Ginny NiCarthy
The Seal Press, 1986
An important and empowering book for women in physically abusive relationships. NiCarthy holds nothing back and covers all aspects of violent relationships, including the decision to stay or to leave, the social and political aspects of violence against women, and family values. Included is an excellent practical section on getting professional help, survival as a single person and parent, responsibility to children, sexuality, and rebuilding. This book offers hope and courage.

The Ones Who Got Away: Women Who Left Abusive Partners
Ginny NiCarthy
The Seal Press, 1987
Thirty-three incredible stories of brave women who left abusive relationships. Powerful and painfully honest accounts.

The Twelve Steps of Phobics Anonymous
Marilyn Gellis, Ph.D., and Rosemary Muat, M.A.
Institute of Phobic Awareness, 1989
Sprinkled with inspirational quotes, this is a guide for those suffering from phobias or panic attacks. The authors share personal stories, review the Twelve Steps, offer insight, discuss current phobia treatment, and suggest ways of managing our lives.

SPIRITUAL

The Bible
A favorite source of strength for people in recovery.

Chop Wood, Carry Water: A Guide to Finding Spiritual Fulfillment in Everyday Life
Rick Fields with Peggy Taylor, Rex Weyler, and Rick Ingrasci
Jeremy P. Tarcher, Inc., 1984
Gently illustrating that the magic we long for is in every moment, these writers have pulled together centuries of thoughts, ideas, philosophies, and traditions. They show that these ancient concepts apply today to the real issues of relationships, family, sex, work, money, play, our bodies, healing, and social action. A rich resource for living a full life.

A Course in Miracles
Foundation for Inner Peace, 1975
A book that will change your way of thinking about the world, God, and reality. It has its own vocabulary and includes a text and daily lesson. Most people read this slowly. It's an excellent source for people who want their beliefs challenged.

Creative Visualization
Shakti Gawain
Bantam Books, 1982
This book offers a clear explanation of creative visualization and many enlightening exercises. It is easy to read and is an excellent resource book for those looking for ways to change the old tapes and behaviors of the past and create a better future through imagery.

Emmanuel's Book: A Manual for Living Comfortably in the Cosmos
Compiled by Pat Rodegast and Judith Stanton
Bantam, 1985
This inspirational book will calm you and perhaps alter your way of thinking about life and its challenges. Easy to read, it offers a spiritually based approach to life. Discusses subjects such as love, the path, healing, fear, relationships, the planet, and the feast of life.

Emmanuel's Book II: The Choice of Love
Compiled by Pat Rodegast and Judith Stanton
Bantam Books, 1989
Here is more wisdom on self, choosing love, illusions, politics, dragons, aging, and more.

A Gradual Awakening
Stephen Levine
Doubleday, 1979
Levine has written a rich and enlightening book about meditation and life. Filled with wisdom, acceptance, and guided meditations.

Living in the Light: A Guide to Personal and Planetary Transformation
Shakti Gawain
Whatever Publishing, Inc., 1986
Gawain guides the reader through meditations and exercises dealing with the higher power within, intuition, our male and

female sides, relationships, work, play, money, health, and more. A good book for those wishing to expand their spirituality.

Love Is Letting Go of Fear
Gerald G. Jampolsky, M.D.
Bantam Books, 1982
This book offers a new look at life, love, forgiveness, judgment, transformation, self-fulfillment, joy, and responsibility. Delightful, easy to read, and recommended when you need a boost.

Ordinary People as Monks and Mystics: Lifestyles of Self-Discovery
Marsha Sinetar
Paulist Press, 1986
This is an affirming and empowering book for people who wish to live life from their hearts. Sinetar tells stories about people who chose individual and unique lifestyles. A helpful book for people who want to change their life course.

Original Blessing: A Primer in Creation Spirituality Presented in Four Paths, Twenty-Six Themes, and Two Questions
Matthew Fox
Bear & Company, 1983
This book is a comprehensive study of spirituality and how to give birth to it within yourself. This work spans continents, time, and the imagination. Highly recommended for people who want to expand their definition of life and spirituality.

The Sermon on the Mount: The Key to Success in Life
Emmet Fox
Harper & Row, 1934
A classic. Although it is based on Christian writings, it is recommended for people of all faiths. Fox was a visionary and had a talent for seeing beyond his time and culture.

The Tao of Pooh
Benjamin Hoff
Penguin Books, 1983
    A. A. Milne's *Winnie the Pooh* serves as an example of the concepts of Taoism in this charming book. More than a lesson in the philosophy of Taoism, it is a commonsense approach to attaining a life of serenity. Affirms recovery by the principles of living in the now, being present and open, and letting life unfold naturally.

Who Dies: An Investigation of Conscious Living and Dying
Stephen Levine
Doubleday, 1982
    This is a compassionate exploration of life and letting go. Gives permission to accept the present and transcend the moment by being in it. Encourages readers to become openhearted.

You Can Heal Your Life
Louis L. Hay
Coleman Publications, 1985
    A popular book in the recovery community, it discusses the concept that thoughts create reality. It addresses how thoughts create illness, how to affirm healing, relationships, work, success, prosperity, and the body. Exercises are included in most chapters. Filled with positive affirmations; good reading for people breaking old patterns.

Zen Mind, Beginner's Mind: Informal Talks on Zen
    Meditation and Practice
Shunryu Suzuki
Weatherhill, Inc., 1970
    This classic book looks at the practice of Zen and is a treasure of insight on living peacefully. A unique book of meditations and essays.

WORKBOOKS

Breaking Free: A Recovery Workbook for Facing Codependence
Pia Mellody and Andrea Wells Miller
Harper & Row, 1989
This companion to *Facing Codependency* provides enough content summaries to make it useful without reference to the original text. Charts, journal suggestions, and ample examples aim at denial of past pain, present codependent behavior, and future recovery.

The Courage to Heal Workbook: For Women and Men
    Survivors of Child Sexual Abuse
Laura David
Harper & Row, 1990
A companion to *Courage to Heal*, this large-format spiral-bound workbook is a powerful tool not only for victims of sexual abuse but for physically or emotionally abused men and women. A gentle tool on the journey through recovery from abuse.

The First Step: For People in Relationships with Sex Addicts
Mic Hunter, M.S., M.A., C.C.D.C.R., L.P., and Jem
CompCare Publishers, 1989
Written by a therapist and a recovering codependent, this workbook contains full journal pages headed by quotations that trace the experience and progression of codependents and sex addicts. Questions on each page lead you through a process of self-examination and acceptance.

A Gentle Path through the Twelve Steps: A Guidebook for All
    People in the Process of Recovery
Patrick Carnes, Ph.D.
CompCare Publishers, 1989
This workbook guides you through the Twelve Steps. It looks at family-of-origin and unmanageability and has a comprehensive guide to the Fourth Step. There are separate sections for the addict and the codependent. Helpful to those going through the

Steps for the first time or to those wanting to review the Steps in more detail.

A Gift to Myself
Charles L. Whitfield, M.D.
Health Communications, Inc., 1990

A condensed version of *Healing the Child Within*, this workbook has affirmations and encouragement built into each entry. Particularly useful for Adult Child and codependency issues.

Old Patterns New Truths: Beyond the Adult Child Syndrome
Earnie Larsen
Hazelden, 1988

Using thoughts and ideas from his other material, Larsen helps the Adult Child get in touch with specific issues, where they originated, and how to change them. There are personal stories throughout the workbook. It is not necessary to read his other books to use this workbook.

The 12 Steps, a Way Out
Recovery Publications, 1987

A companion to *The 12 Steps for Adult Children*, this large-format workbook of lists and questions leads ACAs through a personalized and relevant interpretation of the Steps. For those who want real direction and information in workbook format.

THE TWELVE STEPS
OF ALCOHOLICS ANONYMOUS

1. We admitted we were powerless over alcohol—that our lives had become unmanageable.
2. Came to believe that a Power greater than ourselves could restore us to sanity.
3. Made a decision to turn our will and our lives over to the care of God *as we understood Him.*
4. Made a searching and fearless moral inventory of ourselves.
5. Admitted to God, to ourselves, and to another human being the exact nature of our wrongs.
6. Were entirely ready to have God remove all these defects of character.
7. Humbly asked Him to remove our shortcomings.
8. Made a list of all persons we had harmed, and became willing to make amends to them all.
9. Made direct amends to such people wherever possible, except when to do so would injure them or others.
10. Continued to take personal inventory and when we were wrong promptly admitted it.
11. Sought through prayer and meditation to improve our conscious contact with God *as we understood Him,* praying only for knowledge of His will for us and the power to carry that out.
12. Having had a spiritual awakening as the result of these steps, we tried to carry this message to alcoholics, and to practice these principles in all our affairs.

THE TWELVE TRADITIONS
OF ALCOHOLICS ANONYMOUS

1. Our common welfare should come first; personal recovery depends upon A.A. unity.
2. For our group purpose there is but one ultimate authority—a loving God as He may express Himself in our group conscience. Our leaders are but trusted servants; they do not govern.
3. The only requirement of A.A. membership is a desire to stop drinking.
4. Each group should be autonomous except in matters affecting other groups or A.A. as a whole.
5. Each group has but one primary purpose—to carry its message to the alcoholic who still suffers.
6. An A.A. group ought never endorse, finance or lend the A.A. name to any related facility or outside enterprise, lest problems of money, property and prestige divert us from our primary purpose.
7. Every A.A. group ought to be fully self-supporting, declining outside contributions.
8. Alcoholics Anonymous should remain forever nonprofessional, but our service centers may employ special workers.
9. A.A., as such, ought never be organized; but we may create service boards or committees directly responsible to those they serve.
10. Alcoholics Anonymous has no opinion on outside issues; hence the A.A. name ought never be drawn into public controversy.
11. Our public relations policy is based on attraction rather than promotion; we need always maintain personal anonymity at the level of press, radio and films.
12. Anonymity is the spiritual foundation of all our Traditions, ever reminding us to place principles before personalities.

THE TWELVE STEPS
OF
CO-DEPENDENTS ANONYMOUS

1. We admitted we were powerless over others—that our lives had become unmanageable.
2. Came to believe that a power greater than ourselves could restore us to sanity.
3. Made a decision to turn our will and our lives over to the care of God as we understood God.
4. Made a searching and fearless moral inventory of ourselves.
5. Admitted to God, to ourselves, and to another human being the exact nature of our wrongs.
6. Were entirely ready to have God remove all these defects of character.
7. Humbly asked God to remove our shortcomings.
8. Made a list of all persons we had harmed, and became willing to make amends to them all.
9. Made direct amends to such people wherever possible, except when to do so would injure them or others.
10. Continued to take personal inventory and when we were wrong, promptly admitted it.
11. Sought through prayer and meditation to improve our conscious contact with God as we understood God, praying only for knowledge of God's will for us and the power to carry that out.
12. Having had a spiritual awakening as the result of these steps, we tried to carry this message to other co-dependents, and to practice these principles in all our affairs.

Reprinted and adapted with the permission of A.A. World Services, Inc.

THE TWELVE TRADITIONS
OF
CO-DEPENDENTS ANONYMOUS

1. Our common welfare should come first; personal recovery depends upon CoDA unity.
2. For our group purpose there is but one ultimate authority—a loving higher power as expressed to our group conscience. Our leaders are but trusted servants; they do not govern.
3. The only requirement for membership in CoDA is a desire for healthy and loving relationships.
4. Each group should be autonomous except in matters affecting other groups or CoDA as a whole.
5. Each group has but one primary purpose—to carry its message to other co-dependents who still suffer.
6. A CoDA group ought never endorse, finance or lend the CoDA name to any related facility or outside enterprise, lest problems of money, property and prestige divert us from our primary purpose.
7. Every CoDA group ought to be fully self-supporting, declining outside contributions.
8. CoDependents Anonymous should remain forever nonprofessional, but our service centers may employ special workers.
9. CoDA, as such, ought never be organized; but we may create service boards or committees directly responsible to those they serve.
10. CoDA has no opinion on outside issues; hence the CoDA name ought never be drawn into public controversy.
11. Our public relations policy is based on attraction rather than promotion; we need always maintain personal anonymity at the level of press, radio and films.
12. Anonymity is the spiritual foundation of all our traditions, ever reminding us to place principles before personalities.

Reprinted and adapted with the permission of A.A. World Services, Inc.

THE TWELVE STEPS
OF AL-ANON

1. We admitted we were powerless over alcohol—that our lives had become unmanageable.
2. Came to believe that a Power greater than ourselves could restore us to sanity.
3. Made a decision to turn our will and our lives over to the care of God *as we understood Him.*
4. Made a searching and fearless moral inventory of ourselves.
5. Admitted to God, to ourselves, and to another human being the exact nature of our wrongs.
6. Were entirely ready to have God remove all these defects of character.
7. Humbly asked Him to remove our shortcomings.
8. Made a list of all persons we had harmed, and became willing to make amends to them all.
9. Made direct amends to such people wherever possible, except when to do so would injure them or others.
10. Continued to take personal inventory and when we were wrong promptly admitted it.
11. Sought through prayer and meditation to improve our conscious contact with God *as we understood Him,* praying only for knowledge of His will for us and the power to carry that out.
12. Having had a spiritual awakening as the result of these Steps, we tried to carry this message to others, and to practice these principles in all our affairs.

Reprinted and adapted with the permission of A.A. World Services, Inc.

THE TWELVE TRADITIONS
OF AL-ANON

1. Our common welfare should come first; personal progress for the greatest number depends upon unity.
2. For our group purpose there is but one authority—a loving God as He may express Himself in our group conscience. Our leaders are but trusted servants; they do not govern.
3. The relatives of alcoholics, when gathered together for mutual aid, may call themselves an Al-Anon Family Group, provided that, as a group, they have no other affiliation. The only requirement for membership is that there be a problem of alcoholism in a relative or friend.
4. Each group should be autonomous except in matters affecting another group of Al-Anon or A.A. as a whole.
5. Each Al-Anon Family Group has but one purpose: to help families of alcoholics. We do this by practicing the Twelve Steps of A.A. *ourselves*, by encouraging and understanding our alcoholic relatives, and by welcoming and giving comfort to families of alcoholics.
6. Our Al-Anon Family Groups ought never endorse, finance or lend our name to any outside enterprise, lest problems of money, property and prestige divert us from our primary spiritual aim. Although a separate entity, we should always cooperate with Alcoholics Anonymous.
7. Every group ought to be fully self-supporting, declining outside contributions.
8. Al-Anon Twelfth Step work should remain forever nonprofessional, but our service centers may employ special workers.
9. Our groups, as such, ought never be organized; but we may create service boards or committees directly responsible to those they serve.
10. The Al-Anon Family Groups have no opinion on outside issues; hence our name ought never be drawn into public controversy.
11. Our public relations policy is based on attraction rather than promotion; we need always maintain personal anonymity at the level of press, radio, TV and films. We need guard with special care the anonymity of all A.A. members.
12. Anonymity is the spiritual foundation of all our Traditions, ever reminding us to place principles above personalities.

Reprinted and adapted with the permission of A.A. World Services, Inc.

ALSO AVAILABLE FROM SIMON & SCHUSTER AUDIO:
MELODY BEATTIE ON AUDIOCASSETTE!
CODEPENDENTS' GUIDE TO THE TWELVE STEPS
Featuring the Author,
Melody Beattie
One 60-minute cassette; $9.95

Every day, thousands of women and men share their stories of hope and healing as part of the recovery process. Now you can listen to Melody Beattie share her own experiences and insights in this unique audio program from Simon & Schuster Audio.

In CODEPENDENTS' GUIDE TO THE TWELVE STEPS, Beattie discusses each of the Twelve Steps on the road to recovery and how they can be applied to codependency recovery. If you like tapes, this is an opportunity to hear a compassionate exploration of the behavioral, emotional, and spiritual aspects of recovery, the Twelve Steps, and how you can capture their power in your life.

SIMON & SCHUSTER FOR FASTER ORDERING,
P.O. BOX 10212 CALL TOLL-FREE 1-800-678-2677
DES MOINES, IOWA 50381 (7 A.M.–4:30 P.M. CENTRAL TIME, MON.–FRI.)

CODEPENDENTS' GUIDE TO THE TWELVE STEPS/$9.95 (#90079)

1. Payment method (check one):
   __ Check or money order (no CODs) payable to Simon & Schuster
   __ Visa __ MasterCard __ American Express
   Credit Card number:_____
   Expiration date (mo/yr): ___/___
   Signature (required on all credit card orders):

   _____

2. Ship to:
   Name:_____
   Street:_____
   City/State/Zip:_____

3. Number of copies ordered: __ × $9.95 = _____
   (New York and Iowa residents add
   applicable sales tax):   _____
   Shipping and handling: + $3.95

TOTAL COST: ======

4. Mail instructions: Detach this completed order form. Enclose check or money order or complete credit card information and mail to address above.

PLEASE ALLOW UP TO SIX WEEKS FOR DELIVERY.